FLASH CRASH

■

Also by Liam Vaughan

The Fix: How Bankers Lied, Cheated and Colluded to Rig the World's Most Important Number

A TRADING
SAVANT,
A GLOBAL
MANHUNT,
AND THE MOST
MYSTERIOUS
MARKET **CRASH**
IN HISTORY

..

FLASH**CRASH**

..

LIAM VAUGHAN

Doubleday
New York

www.doubleday.com

Book design by Maria Carella
Jacket image by Jun / iStock / Getty Images
Jacket design by Gray318

Library of Congress Cataloging-in-Publication Data
Names: Vaughan, Liam, 1979– author.
Title: Flash crash : a trading savant, a global manhunt, and the most
mysterious market crash in history / Liam Vaughan.
Description: First edition. | New York : Doubleday, [2020]
Identifiers: LCCN 2020005099 | ISBN 9780385543651 (hardcover) |
ISBN 9780385546355 (open market) | ISBN 9780385543668 (ebook)
Subjects: LCSH: Stocks—United States—History—21st century. | Stocks—
Prices—United States—History—21st century. | Stock exchanges—
United States—History—21st century. | Financial crises—United States—
History—21st century.
Classification: LCC HG4910 .V38 2020 | DDC 332.64/2092 [B]—dc23
LC record available at https://lccn.loc.gov/2020005099

MANUFACTURED IN THE UNITED STATES OF AMERICA

1 3 5 7 9 10 8 6 4 2

First Edition

FOR SUZI AND RUFUS

CONTENTS

FLASH CRASH

■

PROLOGUE

At 6 a.m. on a cold, dark Tuesday morning in April 2015, half a dozen plainclothes police officers, two FBI agents, and two prosecutors from the U.S. Department of Justice rendezvoused at a McDonald's in Hounslow, on the outskirts of London. In a former life, the mock-Tudor building, nestled on a busy round-about near Heathrow Airport, was a pub called the Traveller's Friend. Now it was like any other McDonald's: kindergarten colors, stark lighting, the smell of burning fat and disinfectant. The group exchanged bleary-eyed hellos and commandeered a quiet corner, where they ran through the plan one last time. Then, as the sun crept up to reveal another gray day in suburbia, the officers departed to carry out a mission two and a half years in the making: to capture one of the world's most dangerous and prolific market manipulators.

While the officers and agents edged out of the parking lot, the prosecutors, Brent Wible and Mike O'Neill, settled in and ordered breakfast. It was their investigation, their baby, but since they were on British soil, Scotland Yard was handling the arrest and they'd have to make do with receiving updates by phone.

Their target was a thirty-six-year-old Londoner named

Navinder Singh Sarao, who'd made $70 million from nothing in the U.S. futures markets using a variety of controversial methods and who, in the American government's reckoning, had helped precipitate the most dramatic market collapse in recent history, the so-called "Flash Crash" of 2010.

The Americans had been monitoring Sarao from afar for months, reading his emails, tracing his assets, interviewing his associates, and observing his comings and goings. Yet none of the investigators had met him, and he remained something of an enigma. They knew that Sarao traded alone from his parents' house, and that he prided himself on being a stranger to Wall Street and the world of high-frequency trading, or HFT, which he derided as being full of "geeks." But records showed that he routinely placed bigger bets than the world's largest banks and hedge funds. They'd heard stories of Sarao terrorizing staff at the Chicago Mercantile Exchange, the electronic marketplace where he plied his trade. One employee was left shaken when Sarao, in an accent somewhere between cockney and Asian rudeboy, threatened to cut off his thumbs. Yet Sarao's brokers described him as a pussycat who got lost on his way to their office.

It took the officers five minutes to get to the address, a beige, two-story, semidetached house with a plastic porch and a satellite dish that was indistinguishable from those around it. Sarao's parents had bought it in 1982, a few years after arriving from the Punjab in India. Hounslow has a large Sikh community, and, because it lies underneath Heathrow's flight path, property in the area is cheap. Nav had watched planes roar overhead close enough he could count their windows since he was three years old. Growing up, he'd held running races with his two older brothers and the neighborhood kids where the police now parked their unmarked vehicles. These days, as the DOJ knew from tracking his IP address, Sarao led a more nocturnal existence, trading U.S. markets until around 10 p.m. and then staying up till 3 or 4 a.m. He rarely roused before noon, and when one of the phalanx of officers rang on the doorbell at 8 a.m., Sarao was fast asleep.

Nav's father, Nachhattar, a short man with a gray beard, answered the door. After gathering his composure, he shouted to his son to get out of bed and come downstairs. Nav emerged in the hallway in baggy tracksuit pants and a sweatshirt, strands of thick black hair pointing skyward. "Mr. Sarao, I am with the Metropolitan Police," said the officer in charge of the operation. "We are here to arrest you for fraud and manipulating the market. You do not have to say anything, but it may harm your defense if you do not mention when questioned something which you later rely on in court. Anything you do say may be given in evidence. Do you understand?"

By now the commotion had caught the attention of the neighbors. Nav's mother, Daljit, who was babysitting across the street at her eldest son Rajvinder's house, stumbled home in a daze. Residents peered out through net curtains. Police weren't an uncommon sight in Hounslow, one of West London's poorer neighborhoods, but they rarely arrived so mob-handed, and nobody could comprehend what they might want with the Saraos, a humble, respectable family who kept to themselves and attended the local gurdwara.

Nav was told to shower and grab some clothes while his parents waited silently in the kitchen. When he was finished, the officers began searching the property. Nav's upstairs bedroom was musty and unkempt. There was a single bed, a Labrador-size stuffed tiger, a large TV hooked up to a games console, and a cabinet that contained mail-order pomades and lotions to promote youthful complexion and stimulate hair growth. Against a wall was a framed pair of pink Adidas soccer shoes signed "To Nav, from Lionel Messi." A full-size replica of the Jules Rimet World Cup trophy stood in a corner.

The scene of the alleged crime was a small workstation at the end of the bed that housed Nav's computer setup. There seemed to be nothing state-of-the-art or terribly unusual about it: a desktop with three screens connected to a standard broadband line; a couple of Samsung hard drives; and a slightly dated-looking camcorder. So *this* was where Sarao had amassed a fortune and brought the global financial system to its knees? It was difficult to fathom.

Back at McDonald's, the prosecutors waited for confirmation Sarao had been arrested, then called Jeff Le Riche, an attorney with the Commodity Futures Trading Commission, who was waiting in his house in Kansas City, where it was 3 a.m. The CFTC, the designated regulator for the futures industry, had begun investigating Sarao on a tip-off back in 2012. But as a civil body it has limited powers, so it referred the matter to the DOJ in 2014. Now they were working together. After getting the go-ahead, Le Riche, the head of the CFTC's investigation, fired off a series of prewritten emails instructing Sarao's brokers and off-shore banks to freeze his accounts.

Sometime before noon, Nav was handcuffed and led outside. As they were leaving, he said to one of the officers, "Wait a minute, bruv." There was a football match on television that night, and Nav wanted to run upstairs and record it. "I'm not sure you'll have time to watch that, son," came the reply. The officer was right. Sarao wouldn't set foot back in his home for another four months. By then he would be known around the world as the "Flash Crash Trader" and the "Hound of Hounslow"; the scourge of the markets or a modern-day folk hero, depending on whom you asked.

That afternoon, both the DOJ and the CFTC sent out press releases announcing the arrest. They made for dramatic reading. "A futures trader was arrested in the United Kingdom today on U.S. wire fraud and commodities fraud and manipulation charges in connection with his alleged role in the May 2010 'Flash Crash,'" the DOJ statement said. Sarao "used an automated trading program to manipulate the market," it went on, earning "significant profits" and contributing to a "major drop in the U.S. stock market."

For a multitude of reporters and finance professionals, the announcement was shocking and bizarre. For one thing, the Flash Crash—that apocalyptic half-hour spell when markets around the world collapsed before bouncing back again, and stocks temporarily changed hands at 0.0001 cents—had occurred almost five years ago. Senate hearings, academic papers, and countless articles had followed, but there was little consensus as to what had caused the meltdown. Now, seemingly out of the blue, the American government claimed to have solved the mystery: it was a lone-wolf day trader in London who learned his craft in an out-of-town arcade above a supermarket.

The releases raised more questions than they answered. If what the government was claiming was true, why had it taken the authorities so long to take any action? Why was there no suggestion of market manipulation in their contemporaneous 104-page report on the crash? And what did it say about the stability of the modern global financial system if a solitary individual with a PC and an Internet connection could wreak such havoc? Sarao was accused of something called "spoofing," whereby a trader places a bunch of buy or sell orders, enticing other participants to follow suit, then cancels them before they are executed, with the goal of nudging the market higher or lower. It was a brand-new offense—Sarao was only the second individual to be criminally charged with spoofing, and the first non–U.S. citizen—and a controversial one in financial circles because its victims were predominantly hugely profitable high-frequency trading firms whose modus operandi was to monitor other participants' orders and try to jump ahead of them using lightning-fast computer systems. Some people argued spoofing actually made markets fairer by curbing the rising dominance of those entities Michael Lewis dubbed "Flash Boys" in his 2014 book of the same name. Regardless, since the first days when commodities were bought and sold using hand gestures in the open air, misdirection and gamesmanship had been considered part of the cut and thrust of financial markets. Now, with the backing of the HFT industry, spoofing had been declared illegal. It was as if bluffing had been outlawed in poker.

The U.S. authorities were careful to assert that Sarao's antics had only *contributed* to the crash, but that nuance was lost in the ensuing press coverage. "How One Man Crashed the Stock Market," ran a typical headline. By late afternoon, journalists and TV crews had massed on Sarao's cul-de-sac. Nav's parents were unable to provide them with any answers. "I don't know about computers," Nachhattar told one reporter. "All this is news to me."

The tale that would eventually emerge was a wild one, and beneath it was a bigger story, about how the markets that determine the value of our companies, the cost of our food and fuel, and the size of our pensions had morphed in a few short years thanks to advances in technology that promised much but whose risks may not yet be fully understood. It is the story of the emergence of a new financial elite, whose intellect and superior understanding of the plumbing undergirding the financial system allowed them to cream billions of dollars from ordinary investors while regulators sat comatose at the wheel; and of the human cost when an industry is automated and robots replace people. Most of all, though, it is a story about what happens when one man refuses to accept the cards he is dealt and instead decides to fight back, to hell with the consequences.

ACT **ONE**

CHAPTER 1

WORK WELL UNDER PRESSURE

"Wanted. Trainee Futures Traders," ran the small ad in the Tuesday edition of the *Evening Standard* newspaper. "Applications are invited from graduates who can demonstrate the following skills: highly motivated; analytical approach; disciplined; goal orientated; work well under pressure."

Nav was two years out of university when he sent his CV to Independent Derivatives Traders at the start of 2003. After graduating he'd spent a miserable slog doing telesales for Dial-a-Phone, then taken an admin job on the foreign exchange desk at Bank of America, where the closest he got to trading was booking trades for the posh folks on the floor. By the time IDT invited him to Weybridge in Surrey for an interview, he was unemployed and restless.

Nav might not have known it yet, but he was uniquely well suited to the job. When he was three years old he learned his times tables after stumbling on a Little Professor electronic game. By the time he got to school he could multiply longer numbers in his head. It wasn't that the answers appeared, fully formed, when he saw a question. The trick lay in his memory. Where other children scrawled their workings on a piece of paper, Nav could hold each step, naturally and easily, in his brain. In high school, the problems got harder but he found he still didn't need a calculator. Math and science were his best subjects, but he picked up As and Bs across the board without much effort. Heston Community School was no place for teacher's pets, and Nav made sure nobody mistook him for one. He played practical jokes, was cheeky, and rarely showed up to class on time. Beverley Fielder-Rowe, his form tutor, recalled "a very likeable young man, very intelligent" who was "full of fun." A classmate described him as a "prankster" who "got away with things."

Schoolwork came easily to Nav, but his abiding love was soccer; he and his friends played constantly. In the summer, they cycled to the park in replica kits and kicked a ball until it got dark, stopping only to refuel at the fish-and-chip shop. Nav always insisted he play striker, the glory position, stalking the opposition goal and dispatching opportunities with icy precision. Later on, his attention turned to computer games, particularly the soccer game FIFA. Every time a new edition came out, he devoted hours to perfecting the new moves, eventually ranking in the top seven hundred out of three million players globally. Unusually, Nav didn't support an English team. Being part of a community was less important to him than who was the *best,* and he followed Barcelona.

In 1998, Nav had temporarily left home to attend Brunel, a mid-tier university a few miles from Hounslow, where he studied computer science and math. Like many students, Nav and his friends were broke. But one of their housemates always seemed to have cash. One day, Nav asked him how he could afford such expensive clothes. "Trading," came the response. At the time, the dotcom bubble was in full swing, and Nav's friend had deposited his student loan into a brokerage account and was now funding his studies by buying and selling tech stocks. How hard could it be, thought Nav. He started devouring anything trading-related he could, scouring the Internet for stock tips and plowing through textbooks on financial theory then opening an account of his own and placing some tentative trades.

IDT was based above a Waitrose supermarket. To gain entry, visitors had to walk around the back of the store and up a staircase. Inside were two main rooms, the larger of which, the "trading floor," had around a dozen desks containing computers with connections to the world's major commodities exchanges. On first glance, it didn't scream high finance: the décor was drab, the equipment was dated, and it overlooked a car park. Weybridge, a well-heeled, sleepy town surrounded by golf courses and car showrooms, was also an odd location for a trading firm. Forty-five minutes by train from the skyscrapers of the City of London, the capital's historic financial district, it was literally and figuratively miles from the action.

IDT was one of a burgeoning number of arcades or "prop shops" sprouting up in Britain and the United States. The business model was straightforward and, for a while at least, highly lucrative. IDT would take on a bunch of wannabe traders and teach them the skills they needed to succeed in the markets. Those who thrived were backed with steadily larger sums, while those who failed were cut. Any profits the recruits made after paying a monthly desk fee of around $1,700 were split, with newbies retaining 50 percent and the most successful as much as 90 percent. IDT also creamed off a small sum on each trade, or "round-trip," its traders placed, which quickly added up. The arrangement meant it didn't matter if everyone in the stable was making money as long as they were all buying and selling and there were at least some big winners. As the owner of a rival arcade put it: "During the gold rush, it was usually the ones selling the spades who got rich."

For a generation of ambitious graduates brought up watching *Wall Street* and *Trading Places* but lacking the grades or connections to land a job at JPMorgan, the opportunity was irresistible. The best day traders, they were told by IDT in a rousing speech on arrival, could make their own hours, wear flip-flops to work, and still pull in footballer money. All they had to do was correctly predict whether the market would go up or down more often than they were wrong, and they would be rich and free. The reality, of course, was that it was very difficult to consistently beat the market after costs, particularly when you were so far from the flow of information.

The selection process for Nav and his fellow interviewees was in three parts. First, candidates were given the McQuaig Mental Agility Test, a multiple-choice psychometric exam testing pattern recognition and verbal reasoning. This was followed by a one-on-one session in which they were asked to quickly multiply two- and three-digit numbers in their heads. Those who made it through were invited back a few days later for a two-hour interview, where they were questioned on how they would react to various hypothetical scenarios. IDT was looking for candidates who demonstrated high levels of dominance, analytical ability, sociability, and risk taking, as well as a passion for the markets.

The panel consisted of IDT's founder, Paolo Rossi, his brother Marco, their junior partner, Dan Goldberg, plus whoever ran the firm's training at the time. They were like a dysfunctional family unit. Paolo, the patriarch, was a short, taciturn alpha male who'd made a fortune in London's do-or-die futures pits in the eighties and nineties. At thirty-seven, he owned a mansion in Weybridge on the same gated estate as Elton John. He wore tailored jackets over turtlenecks and drove a new Ferrari to the office, a walking advertisement for what his recruits could hope to achieve. Below him, managing the business day to day, was Marco, who was two years younger, several pounds heavier, and did whatever he was told. He wore sweater vests and drove a family car, and the traders called him Homer Simpson behind his back. A rumor went around IDT that the Rossi brothers, whose parents were Scottish, were actually born Paul and Mark Ross but had changed their names to inject a bit of glamour. It was only half true: the Rossi name did come from an Italian grandparent, but the o had been tacked onto their first names in the pits. Goldberg, who was in his mid-twenties, was the surly adolescent of the family. After working as a runner for Paolo, he was brought over to Weybridge to oversee the traders, a responsibility he carried out with an air of barely disguised disdain. He wore a Mr. Grumpy T-shirt around the office and cursed like a cockney sailor.

Nav sailed through the tests, impressing the Rossi brothers by answering the mental arithmetic questions faster than they could finish looking them up on a calculator. But he failed to make much of an impression during the interview. Stick-thin and shifty, he arrived late wearing a suit that looked suspiciously like it belonged to somebody else. He refused to make eye contact and started sentences with "mate" and "bruv" and "the thing is, yeah." Sarao may have been unpolished, but there were signs of potential. His interest in gaming denoted focus and hand-eye coordination. And he was confident to an almost comical degree. When the panelists asked him what he hoped to achieve in his career, he replied, straight-faced, that he wanted to be as rich as Warren Buffett and start his own charity. In the end, Nav made the cut and was offered a slot on IDT's second-ever batch of intakes.

IDT'S ROOTS, like those of most of the British futures arcades, can be traced back to 1982 and the opening of the London International Financial Futures and Options Exchange, or Liffe (pronounced "life"). Futures are financial contracts in which one party agrees to sell an asset, say one hundred bushels of wheat, to another for delivery at some future date. Their original purpose was to allow businesses to hedge potential risks. A pig farmer, for instance, who knows she will need to feed her livestock in six months' time may agree to buy some wheat for a set amount today, eliminating the risk that the price soars between now and then. Of course, it's possible that the price will go down and she'll miss out on some potential savings, but the stability and predictability she gains by fixing the cost now make the deal worthwhile. Before long, a second class of investor, the speculator, started turning up at the pits. Speculators buy and sell futures using their own funds with the sole aim of turning a profit. If, for example, a speculator believes the price of wheat will go down because he's heard there will be a bumper harvest, he'll sell some wheat futures now in the hope of buying them back at a later date for less. He has no interest in ever actually taking ownership of any wheat; it's just another type of asset on which to place a wager, no different from buying gold or General Motors stock.

For more than a century, futures were principally traded at the Chicago Board of Trade and the Chicago Mercantile Exchange, but in 1979 Margaret Thatcher was elected prime minister of Britain, ushering in an era of buccaneering capitalism and deregulation. Three years later, a European market focused solely on financial futures—instruments tied to the future value of bonds, equities, foreign exchange, and interest rates as opposed to commodities like wheat or copper—was born. Liffe started out at the Royal Exchange, a grand, cavernous, rectangular coliseum directly opposite the Bank of England. When it was built as a venue for merchants to congregate, in 1571, financial traders were banned because of their "rude manners." Four hundred years later, they had taken over.

The first participants through Liffe's doors were given the honorific "Day One Traders." They included David Morgan, a serial entrepreneur who owned a boutique on Carnaby Street and, according to the legend, made a fortune selling dried fish to Nigeria in the 1970s. Morgan was a small, regimented man with a suave bearing and a tightly clipped mustache that earned him the nickname Colonel. Traders saluted him as they passed. Morgan wasn't the greatest trader himself, but he could recognize potential in others and started backing new recruits, many of them high school graduates from working-class backgrounds. They adored him, happily sacrificing a share of their profits for the opportunity to make a fortune.

Paolo was among them. Brought up with his brother in south London by their mother, a housewife, and father, a police detective, Paolo found school easy and took his math exam early, but he was restless, and when his friends went off to university, he landed a junior role at the Bank of England. After a couple of fusty years behind a desk learning about interest rates and yield curves, he got a position at a merchant bank, where he worked in a department that used futures to hedge its portfolios. One day a broker invited him on a tour of Liffe. They met by the Royal Exchange's towering stone columns at 1:25 p.m., five minutes before a big economic announcement was due to be made.

"Even now, thinking about it, the hairs on the back of my neck stand up," Rossi recalls. "You walk in there and the first thing that hits you is the electricity. And then the noise. Everyone is shouting at each other. All arms and hands in the air, people trying to get people's attention, girls in booths screaming. It was like going from total silence straight into Wembley Arena for the FA Cup final. I instantly knew I wanted to be there."

Inside, business was organized around a dozen or so crammed, sweaty, lightly sloping pits where the buying and selling took place. For eight frantic hours a day, traders carried out a relentless stream of orders relayed to them in hand signals from booths running around the edges of the room. Then, when the market closed, the place would empty out and the pubs would fill up. Liffe's ecosystem was made up of three broad species: brokers from firms like JPMorgan and Goldman Sachs, who wore multicolored jackets and acted as intermediaries, executing orders that came in by phone from customers including global corporations and pension funds; runners, who sported yellow and ferried around messages while trying to avoid projectiles and abuse; and, at the top of the food chain, the red-jacketed "locals," speculators who carved out a profit buying and selling for their own accounts. They had a reputation for being ruthless, but in always standing ready to take one side of a trade or the other, they provided that essential quality to any market known as "liquidity."

Rossi quit his job and took a pay cut to take up as a runner with David Morgan Futures. Within two years he was trading and by the age of twenty-six he was a local, buying and selling German government bond futures in the "bund" pit, the biggest and most aggressive of them all. Before long he started his own firm, backing a new generation. Recognizing the stars of the future wasn't easy. The atmosphere could be confrontational—

according to myth, a Chicago trader was once left sprawled on the floor after having a heart attack while business carried on around him—and owners often hired beefy individuals or former athletes who could hold their own in a crowd. But some of the most successful, like Rossi, were soft-spoken and physically unimposing. A grasp of economic theory was less important than mental acuity, decisiveness, stamina, a thick skin, and the power to influence others. It helped, too, to have a healthy disregard for the value of money.

Rossi's approach was to trade constantly in an effort to pick up information and build a holistic picture. "Sometimes you don't have a view, but if you take a position, even it's just one lot [a 'lot' is a single contract], you can learn something. Don't just stand there. Buy or sell it, how does it feel? You'd be amazed how many times you buy a one-lot and think, 'I hope it goes up,' and then you see it's never going up and you end up selling ten lots. So that one lot helped you make a decision and you go from there."

Relationships were crucial. Brokers with big orders to fill went to preferred traders first, and some eagle-eyed participants sought to jump ahead of incoming orders—an illegal but inescapable practice known as "front-running." The ultimate goal, though, was to become so big you could bully the market simply by taking a position and watching the minnows line up behind you on the assumption that you knew something they didn't. The risk of ruin was ever-present, but the rewards for those who reached the highest echelons were great. "I remember when I made my first million," says Rossi. "I was twenty-six and I said to one of my mates: 'The next hundred grand I make I'm treating myself,' and I did. I bought a Ferrari."

The next decade was all fast cars and fast living for Rossi and the other traders, who were christened "Maggie's Boys" owing to their affiliation with Thatcher. The press called them yuppies, but in another life many of them would have been plasterers or carpet fitters. For a while, they seemed invincible. In 1997, a statue was erected outside Liffe's new premises immortalizing the futures trader in all his pomp: a man (even in 2018, only an estimated one in eight traders were women), mobile phone in one hand, tie loosened, the hint of a smirk on his lips. Today it sits in a museum, a fitting metaphor for the pit trader's fate.

Most historians of financial markets agree that the first time a security was bought using a computer was December 1969. However, New York technology company Instinet's primitive share-dealing system was so far ahead of its time it would struggle to gain traction for the next two decades. Computers could line up buyers and sellers more quickly and cheaply than men in bright jackets, but they were also susceptible to malfunctioning and were less adaptable to the kind of freak occurrences that markets tended to throw up. With so much money at stake, entrusting multimillion-dollar orders to a machine wasn't worth the risk—at least not according to the vested interests at the banks and brokerage firms that were happy with the status quo.

It took the crash of October 19, 1987, to force a shift. On what came to be known as Black Monday, the Dow Jones Industrial Average dropped 23 percent, wiping a trillion dollars off the wealth of ordinary Americans. The postmortem revealed that many brokers, desperate to contain their losses, had stopped answering their phones when clients called. The industry's reputation took another battering a couple of years later when the FBI indicted forty-six brokers and traders from the Chicago futures exchanges for fraud and front-running. The trusty market makers had floundered, and before the decade was out new systems proliferated allowing dealers to transact with each other electronically. For a long time, "open outcry," with its runners and hand signals, existed concurrently with electronic systems. In the end, though, the spread of home computing and the Internet brought the plucky pit trader to his knees, eradicating the need for buyers and sellers to gather under one roof and opening markets to a new breed of stay-at-home investor. At Liffe, the end came slowly and then all at once.

The first shot of what came to be known as the "Battle of the Bund" was fired in 1990 when Frankfurt-based Deutsche Terminbörse launched an electronic trading platform for futures. At first, Liffe ignored the threat. Then, when volumes started sliding, it dug in, extolling the virtues of open outcry and overhauling its fee structure. But when DTB announced it would let traders use its platform for free, there was an exodus. Liffe's share of the all-important bund market went from 70 percent in 1996 to 40 percent a year later to less than 10 percent a year after that. Every morning fewer and fewer traders showed up until finally, in August 1998, the bund pit was closed for good. Other markets quickly followed.

Rossi tried to offer a home to some of the diaspora, but few successfully made the transition, and an army of former pit employees found themselves displaced. Buying and selling futures on a screen should theoretically have been no different from doing it face-to-face. In reality, they were completely different jobs with different skill sets. For one thing, trading online was anonymous, which eradicated the importance of social dynamics and democratized the playing field. Brute force was no longer an asset when nobody could tell who they were dealing with. And the speed of transacting rocketed, rewarding fast reaction times and nimble fingers. Rossi cut his old stable loose, took a year off, and then started again.

NAV AND the rest of IDT's new recruits gathered in Weybridge for the first time in May 2003. Combined with the first intake, there were around a dozen traders on the roster. Looking around the room, it was clear they were a diverse and well-educated bunch, albeit entirely male. There was Vikash Rughani, a plummy-voiced cricket fanatic with a master's from Henley Business School; Shiraz Hussain, a quiet, industrious type; Chris Morris, a tall, well-mannered Brit who probably should have been working at a high-end bank in the City; Petros Josephides, a grinning, barrel-chested Cypriot with a booming voice; and IDT's golden boy, Bradley Young, a gregarious Aussie who could walk into a bar knowing no one and leave with a girl on his arm and ten new best mates for life.

"Nav was from a very different background to the rest of us," recalls one of the recruits. "We were all middle-class, educated, pretty international, and then there's this kid from a very working-class background. He wasn't professional. He couldn't hold a conversation and come off like a normal person. When he spoke he made these weird comments. We used to call him 'The Chav.'"

For eight weeks, Nav's group was taken through the theoretical underpinnings of trading in IDT's pokey classroom. A former Liffe trader led classes on economics, markets, financial products, and risk management, and set homework assignments reading classic texts like *Market Wizards, Reminiscences of a Stock Operator,* and *Steidlmayer on Markets.* Goldberg gruffly explained the nuts and bolts of placing and canceling trades using the trading software. Paolo regaled the group with war stories. They learned how to read charts and gauge market profile, and discussed the importance of psychology by examining the crowd effect, the history of various market crashes, and seventeenth-century Holland's tulip mania. During the training period, the rookies were paid £500 (around $800 at the time) a month, a large chunk of which was taken up just making their way to the hinterland of Weybridge. To make ends meet, they waited for sandwiches to be discounted in the Waitrose downstairs and ate them in the vacant office next door. Still mostly in their early twenties, the recruits had few responsibilities outside IDT, and they became close quickly. "It was like the army," says one member of the group. "We were all in it together with no money and these big dreams." But while Nav would joke around in class, he split off from the rest of the group at the end of the day when they went to the pub to unwind.

After a couple of months, the new intake was let loose on a simulator, buying and selling futures at live prices. Each morning they were given a new challenge: one day they could place only one trade; the next they were given unlimited transactions; sometimes they traded futures tied to stock indices; other times, they practiced on the bund. It was amazing how easy it was to make money when they had no skin in the game, and before long they were desperate to test their skills with real cash. Only Nav seemed content to keep watching the market and its eternal possibilities.

In his group, Josephides showed the best results on the demo and was the first to be unleashed with real money. With a big smile plastered across his face, he began taking positions using the interface. But this time, unlike over the past few weeks, every time he placed a trade the market seemed to move against him. His classmates watched as Josephides's account fell below zero, then sunk lower and lower. By 4:30 p.m., when the market closed, he was in the hole for £2,000—money he would have to pay back to IDT before he could realize any profits. It was a painful lesson in hubris, and one they would all learn many times over.

■

CHAPTER 2

THE BOY PLUNGER

Everyone knew not to disturb Nav when he was trading. For eight hours a day he sat at a lone desk at the far end of the trading floor, his face inches from his screens, in what appeared to be a catatonic state. To block out the world, he wore a pair of red, heavy-duty ear defenders of the type favored by road workers. He didn't communicate with anyone. Only his fingers moved. Nothing existed beyond him and the market.

Professor Mihaly Csikszentmihalyi from the University of Chicago coined the term "flow" for the kind of transcendental experience that takes hold when an individual is completely immersed in a task. It arises when we use skill to tackle something challenging, like chess or yoga, and is characterized by a sense of deep concentration, mastery, and contentment. Time distorts, hunger and tiredness dissipate, and any sense of the self dissolves into the ether. For a few blessed moments we forget who we are and simply react. Performance coaches strive to cultivate flow, but for some—those Csikszentmihalyi describes as "autotelic personalities"—it comes naturally and isn't tied to any yearning for money, status, or validation. The doing is its own reward.

Before Nav joined IDT, he found he was able to play computer games for longer and with greater concentration than other people. He would wager hundreds of pounds a match on FIFA online, beating players in the top one hundred globally. That single-mindedness had some drawbacks. Nav was absentminded to the point of hazardousness. He regularly fell off the small, 125cc motorcycle he'd bought to drive to work, and was known to sit down and start trading with his helmet still on his head. But when it came to trading futures, Nav's hyperfocus was a gift.

Three years into his time at IDT, the distractions had increased. In 2005, after outgrowing its Weybridge digs, the firm had relocated to Woking, a less salubrious commuter town a few miles to the northwest. Paolo and Marco changed the company's name to Futex and rented an entire floor of the Cornerstone, a hulking 1980s concrete-and-brick box on the same block as a public toilet and a boarded-up pub called the Rat & Parrot. They ramped up hiring, taking on two classes of ten people a year, and lowered the entry requirements for new recruits. The training program was also condensed. Within a couple of years there were forty or so traders of wildly varying abilities and backgrounds panning for gold and racking up commissions from first thing in the morning until late at night.

The office had a reception area, a breakout room, a kitchen, and a classroom with a poster of Muhammad Ali. Paolo and Marco had their own offices. Everyone else sat on the trading floor, which was made up of a dozen or so rows of desks, divided down the middle by a walkway whose principal feature was a slightly sad-looking houseplant. The atmosphere ebbed and flowed with movements in the markets and news relayed through loudspeakers known as squawk boxes. It grew particularly febrile ahead of key economic announcements, such as employment figures, when Goldberg patrolled the floor shushing the trainees like an angry librarian. When the figure hit, the room exploded. The most experienced traders set the tone. Young, who by now wore flip-flops and board shorts to the office, had a habit of barking strings of Aussie-tinged expletives when things weren't going his way. "I've done my fucking arse!" was a particular favorite. One trader was evicted after punching a wall.

Nav found all this negativity and posturing counterproductive. "You'd hear people say stuff like 'I don't want to be trading,'" he later told a friend. "Those things make you demoralized. If you don't stop them going in then they'll have an effect on you." Nav believed his emotional state was critical to his success, and he guarded it fiercely. "You've got to make your mind strong," he explained. "A lot of people subconsciously take out their self-loathing in the markets. Make your self-esteem high. Make yourself feel like you're deserving of the money!" Nav's solution was to extricate himself entirely, taking a desk by the toilets at the far end of the floor, three rows from anyone else.

At Futex, the number of screens you had was a mark of honor. It was common for traders to have eight or ten, crammed with charts, news reports, and flashing prices, as though they were guiding a spaceship. The thinking was that, by having a comprehensive view of the world, you would be able to make better decisions. Plus, it looked cool. As with so much else, Nav took the opposite approach. He stripped back his setup to just two screens, enough to fit the limited tools he needed to make money.

By now Nav predominantly traded the S&P 500 "e-mini," a futures contract that tracks the Standard & Poor's 500, the bellwether index comprising five hundred or so of the largest companies on the New York Stock Exchange and NASDAQ. As the share prices of U.S. businesses rise and fall, so does the S&P 500, distilling the fortunes of corporate America into a single figure. To coincide with U.S. opening hours, Nav arrived at the office just before 2 p.m., when most people were returning from their lunch break, and logged off after 9 p.m., when it had cleared out. More than $200 billion of e-minis are bought and sold on the Chicago Mercantile Exchange's (CME) electronic platform every day, and trading volumes in the contract far exceed the amount of buying and selling that goes on in the underlying stocks. It is among the most liquid markets in the world, used by banks, companies, hedge funds, and asset managers to speculate on the prospects of the U.S. economy or hedge other investments.

Nav, like most traders at Futex, had very little interest in the outlook for corporate America, per se. He'd never visited the country, and he preferred reading soccer websites to the *Wall Street Journal*. He wasn't an investor like Warren Buffett, seeking out undervalued companies by scouring financial reports and sales figures; and he wasn't an economics expert, hypothesizing over what the complex interplay of geopolitical events and interest rates might mean for the markets. His horizons were much shorter. Nav was what's commonly referred to as a "scalper," a trader who hops in and out of the market throughout the day, notching up small wins and positioning himself to clean up should there be a big swing one way or the other. At the end of almost every session, he made sure he had no outstanding positions— that he was "flat," in the idiom of the trader. The next day he started afresh.

The value of a single e-mini contract—the minimum one can wager—is calculated by taking the current value of the S&P 500 and multiplying it by $50. In mid-2007, when the S&P 500 was trading at around 1,500, a single contract, or "lot," was worth $75,000. The market moves in increments of 0.25, known as "ticks," and, regardless of the current price, every 0.25 move is worth $12.50 per contract (0.25 x $50). So if a trader buys 100 lots at 1,500 (at a cost of $7.5 million), waits for the price to notch up a tick, and then sells, she will walk away with $1,250. Of course, not everyone has $7.5 million sitting around, which is where brokers come in. Brokers act as an intermediary between a trader and the exchange. Even in extremely volatile conditions, the S&P moves around by only a few percent in a day, so rather than requiring their customers to put down the total size of their position, they ask for a smaller sum, known as "margin," which is calculated to cover any potential losses. Even so, losses can quickly mount up. As a result, futures markets are almost exclusively inhabited by professionals.

At any moment on any financial exchange there are two live

prices: the current selling price, known as the "best offer," which is the minimum anyone is willing to accept; and the current price to buy, known as the "best bid," which is the most anyone is willing to pay. The difference between the two is known as the "bid-ask spread," and in the S&P 500 e-mini, where the volume of trading is huge, it is rarely bigger than a tick for long.

To buy an e-mini on the CME's electronic exchange, Globex, a trader must place an order, of which there are two main types. If she's willing to trade at the current "best offer"—let's say it's 1,500.00—she'll submit what's known as a "market order," and the transaction will happen immediately. However, if she wants to pay less, she can place a lower bid, at 1,499.00, say, and hope that the market comes down four ticks. This is referred to as a "limit order." It can be canceled at any time. Once the trader's buy order of either type is executed, she is described as being "long." To exit the trade, she simply sells the same quantity of e-minis, hopefully for more than she paid, after which she'll be "flat" again. A trader can also "short" the market, or bet that the price will go down, by carrying out the process in reverse, selling some e-minis and then buying them back. (In trading, it's possible to sell something you don't actually own as long as you make good on it.)

The single most important thing on Nav's screens was a display called the ladder, which shows trades occurring and orders entering and leaving the market in real time. Also known as the central limit order book, it looks like an Excel spreadsheet with three columns whose contents are constantly shifting. The central column contains twenty price levels, ordered from high to low. They range from nine ticks above to nine ticks below the current "best offer" and "best bid." Next to each level is a figure showing the number of orders waiting "in the queue" to trade at that level. Taken as a whole, the ladder provides an indispensable window into a market's supply and demand at any given moment.

Adjacent to the ladder on Nav's screens was a simple price chart that plotted the e-mini's rise and fall, which he used to gauge the overall mood of the market and find patterns that might repeat themselves. "It's a graphical image of people's fear and greed," he

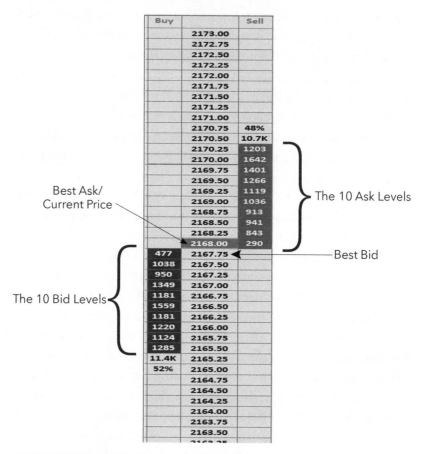

The ladder shows trades in real time as they're entering and leaving the market, offering an invaluable window into a market's supply and demand. In this case, traders have placed orders to buy a total of 477 contracts at 2167.75.

explained to a trader who asked him why he monitored it so closely. "That's what you're trading, people's fear and greed. And they repeat themselves again and again. If it's an individual, some may have more greed, some fear. As a collective, everything rounds off to something you can measure."

To some, staring at numbers and charts on a screen all day might sound dull, but for those who put in the time to understand its mysteries, the ladder can become highly addictive—a vast, confounding, ever-changing, zero-sum game played against some of the sharpest minds in the world for potentially limitless rewards. Every win releases a dopamine rush. Every loss is a blow. Adrenaline and cortisol course through the veins. In the words of Paolo Rossi, "When you're trading, you're alive."

Scalpers analyze the ladder for clues as to whether prices will rise or fall. To take the most basic example, if the total number of resting offers significantly outweighs the number of bids, supply would seem to outstrip demand and it might be reasonable to conclude the price will go down. However, there are myriad other factors to consider, including the speed with which prices are moving and the proximity of the resting orders to the best bid or offer. There's also the question of who placed the orders and why. An international pension fund buying up e-minis incrementally over several hours as part of a billion-dollar transaction, for example, is likely to have a much more significant impact on prices than a bunch of speculative scalpers who are constantly placing and canceling orders to earn the odd tick. Since all trading on the CME is anonymous, it's impossible to know for sure, but good traders are able to build a sense of who they're up against and react accordingly.

To confuse matters, the bids and offers in the order book don't necessarily reflect buyers' and sellers' true intentions. Rather than entering one huge bid and tipping the world that it's in the market for e-minis, the aforementioned pension fund would likely break up its order into small chunks, perhaps using a feature available on the CME called an "iceberg." Another trader might try to create as much noise as possible, entering more bids into the ladder than he really wants filled, with the goal of enticing opportunistic traders to join him and push the price higher. Like the red-jacketed locals in the pits, he is seeking to use his perceived bulk to boss the market around. This perpetual gamesmanship helps explain why nine in every ten orders placed in the futures markets were canceled before they could be filled.

In the same way poker players try to deduce their opponents' hands from their betting patterns or the twitch above their left eye, traders will use pattern recognition and statistical analysis to fill in some of the gaps in their knowledge. Fifty offers keep appearing on the sell side of the market exactly ten minutes apart? Maybe it's an algorithm that can be exploited. Someone keeps placing bids of 139 lots? Perhaps it's a complacent day trader who hasn't bothered to mix up his order size. With hundreds of market participants active at any time, the permutations are endless. Like a jazz musician who's learned his scales and is now free to improvise, Nav was able to subconsciously evaluate the ladder and perform complex calculations in real time. *The last twelve times I saw the price move this way, this other thing happened 85 percent of the time. I'll buy.* The lightning-speed mental arithmetic that had amazed the Rossis during his interview kicked in, and with his left hand hovering over his keyboard and his right hand on the mouse, he bought and sold futures at an astounding rate. "I know it sounds ridiculous, but he was like one of the robots in *West World* or Neo from *The Matrix* or something," recalls Leif Cid, who spent time at Futex in 2007 and 2008. "He didn't just observe the market. He was *inside* it."

Four years after joining Futex as a novice, Nav had built up a bankroll of $400,000 and acquired something of an aura around the trading floor, where most didn't survive a year. On a good day he would make $20,000 or $25,000 before casually yanking off his ear defenders, putting on his helmet, and driving his wobbly motorbike back to Hounslow. New recruits were told to watch out for the quiet guy with the beaten-up brown leather jacket who arrived at 2 p.m. each afternoon to trade the U.S. market from the back of the room. They crowded around the risk manager's computer to rubberneck at the size of his positions. While they were flailing around with one and two lots, Nav routinely staked hundred-lot orders, representing more than $7 million of his broker's funds. At that level, his account rose and fell by $1,250 each time the e-mini moved a single tick. Every few hours, Nav stood up and bounded over to the kitchen, where he filled a jug with milk and drank it straight from the lip like a ravenous animal. His colleague Cid and his luckless friends would follow him in and ask what he thought about the markets that day. Nav tried his best to impart some wisdom, but much of what made him special couldn't be taught. Cid hung around anyway, "as if by osmosis it would rub off on me."

Some of Nav's decision making was perplexing to the other traders. One of the first lessons they'd been taught about placing a trade of any size was: always use a stop-loss. A stop-loss is a standing instruction to automatically buy or sell once the market reaches a certain threshold. A trader buying e-minis because he thinks the S&P 500 will rise, for instance, might place a stop-loss at twenty ticks below what he paid to limit his potential downside. It is widely considered an essential tool to avoid catastrophic losses—a safety net to ensure that, should the bottom fall out, you won't plummet to your doom. Nav shunned them, saying he preferred to "let it breathe." That philosophy, while highly risky, meant that trades veering into losing territory had the opportunity to reverse course. If Nav had a high degree of conviction about a position and he didn't want to be put off by moment-to-moment fluctuations, he would leave his desk and start yanking himself up and down on a pull-up bar he'd fitted in one of the doorways. Other times he could be found lying on the sofas by reception playing the soccer management game *Championship Manager* on his phone. "You'd go over and say, 'What the fuck are you doing? The market is going crazy.' And he'd say, 'It's my time analysis,' " recalls Josephides. "Nobody knew what the hell 'time analysis' was, and it became this running joke: Nav's doing his 'time analysis' again."

From the start, Nav pushed for more capital to trade with. Whenever he hit a new milestone, he would stride down the walkway to Marco's office, close the door, and demand higher risk limits. For the Rossis, it was something of a bind. On the one hand, Nav was one of a handful of golden geese. The money he generated through the profit-split arrangement was enough to fund a dozen new recruits. On the other, they didn't want to give Nav enough rope to be able to bring down the entire firm. Usually they found a compromise, but not before Nav told Marco what he thought of him loudly enough for half the trading floor to hear.

The lack of stop-losses, the huge positions, the "time analysis"—they were all symptomatic of another element of Nav's makeup that elevated him above the crowd: a near-total imperviousness to risk. His attitude didn't change if he had taken a position of one lot or one hundred. If a trade was right, he reasoned, it was right, so there was no point in holding back. "If you don't care about the money it's a lot easier," he later told a friend. "Look at it like a computer game; you're playing to win but it's a bonus if you get paid. If it wasn't fun I'd have stopped doing it." There were days Nav lost tens of thousands of dollars and nobody on the floor had any idea. Traders who lost a fraction of the sums he did would curse their luck, berate the irrational morons in the market, and tell sob stories for days. Some shut down their computers, ashen-faced, and never traded again. But Nav's demeanor barely changed. It was as if the caveman part of his brain, that primal instinct to guard what he'd gathered at all costs, was missing, freeing him up to put it all on the line again and again. "The way I see it is, I haven't lost an arm or lost a leg," he rationalized. "You're never getting them back. Then I'll be crying. But I know I can make the money back tomorrow, or if not tomorrow, I can get in my head for two or three months and make it back. Why worry about losses? Everyone loses, bruv. You've just got to deal with it."

Nav's swashbuckling exploits in the market stood out because they were so at odds with the way he lived his life. He barely withdrew anything from his trading account to live on, preferring to let it accumulate like a high score. He'd long ago ditched his ill-fitting work attire in favor of tracksuit pants and cheap sweaters that he wore for days on end. For lunch, or, more accurately, dinner, he ate supermarket sandwiches or a Filet-O-Fish from McDonald's. He barely drank, didn't smoke, had no love life to speak of, and when the rest of the office decamped to O'Neill's pub every Friday, he stayed behind to continue trading. One Christmas, Futex took the team to a well-known nightspot in central London. Nav was refused entry because, despite repeated reminders to dress up, he arrived in his trademark yellow Fila-branded sweatshirt and sneakers. Eventually, he snuck in and spent the rest of the night hiding from the doormen. For old-school traders like Paolo, who proudly displayed their success, it was bewildering. What was the point of making all that money if you were never going to spend it?

The closest thing to a bible for traders is *Reminiscences of a Stock Operator* by Edwin Lefèvre. Published in 1923, it recounts the early life and wisdom of Jesse Livermore, a trading guru who went from watching prices on a bucket shop ticker tape at fourteen to making and losing a fortune many times over. At Futex, wet-behind-the-ears graduates and grizzled veterans alike mined well-thumbed copies for insights. It was said that Livermore, who was given the nickname the "Boy Plunger" for his habit of profiting from financial crashes, could "read the tape"—that is, he could look at price movements in a security or future and accurately predict where it was heading based on his careful study of past behavior. The reason for the move was almost incidental, he maintained. What mattered was that it would move and which way. "There is nothing new in Wall Street," wrote Lefèvre, channeling Livermore in a famous passage. "There can't be because speculation is as old as the hills. Whatever happens in the stock market today has happened before and will happen again. I've never forgotten that. I suppose I really manage to remember when and how it happened. The fact that I remember that way is my way of capitalizing experience."

Sarao may not have reached the same heights as Livermore, and his lifestyle was certainly more abstemious than the freewheeling, three-times-married American playboy, but, years later, his peers at Futex would point out some striking parallels. Both started out with nothing on the fringes of finance and had photographic memories; both could divorce emotion from their decisions and were willing to risk ruin for a shot at glory; both prided themselves on the conviction of their calls and hated discussing trading with anyone else lest their instincts be contaminated. They would both also end up inextricably linked to market crashes. Livermore, who earned $100 million shorting stocks in 1929—the equivalent of more than $1 billion today—ended up squandering it all and shooting himself in the head in the cloakroom of the Sherry Netherland Hotel in Manhattan in 1940. For those paying attention, Livermore's life is a cautionary tale about the dangers of blind obsession and the perils of tying your destiny too tightly to the whims of the market. The traders at Futex only ever talked about his legendary skills.

∎

CHAPTER 3

THAT'S A FUGAZI

A few weeks before Nav joined Futex, a post titled "Elliot and Gann analysis exposed" appeared on a popular day-trading forum. Its author was a newcomer to the boards who called himself "That's a Fugazi" and used a picture of the Joker as his avatar.* On the brief bio attached to his profile, he described his trading style as "WINNING—period. Losses do occur, but only as often as the soccer World Cup." Under "list of markets traded," he wrote: "I'd trade fruit and veg as long as it made wonga." The signature that ran along the bottom of his posts read: "OH SHEEP COME JOIN THY SHEPHERD IN THE LAND OF THE RICH AND BEAUTIFUL!"

When Nav created his online alter ego, he was a newcomer to trading, twenty-four years old and still buying and selling individual stocks rather than the index futures that would make him rich. His idiosyncratic way of seeing the world and preternatural confidence, though, were evident from the start. Indeed, his opening gambit on the site was a repudiation of two of the godfathers of trading theory. Ralph Nelson Elliott was a Kansas-born

---

* Nav's forum username has been changed.

accountant who, in 1938, published a book called *The Wave Principle* that posited that markets move in discernible and therefore predictable wave formations based on the ebb and flow of crowd sentiment from optimism to pessimism. According to Elliott, while markets might appear to be random, they are in fact governed by recurring patterns grounded, like much in nature, on the Fibonacci sequence. Sarao was unconvinced: "I am well versed in Elliott waves—indeed I have the E-wave bible and have made some astounding predictions based on it. Yet I soon realised, after throwing away my rose-tinted glasses, that 70% of the time a chart can fit numerable e-wave patterns of [sic] no pattern at all. Which means one is up the proverbial creek if one is limited to that technique."

Writing around the same time as Elliott was William Gann, a Bible-toting son of a Texas cotton farmer who sought to apply principles gleaned from geometry, astronomy, and astrology to forecast cycles in commodities markets. Nav gave Gann even shorter shrift: "Well let me tell you all that literally a 12-year old kid could use this method, it's a simple method of algebra, an intellectual mind like mine does not even require a calculator for this one . . . I challenge anyone here to name a way Gann has helped them make money."

Nav wasn't the first person to question the principles of technical analysis, a school of trading that uses charts and statistics rather than economic fundamentals to try to predict the direction of prices. Elliott and Gann had both been dead for half a century, and their respective methods had been so widely pulled apart they had reached the status of sacred cows in some quarters. But his blunt assuredness was striking for someone who had barely formally studied finance and whose trading experience was confined to buying and selling a few stocks. It was akin to an economics freshman discounting the work of John Maynard Keynes or an unpublished writer ripping into Charles Dickens. One of Nav's objections, beyond his contention that Elliott's and Gann's methods didn't work, was the idea that the universe and everyone in it were governed by some overarching natural law. "Which means that in essence EVERYTHING HAS BEEN WRITTEN BEFOREHAND," he wrote. "You need to believe EVERY- THING [sic] LITTLE THING IS DESTINED. That we are mere robots without any free will or choice." Nav prided himself on being a freethinker who formulated his own views about the world based on the abiding principle "Do Your Own Research," or DYOR. "I wish I could tell you, (the sheep) the way to unlock yourselves from following the herd," he wrote in a follow-up post. "[M]ost of you are doing it without even knowing it, we are all programmed form [sic] birth to follow society in fashion, values etc etc and must atune our minds to think independently."

That's a Fugazi's critique proved predictably contentious. Some of the forum's members jumped to Elliott and Gann's defense. Others mocked Sarao's unpolished delivery. "Please accept my sympathy by the way, as it sounds like your bedsit floor must have collapsed," wrote one. "I'll have a pint of whatever Mr. Fugazi is drinking," wrote another. Nav failed to see the funny side and accused them of lacking the intellect to understand what he was saying. "SHEEP ARE HOSTILE WHEN ENCOUNTERING BRILLIANCE," he wrote. The exchange set the tone for Nav's activity on the forum over the next few months. Under the guise of talking about trading he would abuse his fellow posters and make outlandish claims about his own talents. He posted a poll titled "Can Fugazi tell the future??" with options that included "Maybe, but it's kinda scary to face up to what he predicts" and "No more need for crystal balls, he knows it all." He also claimed to run a seminar on "trading and LIFE," but when pressed about how to sign up, he declined to provide any details.

At first, the other forum members found That's a Fugazi's posts, with titles like "Proof of pure unadulterated genius," amusing. They were full of references to "mugs," "moola," and "tings," which earned him the nickname "The Sage of Peckham," a working-class neighborhood in London. One poster asked if he was Ali G. But by the summer the entries had started to take on a darker hue. With the Iraq War raging and 9/11 fresh in the mem- ory, Nav claimed he could foresee terrorist attacks thanks to his

unparalleled ability to read financial markets, "the most powerful predictive tool in the world." When fellow posters complained
he was being insensitive, he wrote: "Unlike the majority, I prefer
to face the truth no matter how horrible it is, and until civil war
breaks out in the UK and elsewhere as it will in the next 15yrs, the
future will be a scary and horrible one."

By now Nav had been at Futex for a few months, and a clear
chasm existed between his larger-than-life online persona and
the enigmatic young man who made his way to Weybridge each
day to learn to trade futures in the real world. At work, Sarao
was hardworking and quiet; not exactly lacking in confidence but
somewhat awkward and preoccupied. Then, each evening, when
his fellow recruits headed off to the pub, he returned to Hounslow and unchained the increasingly megalomaniacal Fugazi once
more. "Hello all, I know you missed me but you won't admit it,"
he wrote one day that summer, before assessing the statistical
likelihood of a biological or nuclear terrorist attack (80 percent)
and the assassination of George W. Bush (20 percent).

"I am going to be accused by many a sheep of being part of
Al-Qaeda," he went on. "This is the typical retort when one is
stuck of ideas. First let me expalin [sic] to you that I am not Mus-
lim, so that kinda rules me out I guess. It's funny, the hypocrisy
that lives in this world. I mean I'll get dirty looks in the street for
being brown skinned, yet there have been more white caucasian
people convicted of Al-Qaeda attacks than of my community."

Eventually, That's a Fugazi overstepped the mark. The
forum's administrators warned him about trolling and his fellow
posters turned against him, blocking him from their feeds. "Anyone who seeks to gain by boasting of 'predicting' terrorist attacks
is beneath contempt," wrote one. Nav denied he was seeking to
gain anything and suggested his critics had been "brainwashed by
mass media." Later that day he wrote: "apologies for the harsh
tone. BUT THE SOLE REASON THIS WORLD IS IN THE
STATE IT IS, IS BECAUSE NONE OF YOU CAN BE BOTH-
ERED TO FIND OUT ABOUT THE WORLD YOU LIVE
IN." For a couple of months, Fugazi disappeared from the boards

before returning with a new thread about how he'd switched from trading individual stocks to index futures like the e-mini. "As you can guess I'm doing rather well," he wrote. But where the early posts had garnered dozens of responses, this time nobody bothered to reply. Amid the silence he pleaded: "Come back to your master oh herd, thou art nothing without Him."

CHAPTER 4

THE TRADE I

After years of patiently building up his account, Nav pulled off a trade at the start of 2008 that would catapult him into the big time and go down in history at Futex. The global financial crisis, which had started to make its presence felt the previous spring, was gathering pace. Markets lurched around on news of the precarious state of the economy and the measures governments and central banks were taking to shore up the system. Where the S&P 500 might previously have moved forty or fifty ticks in a day, it was now not uncommon for the index to jump around in a range of 5 percent, more than five times as much. The turmoil may have been disastrous for the wider economy, but it was a boon for traders like Nav who thrived on the action. Sentiment had swung firmly from exuberance to panic, and there was easy money to be made. Every time a bank reported big losses or a hedge fund announced it was folding, the market reliably tanked. Quick-fingered scalpers had only to wait for news to come out of the squawk box, ride the downturn, and get out a few moments later before the rest of the world caught up. Order books were full of forced sellers who had no choice but to offload assets to raise cash or hedge their mutating portfolios. There was always a heightened risk of disaster in such volatile markets, but life was generally sweet for Paolo's squadron of day traders.

Late one afternoon in early January, Nav was at his desk at the Cornerstone when he noticed something odd in the DAX, an index that tracks Germany's thirty biggest companies. Despite the swirling negativity, there was a glut of buy orders waiting in the order book; and whenever the bids were hit, Nav observed, they quickly replenished. The result was that, over the course of the evening, while most U.S. and European markets remained depressed, the German index actually crept higher. Somebody out there appeared to have an insatiable appetite for DAX futures in the face of strong signals that prices should be going down. Nav stood up and went to speak to Brad Young.

"It's the Chinese, I fucking know it," Young barked when Nav asked him what he made of the mysterious buying. Residing as they did on the fringes of the financial firmament, traders at Futex were inclined to indulge in conspiracy theories about sinister forces controlling the markets. If it wasn't the Chinese, it was the Plunge Protection Team or Goldman Sachs or the Bilderberg Group. Young's theory this particular evening was that the People's Republic of China had become so rattled by the turbulence in the U.S. financial system it had decided to shift some of its vast resources into Europe. It wasn't completely outlandish. China regularly intervened in the foreign exchange markets to stabilize its own currency. Plus, whoever was buying up the DAX had significant firepower. For long periods there were hundreds of millions of dollars' worth of bids sitting in the order book.

Nav rarely discussed his trading strategies with other people. Partly that was due to fear that he would be pushed off his game, but he had also developed a finely honed bullshit detector. He'd long since decided that the trainers who came and went at Futex were full of crap. If they really knew what they were talking about, why were they wasting their time on a bunch of noobs? Even Paolo, legend of Liffe and the firm's founder, received a roll of the eyes when he tried to offer Nav any words of wisdom. But to Nav, Young was different. He didn't just talk a good game.

He backed it up, risking tens of thousands of dollars when he felt good about a trade. And unlike Nav, he was a DAX specialist.

Young grew up catching waves in a surf spot one hundred miles north of Sydney. After spinning up a bankroll buying and selling equities in between classes, he had moved to London to do some traveling and try his hand at trading futures. Outwardly laid-back, he had a fiercely competitive edge and a burning obsession with the markets that rivaled Nav's. Back at Weybridge, their relationship had gotten off to a rocky start. Fed up with the state of the kitchen one day, Young had spent hours cleaning up, only for Nav to put a fish pie in the microwave without a lid. When the pie exploded, spraying the kitchen in gunk and leaving the cramped office stinking of fish, Young lost his temper and started shouting at Nav, who hurled obscenities back. After a tense few seconds, they both cracked up laughing. Since then a friendly rivalry had built up between Futex's two stars. Still, while Nav had some cachet around the floor, Young was the one the rookie traders really wanted to be like, showing up to work dressed like he was going to the beach and going on exotic holidays every few months. If the team went to the pub early on a Friday, Young left his credit card behind the bar, asking only that they return the favor one day when they had some success of their own. Once, after a particularly profitable week, he ferried them all to a swanky bar in Kensington for a night out. Young was the living embodiment of why many of them got into day trading in the first place: a charismatic, happy-go-lucky master of his own destiny who made a shedload of money without answering to the man.

Nav and Young agreed to keep watching the DAX and went home for the night. The following morning they saw that the index had opened 90 points lower, a substantial drop. Whoever was propping up the market had seemingly given up and gone to bed. Over the next few hours, DAX futures continued to tumble in line with markets around the world, but by late afternoon the wall of bids had reappeared and prices started to edge up again. It was surreal. During the regular trading day for stocks, from

9:00 a.m. to 5:30 p.m. Central European Time, German futures followed the global downward trend. Then, when the country's stock market closed and volumes thinned out, DAX futures, which keep trading until 10 p.m. CET, began edging higher, like a salmon swimming against the stream. It wasn't clear who was behind the phenomenon or why. As Jesse Livermore had noted back in 1923, it didn't really matter. The important thing was that there was a trend that could potentially be exploited.

That night, before heading home, Young and Nav devised an experiment. Both of them would sell a few DAX contracts and see what happened. If the market took a tumble, as it had the previous night, they would buy back the same number of contracts the next morning, closing out their position for a profit. If it didn't, they would take the hit and move on with their lives. Generally speaking, it was frowned upon at Futex to leave a position open overnight because you couldn't react quickly if the market moved against you. They needn't have worried. The following morning the DAX opened 65 points lower, earning them more than $10,000 apiece. By day three, the traders around them had started to take notice. There still hadn't been anything in the press that might explain the move, but the pattern was clear. Half the office followed their suit, hoping to piggyback on the nightly deviation between the German index and markets around the world. Once again, the market rallied before collapsing overnight, this time by 80 points.

Nav and Brad had struck gold. For two weeks, they repeated their overnight trade, placing steadily larger positions before heading home to bed and praying their good fortune would hold. Time and again it did, and by the second week of January, Nav had gone from shorting a handful of contracts to betting two hundred lots a night, a $15 million position that yielded six-figure profits. Young made a decent return but couldn't resist the urge to keep trading the DAX throughout the day, and he ended up giving back a lot of his winnings. Nav, in classic style, just "let it breathe," betting the most he could, then leaving the market alone and going back to scalping the e-mini. The strength of his conviction never faltered, and by the middle of January his account balance had ballooned to more than a million pounds.

ON SATURDAY, January 19, 2008, a thirty-one-year-old French trader named Jérôme Kerviel stood outside Société Générale's imposing headquarters on the outskirts of Paris and texted his boss: "I don't know if I'm going to come back or throw myself under a train." Waiting for him in a conference room inside were the head of the bank's investment banking division and various other executives who had spent the past twenty-four hours frantically scouring Kerviel's trading records after uncovering evidence of what they suspected to be a massive fraud. Over the next several hours, Kerviel confirmed their fears. Starting in 2005, he confessed, he'd been secretly placing unauthorized trades worth hundreds of billions of dollars. Unlike most of the firm's elite traders, Kerviel, the son of a blacksmith and a hairdresser from Breton, had started his career in an administrative function, and it was there that he'd learned how to cover his tracks using a combination of fictitious transactions and forgery. He'd escaped detection because, for the most part, he'd been successful. In 2007 alone, he said, he'd made a profit of around $2 billion by correctly predicting the impact of the impending financial crisis. Bizarrely, he was never able to claim credit for his success, because nobody else knew about it. The story might have ended there, except Kerviel had recently embarked on his most ambitious foray yet.

Between January 2 and January 18, the trader had accumulated a long position of $70 billion, double the market capitalization of the entire bank. As his colleagues left the trading floor each evening, Kerviel had stayed behind manically buying futures tied to the DAX and other indices, convinced that the worst of the crisis was over and that the markets would rebound. But his winning streak had come to an end. Kerviel's wave of after-hours buying only ever propped DAX futures up for a few hours each night. Then, like some horrific Wall Street version of *Groundhog*

Day, he awoke each morning to find gravity had kicked in and the market had sunk back in line with the rest of the world. As Kerviel made his confession, Société Générale's management ordered one of his colleagues to close out his positions. By the time the employee was finished, the bank had lost $7.2 billion. News of the incident rocked global markets and helped push the DAX 12 percent lower in two days, wiping hundreds of billions of dollars off the value of Germany's biggest companies.

Reading about events at Société Générale, the traders at Futex quickly worked out that Kerviel had been the one behind the DAX's strange maneuverings. It wasn't the Chinese after all. One of Europe's biggest banks had been brought to the brink by a lone trader with oversize ambitions and inadequate oversight. Later, Kerviel was sentenced to three years in jail and ordered to pay back the entire $7.2 billion he lost, the biggest fine ever levied on an individual. His desperate buying spree placed him among history's most notorious rogue traders, a name uttered alongside the likes of Nick Leeson of Barings Bank and Kweku Adoboli at UBS. It also gave a young day trader from Hounslow the capital he needed to take his trading to new heights.

CHAPTER 5

■

RISE OF THE ROBOTS

The more money Nav made, the bigger the positions he took, as if he were climbing the levels of the ultimate computer game. In a matter of a few months, he'd gone from placing fifty- and hundred-lot orders to five hundred lots, more than anyone else at the firm. At that size every tick, or 0.25-point move, of the S&P 500 was worth $6,250. Becoming a bigger player had its advantages, but lately the markets had left Nav feeling unsettled. Beginning in around 2007, the ladder had become slippery and harder to read. Orders flashed then disappeared like phantoms, prices moved in unfamiliar ways, and spoofing—the placing of bogus orders with no intention to actually buy or sell—had become rife. Nav's opponents seemed to him to be so adept at predicting his next move that he became convinced they could "see through the ladder" at who they were trading with. This sense of being persecuted coincided with the emergence of a new breed of participant engaged in something called high-frequency trading, or HFT.

HFT involves rapidly buying and selling assets using state-of-the-art technology to profit from extremely short-term price moves. The term is somewhat vague and ill-defined, but it's used by some academics focused on futures to refer to a relatively small number of very active entities that trade large quantities of contracts without ever accumulating a sizable position, and that end each day flat. At the heart of HFT are algorithms, or "algos"— sets of rules instructing computers to react to shifting market conditions with very little human intervention. These can be as simple as "if the price of x moves by y, buy z," and as complicated as anything a roomful of nuclear physicists could come up with. Like human scalpers, HFT practitioners make decisions based on short-run shifts in supply and demand and the relationship between correlated markets, as opposed to any fundamental sense of the value of a share or commodity. But while the quickest-drawing day traders may be able to react to new information in a fifth of a second, the speed of HFT is measured in microseconds—millionths of a second.

The first HFT firms, such as Getco and Jump Trading, were started at the turn of the millennium by former traders from the Chicago pits who, instead of opening arcades and backing human traders as Paolo Rossi had done, hired teams of coders and math PhDs to program computers that could trade autonomously. Before long, they had descended on the markets like a plague of stinkbugs. In 2003, HFT firms barely registered in U.S. futures markets, but by 2008 they were involved in one in five trades and by 2012 as many as 60 percent. For a long time, HFT existed outside the mainstream consciousness. Its practitioners were small, privately owned, lightly regulated (most operated through licensed brokerage firms), and highly secretive. Even Wall Street was behind the curve. It was only during the financial crisis, when the leading HFT players started reporting profits in the nine figures, that people began to sit up and take notice. Articles appeared in the business press with headlines like "Rise of the Algos" and "Robot Wars." Stanford and MIT graduates bypassed Manhattan and Connecticut's hedge fund country and packed their bags for the Windy City. The draw was obvious. In 2008, while much of the financial sector was in a battle for survival, Jump, a firm of a few dozen employees, made $316 million. The same year, Citadel, owned by one of America's wealthiest and most secretive investors, Ken Griffin, pulled in about $1 billion in a unit devoted to HFT.

In spite of this flurry of attention, few people outside the close-knit industry really understood what these firms did or where the money was coming from. A bedrock principle of economic theory is that, the higher the returns of an investment, the riskier it will be, yet somehow the academics at these outfits, many of whom had no background in finance, had found a way to subvert that. By combining speed and statistical analysis with a unique understanding of the architecture underpinning electronic markets, they achieved the holy grail of investing, making large and consistent profits while taking very little risk. Hard data on HFT was hard to come by and firms were under no obligation to reveal their strategies, even to the regulators who, for a long time, seemed willing to take on trust that participants were acting responsibly. The only repository of real-time trading data was the exchanges themselves, private enterprises that straddled a curious line between seeking to attract the HFT firms' business and being responsible for policing them in their role as "designated self-regulatory organizations." Since HFT is predicated on vast numbers of transactions and exchanges collect a commission on every trade, their interests were closely aligned. Indeed, the explosion of HFT helped make the CME Group, which had only recently gone public, one of the most profitable companies in America. This symbiotic relationship was perhaps best illustrated by the revolving door between the top firms and the exchanges where they operated. Virtu Financial Inc.'s director, John "Jack" Sandner, was the longest-serving chairman in the CME's history. William Shepard, another longtime CME Group board member, is reported to own a sizable stake in Jump. The high-frequency trading industry and the CME Group were not just on the same side of the fence. They were the same people.

Executives at the likes of Jump, Citadel, and Hudson River Trading pointed to the higher number of trades in general, and the shrinking gap between asking and buying prices, as evidence that their activities were improving the marketplace by making transacting cheaper and less volatile for everyone. But trading is a zero-sum game, and if HFT firms were winning, somebody had to be losing. In a research note suggesting institutional investors and pension funds were the ones getting stiffed, New York consultancy Pragma Trading wrote: "Given that HFTs are very short-term intermediaries between the directional traders who are actually trying to accumulate or unwind a position, it is hard to see how they can simultaneously be saving investors money and pulling billions out of the markets in trading profits." The small number of researchers who did manage to examine HFTs' methods found evidence of practices including "momentum ignition," a kamikaze attempt to incite abrupt market moves; "wash trading," or trading with yourself to push the market around or pick up rebates; and "quote stuffing," whereby entities flood the market with huge numbers of orders in a short space of time to cause delays. It was impossible to know just how widespread any of this was since the regulators, by their own admission, lacked the technology and expertise to monitor what was happening in their purview. There were also questions about what such a fundamental shift in the makeup of the markets might mean for stability. "What happens if a major event causes turmoil in the market? Will these HFTs simply shut down their computers and walk away since their model has been corrupted?" wrote Joe Saluzzi from New York brokerage firm Themis in a strikingly prescient 2009 blog post. "Where will all that LIQUIDITY that they claim they provide go when the market doesn't suit them? A major vacuum will be formed in the market as multiple parties run for a much smaller than expected exit."

For day traders like Nav, there were more pressing concerns. HAL 9000. The Matrix. Skynet. Dolores. The existential threat posed by robots has been rooted in the human psyche since the dawn of computers. For Nav and his peers, the fear wasn't that they would upend the financial order altogether, but simply that these ultrafast, highly sophisticated machines would be able to scalp better and more efficiently than they could, crowding them out of the market. A poster on one of the trading forums drily captured the prevailing mood. "One day, years from now," a trading desk "will typically consist of three things. A man, a dog, and a computer. The computer's job will be to trade. The man's job will be to feed the dog. The dog's job will be to bite the man if he goes anywhere near the computer."

The exact strategies HFT firms employed were diverse and constantly changing, but at the heart of many of them were three elements: an ability to predict which way the market was about to move; the speed to capitalize on that move; and a novel way of minimizing losses when they guessed wrong. The first element involved statistically analyzing changes in the order book and elsewhere for information that indicated whether prices would rise or fall. Inputs might include the number and type of resting orders at different levels, how fast prices are moving around, and the types of market participants active at any time. "Think of it as a giant data science project," explains one HFT owner. For years, Nav had used his superior pattern recognition and recall skills to read the ebbs and flows of the order book until it became second nature, but even the most gifted human scalper is no match for a computer at parsing large amounts of data.

When it came to speed, the leading HFT firms invested hundreds of millions of dollars in computers, cable, and telecommunications equipment to ensure they could react first in what was often a winner-takes-all game. Exchanges charged tens of thousands of dollars a month to allow customers to place their servers next to the exchange's to minimize any lag in receiving data. The result was, in the words of Eric Budish at the University of Chicago Booth School of Business, a "never-ending socially-wasteful arms race for speed." Only the top-tier firms could afford to keep up, meaning barriers to entry were high. And the exchanges gave their most valued customers sweetheart deals that slashed their cost of trading to a fraction of other participants'. Point-and-click traders had no chance. By the time a human being had seen, processed, and reacted to a buy signal or news of an interest rate cut, the market had entirely absorbed the information and any value had evaporated. Tried and tested arbitrage strategies, whereby traders look for two closely correlated securities to temporarily fall out of kilter and bet they will come back in line, were fruitless in the face of machines that could identify and profit from anomalies tens of thousands of times quicker than they could.

The final element of HFTs' success was an understanding of the plumbing underpinning electronic markets. The CME's platform, Globex, is what's known as a "First In First Out," or FIFO, market. That means that whenever a trader places a limit order (that is, an order away from the current price), it joins the back of the queue, behind any other orders at that level. If the best bid in the market is currently $99.00 and you want to sell when it reaches $100.00, for instance, your order will be placed last in line behind any other traders currently looking to sell at $100.00.

HFT firms monitor these queues for opportunities to benefit from what is essentially a risk-free option. Consider an example: HFT firm AGGRO decides the market is statistically likely to fall and so places an order to sell ten e-minis at the current price (the "best ask"), again let's say $100.00. As AGGRO's ten-lot order makes its way to the front of the queue, new orders join at the same price; by the time AGGRO's e-minis are purchased, or "hit," another one thousand lots are waiting in the $100.00 line for a buyer. At this point, there are two possibilities. If the market falls, as AGGRO predicted, the firm can buy ten e-minis at a lower price, say $99.50, and walk away with a profit. If it starts to appear, however, based on fresh information entering the order book, that the price is actually going to *rise,* AGGRO can quickly turn around and buy ten e-minis from somebody further back in the $100.00 line, exiting the trade without taking a loss. By consummating trades only when they knew they could extricate themselves with little or no loss when they got it wrong, HFT firms largely eradicated losses. They also helped create a situation in which, by 2010, the overwhelming majority of all orders on the CME were canceled before they were consummated.

With all this to-ing and fro-ing, it's easy to understand how day traders like Nav came to believe they were being targeted. Every time they placed or canceled an order, even if it was only a handful of contracts, the market moved. "I remember clearly the first time I noticed the HFTs," recalls one of Futex's senior traders from that era. "It was the start of a new year, we logged on, and the order book just seemed subtly but discernibly different, like an update on your phone or something. I was on a bank of twelve desks and we all just looked at each other and said, 'What is going on?' And from then on it became much harder." At arcades around the world, algos became like bogeymen, blamed for anything and everything that went wrong. If a trader took a position and the market moved against him, it wasn't a bad trade, it was the "fucking algos picking me off." Rumors abounded about illicit deals between the exchanges and the HFT giants, but the truth was that the robots didn't need to know their opponents' identities to thrive. Fast machines, cheap commissions, and probability were enough.

The ascendancy of HFT squeezed many human scalpers out of the market. Some adapted by trading over longer time horizons, leaving positions running for hours or days rather than seconds. Others took to actively seeking out and trying to exploit algorithms, which quickly became ubiquitous among banks and asset managers as well as HFTs. In 2007, Svend Egil Larsen, a self-described algo hunter from Norway, noticed a flaw in the way an entity reacted to trades in certain stocks and set about taking advantage. He made a modest $50,000 but was later charged, along with a colleague, with market manipulation. The alleged victim in the case was a broker called Timber Hill, one of a raft of companies owned by the Hungarian-born electronic trading pioneer Thomas Peterffy, a man whose personal wealth is estimated by *Forbes* at $17.1 billion. Larsen was originally found guilty and given a suspended sentence, but the conviction was overturned on appeal. "We feel like Robin Hood, or David beating Goliath," he told the *Financial Times*.

Most day traders harbored a degree of resentment toward the HFTs, but for Nav, who had a fierce antiauthoritarian streak, it tapped into something deeper. How could he compete with a bunch of faceless billionaires who never lost? And how was that fair? The markets were supposed to be the ultimate meritocracy. It didn't matter what you looked like behind your screens, or where your parents came from. If you made the right moves, you got the rewards. Except, Nav was increasingly coming to believe, that wasn't true. Like so much else in life, the players destined to win were the ones with the most money and the right connections. In reality, Nav didn't know who his opponents were, and it would later transpire that some of those he complained about the most were actually gifted human scalpers with limited technology just like him. But to his mind, they were all cut from the same cloth: privileged elites with better equipment hell-bent on trying to take him down.

With his math skills, his aptitude for pattern recognition, and his lateral way of thinking, Nav might have made a highly prized employee for an HFT firm. Instead, he made a decision that, as an already successful and wealthy trader, he didn't have to make. On June 4, 2007, after three years of silence, That's a Fugazi filed a new post. It was titled "S&P 500 Futures Corruption," and it read:

> For all those that trade the e-mini S&P 500 with a ladder (where you can see the bids and offers), you must have realized now how some market participants have an unfair advantage over the rest. I'm mainly referring to the two spoofers . . . who are there everyday and seem to push around the market. Now, I'm not one to complain about spoofing I mean hey it happens in every market, but these two S&P spoofers CANNOT BE HIT. I've tried many times gentlemen and they simply can't. Hence, they contravene the rules, as per CME themselves and should be eliminated from the market . . . I've spoken to CME about this and they simply refuse to accept that it is going on, even though you only need to watch the ladder at any time during the day to see that it is. It's a clear example of letting the big guys get away wth blue murder at the expense of the small guys.

The post went on to suggest that traders should consider boycotting the e-mini to force the exchange to take action before concluding:

> I'm half thinking of asking CME directly how I can get the equivalent software which allows you to spoof without being hit, because I do a fair volume myself, but I feel it would be wrong. THE MARKETS SHOULD BE ON A LEVEL PLAYING FIELD FOR ALL.

Fugazi's language was less combative than in his earlier posts, but still nobody replied. Four days later, he posted an update:

> Oh one final caveat. I am working on a program on TT* to get the exact same cheating software. If you cant beat em you may aswell join em eh? Europeans have a pathetic attitude of accepting whatever authority throws at them—they never fight back. With the volume I do I know the exchange will turn a blind eye. And just imagine how easy trading will be since one is already cleaning up whilst playing by the rules. Tis been a sweet week.

There, on a popular public forum, Nav laid out the seeds of a plan that eight years later would culminate in his arrest for manipulating the market and helping cause one of the biggest intraday financial crashes in history. If anyone was paying attention, they might have been able to talk him out of it or notify the authorities. But, like the boy who cried wolf, he'd run out of credibility, setting him on a path disciples of Elliott or Gann might suggest he was destined to travel.

---

* Trading Technologies is a trading software provider.

■

CHAPTER 6

END OF AN ERA

On a spring afternoon in 2008, traders at Futex returned from lunch to find Nav leaning back in his chair with his hands behind his head. For hours he didn't touch his computer. A rumor made its way around the office: "He's on strike."

After five years, Nav had fallen out of love with Futex. He was fed up with the schlep to Woking and the distractions that awaited him when he got there. He was tired of begging for bigger limits. But most of all, he was sick of giving his money away. When he joined the arcade, he'd signed a contract agreeing that, in exchange for Futex staking him, he'd give up a share of his profits, a monthly desk fee, and a commission on every "round-trip." The profit split started at 50/50 and went up on a sliding scale depending on how much he had in his trading account. Now that Nav had accumulated more than £1 million ($1.6 million) he was entitled to 90 percent of everything he withdrew, the maximum available.

For fledgling traders, Futex was an attractive proposition. They were given capital to try their hand and didn't pay anything back until they were profitable. If they failed, as most did, they could walk away owing nothing. The flip side was that those who *did* make it subsidized everyone else. By now, Nav was routinely earning $50,000 a day, which meant giving $5,000 to the Rossis. And, with his frenetic style of trading, he could easily hand them an additional $2,000 in commissions. "A lot of these people, it was their first job, just out of uni, twenty-two, twenty-three years old," says one former trainer at Futex. "They keep them very much within those four walls, and because they're down in Woking they rarely speak to anyone else within the City. But then they speak to other prop houses and realize what a shitty deal they have."

Nav's 90/10 split was generous by the standards of most other traders on the floor, but he wanted 95 percent. When the Rossis refused, he shut down his trading software knowing he'd be severely crimping the company's cash flow. It was the culmination of a feud that had been escalating for a while. A couple of years earlier, Nav had decided to quit trading FTSE 100 futures, the UK equivalent of the S&P 500 e-mini, where he was regularly making £2,000 a day, to try his hand at some bigger markets. After a shaky start, Paolo took Nav aside one day and suggested he go back to the FTSE. "Five hundred grand a year, that's more than enough for you," Rossi said.

"How do you know what's enough for me?" Nav replied, incensed that Paolo of all people would try to clip his wings.

On another occasion, Nav had gone home one night after placing a two-hundred-lot trade. The next morning, he was woken up by a call from Paolo telling him he'd lost a million dollars, virtually everything he had, he would later recount to a friend. Nav was shocked. "Just get me out," he said.

"Nav, calm down," Paolo chuckled, according to Nav's recollection, "you're a hundred and twenty ticks onside!" Nav's overnight trade had earned him hundreds of thousands of dollars. "This is a lesson for you: always have a stop in the market. One of these days something like this will happen and you'll get rolled over."

It was an incredible result, but Nav couldn't get past Paolo's attempt to scare him into exercising better risk management. When he arrived at the office, he remembers marching into the owner's room and shouting: "Are you still gonna take my money after that little escapade? Putting me through that and then charging me two hundred thousand dollars for it?!" Nav was on an 80/20 profit split at the time. "What a wanker," he complained to the friend. "The guy's got no shame."

It didn't help that Paolo was so blatant about how much money he had. Futex's website had a page titled "Futex Lifestyle," which could more accurately be described as "Paolo Rossi Lifestyle." There were photos of Rossi at the Wimbledon final and watching Champions League soccer. Once, when his Ferrari had come back from the garage and the Lamborghini he'd been given as a replacement hadn't yet been taken away, he posted a picture of them both with the caption "some tough choices." One of his cars had the license plate R9ssi and he was a member of Queenwood, one of the UK's most exclusive golf clubs, where he shared the fairways with Hugh Grant, Catherine Zeta-Jones, and golf pro Ernie Els. "All that material stuff is pointless and attracts the wrong people," Nav said to his colleagues with disdain. "Trust me. It's a mirage."

But Paolo wasn't the only one displaying his success. In August 2007, a magazine called *Trader Monthly* published its annual "30 Under 30" list of the most successful young traders. It included the following entry:

> Legend has it that just outside London in the small, affluent city of Woking resides a pure prop trader who works two hours a day, two days a week—and still makes twice as much as anyone else at his clearing firm. The legend, it turns out, is true—and that gifted trader has the 30 Under 30–appropriate surname Young. "He wears jeans, his lucky jersey and no shoes," says one colleague. "He even puts on trades and sleeps at his desk."
>
> [Bradley] Young, an Aussie who spends more time on vacation than he does trading, has been known to pull down $250,000 a week even after the bosses at Futex exact their tribute . . .

Says Young: "From the very first day I traded a futures contract, I've always believed that I was going to be one of the greatest traders of all time. As each day passes and my career progresses, this belief becomes stronger."

Trader Monthly was launched in 2004 and quickly became popular on trading floors around the world, mixing profiles of Big Swinging Dicks with articles on classic cars and how best to disguise one's strip club receipts when claiming expenses. Like its readership, it was male, crude, and brash. But the "30 Under 30" feature took off and was frequently picked up by the mainstream press. CNBC interviewed inductees like they were celebrities. For Brad to be anointed was major kudos, even if the stuff about him barely turning up to the office was untrue.

A couple of months later, Nav emailed the editor:

> Good evening,
> I have recently been introduced to your magazine and must congratulate you, since it is one of the better publications I have seen on the art of trading. I read with interest your top 30 under 30 list and was wondering what criterion someone would need in order to be part of it. I am a local who works on a 90/10 split. I trade the e-mini SP 500 and on volatile trading days I do on average 10,000 round turns or about 1% of the SP 500's total daily volume. If I trade well on a volatile day I normally make circa $133,000. On quiter [sic] days I look to make between $45,000 and $70,000.
> It's been an extraordinary year in my trading career. You must understand that for me to be in the top 30 is not a vanity thing. I prefer to keep a low profile and indeed hide my P&L's from my trading colleagues. However, I am looking to set up a trading arcade of my own and maybe the publicity would be a good thing for the arcade. Maybe we can do something in the future.
> Best regards,
> Navinder.

Nav never did feature in *Trader Monthly,* and he didn't start his own arcade, but he was beginning to outstay his welcome at Futex. Once a major generator and a great advertisement for the firm, he was increasingly looking like a liability. He came to the office less and less frequently, and when he did turn up, he caused trouble. At one point, he complained that his bank was stealing money from his trading account. When the Rossis told him he was mistaken, he questioned whether they were in on it. Nav's nosebleed stakes were giving management sleepless nights and, if he took home any more than 90 percent of his profits, the economics no longer stacked up. Earlier in the year Nav had paid to "lease a seat" at the CME—essentially, a form of membership with privileges—which slashed the fees he paid the exchange per trade, in turn eating into Futex's commissions. The firm also suggested it had received warnings from Her Majesty's Revenue & Customs that Nav wasn't paying his taxes.

Matters came to a head in the summer of 2008 when Nav told Futex he was leaving and wanted his capital, a sum of around $3 million. At first Paolo resisted, telling Nav he'd return the money in installments until he was confident the tax authorities were happy. When Nav instructed a lawyer to begin legal proceedings, Paolo caved, but ties between the two men were severed for good.

"At the best point our relationship would have been mentor-student, at the worst point you're dealing with a mentality that if you hold him back, he feels like you're against him," says Rossi. "If you don't give him the limits he wants, you're against him, if you're taking a clearing fee, you're against him. He's got this mentality that everyone is ripping him off. But we nurtured him and at Futex he knew everyone. It was like a brake on his worst instincts. When he left there was no one to look out for him."

■

CHAPTER 7

THE TRADE II

Nav's first task on leaving Futex was to find a new broker. Every independent trader is required to trade via a regulated brokerage firm, which acts as a kind of conduit to the exchanges, covering any losses and monitoring their clients' activity. In April 2008, Nav called GNI Touch, an offshoot of Man Financial Group (later renamed MF Global), the world's biggest futures brokerage firm. At the time, he was still locked in the dispute with Futex and had only around $750,000 to put down as margin. The fee that brokers charge their customers per round-trip ranges from a few cents to a couple of dollars, depending on the volume they trade. "Whenever we take on someone new, ninety-nine percent of the time they'll inflate what size they do and how much profit they make, and not just by a little bit," says a former senior member of GNI's futures desk. "They'll say 'I do a hundred thousand lots a month,' and it's actually more like five thousand."

When Nav said he did ten thousand round-trips a day and regularly made $110,000, the GNI executive chuckled to himself and offered him rates commensurate with a trader who does one-fifth that amount. A few days later, he found out Nav was telling the truth when an engineer drove to Hounslow to set up the software and a connection to the exchange in Nav's bedroom, allowing his brokers to watch him remotely. Astounded, GNI slashed Nav's fees accordingly. Once a trader is up and running, there's not actually much for a broker to do. A big part of the job is maintaining relationships, and it's not unusual for a company like Man to throw back 20 percent of whatever it collects from a customer in fees on lavish meals, nights out, or tickets to events. Man had a box at Wembley Stadium and another at the O2 Academy concert hall. But Nav wasn't interested. "He never wanted any entertainment and kept contact to the absolute minimum," says the ex–GNI broker. "His ambitions were clear: he wanted to be the largest trader in the market and was totally uninterested in material gain. The profits just allowed him to trade bigger."

Nav started trading from home just as the financial crisis was peaking. With so much volatility, there was still easy money to be made, even with the proliferation of the algos. Markets lurched around with every fresh piece of bad news or government attempt to restore calm, and many of the moves were predictable and overblown. In such frenetic markets, it was easy to miss things and Nav thought he might benefit from being surrounded by other people, so he rented a desk for $2,300 a month at an outfit called CFT Financials, where, unlike at Futex, he didn't have to give up any of his profits. Located a short walk from the Tower of London in the old financial district, CFT was founded by a high-rolling day trader known as "Braveheart" who graced the inaugural cover of *Trader Monthly* leaning on the hood of a vintage car with a model in his arms. The thirty or so traders at the firm were generally older and more experienced than those at Futex. No one was screaming obscenities or playing football in the car park. Still, when Nav arrived, the atmosphere was abuzz. Bid-ask spreads had burst wide open, reflecting the heightened level of risk, and there were opportunities to make weekly salaries in a day. To capitalize, Nav worked from morning until night, trading European markets first and then switching to the e-mini. After a few weeks, he made his second career-defining trade and, like the last one, it had less to do with scalping than with sheer conviction and intuition.

On Thursday, November 20, 2008, the S&P 500 closed at 752 points, its lowest level in more than a decade. Two months had passed since the collapse of Lehman Brothers and, with the financial system still teetering, reports suggested the U.S. government and the Federal Reserve might have to adopt more drastic measures. Arriving in the office on Friday morning, Nav started loading up on S&P 500 futures, reasoning that markets had only one way to go. Sure enough, after a shaky few hours, U.S. stock prices started to climb. The following week, they rallied even harder when the Treasury Department announced it would inject $40 billion into Citigroup. Believing the market had further to go, Nav added to his long position until every dollar in his account was on the line.

Watching on from GNI's offices, Nav's brokers were growing nervous. Not only was Sarao sailing close to the trading limits they'd set him based on the margin he'd put down, but he hadn't placed a stop-loss to limit his potential downside. If the market suddenly tanked, the firm could take a serious hit. Eventually, the senior broker on the desk came to the conclusion he had no choice but to call Nav and ask him to top up his account. When Daljit, Nav's mother, answered, the broker asked her to wake him up. Nav came to the phone sounding irritable. Before the broker could finish explaining why he was calling, Nav growled, "What are you talking about, bruv? Look at the market!" The broker had failed to notice that the S&P 500 had been on another tear. Before he had a chance to apologize, Nav told him he was going back to bed.

Later that day, the Federal Reserve announced it was allocating $800 billion to ease the flow of credit around the system. It was the bazooka the markets had been waiting for, and by the time the market closed in New York, the S&P 500 stood at 857 points, marking a rally of 100 points in three days. It was a staggering rise of a magnitude that comes along only every few years. At that point, Nav could have cashed out for a hefty profit, but once again he doubled down, putting his winnings back on the line. Rather than waiting and watching, he took himself out of the office to a nearby McDonald's, where he drank four milk shakes in a row. It was the ultimate manifestation of his "let it breathe" philosophy. By the time he exited his position two days later, the index had risen a further 39 points. Over the course of a week, the S&P 500 had gained more than 19 percent, and Nav had ridden the tidal wave to the shore, earning himself around $15 million.

"People think it's gambling, but it's almost the opposite of gambling," reflects one day trader. "The package gets voted in and it's like having two aces in poker, but you have to have massive balls. Shall I go all-in or not? The market has only one way to go. But you have to be willing to put everything on the line."

A few days later, the senior broker called Nav to congratulate him on his win and ask what he planned to do with the money. When Nav replied, "Trade it," the broker warned him about the danger of viewing profits as an abstract number, a lesson he'd learned to his detriment in the pits. The broker advised Nav to buy himself something nice, but Nav said he didn't need anything and steered the conversation back to his favorite subject: the menace of high-frequency trading. Since joining CFT, Nav had become more convinced than ever that the HFT firms could see who was behind orders, and he complained about it to his brokers ad nauseam. He had also come to believe the robots were able to see where stop-losses were sitting—potentially valuable information that would allow them to trigger flurries of buying and selling. Even now, on the back of a life-changing win, Nav was preoccupied with how he was being cheated. Sensing he was wasting his time, the broker wished him well and hung up.

Around this time, Nav did treat himself to one indulgence: a Volkswagen Golf. The traders at CFT smiled as he talked enthusiastically about overtaking other cars in what was essentially a run-of-the-mill hatchback, after earning more in a week than the annual salary of Goldman Sachs's CEO. His interest in the vehicle waned when he picked up a couple of parking tickets, and within a few months it was rusting on a driveway, where it would remain, untouched, for years. Eventually it was towed away for scrap. After factoring in depreciation and running costs, Nav told anyone who would listen, owning a car was a bad trade.

CHAPTER 8

■

A BRIEF HISTORY OF SPOOFING

Nav's wager on the financial crisis left him with more firepower than ever, but the reality was that scalping the market was becoming harder and harder for human traders. More than a year had passed since That's a Fugazi had revealed his intention to build a program to compete in an increasingly automated world, and he was now ready to put it into action. Nav's grand vision was to induce other participants to trade how he wanted them to. It was only a more sophisticated version of what traders had been doing, one way or another, for centuries.

When Daniel Defoe wasn't writing novels like *Robinson Crusoe* and *Moll Flanders* or spying for the monarchy, he spent his days in eighteenth-century London working as a merchant, buying and selling wine, hosiery, and perfume. A prolific social commentator, Defoe turned his gaze in 1719 to Exchange Alley in the City of London, a narrow, gray-stone street near the Bank of England where, in rowdy coffeehouses, some of the earliest recorded trading in stocks and commodities took place. "'Tis a trade founded in fraud, born of deceit, and nourished by trick, cheat, wheedle, forgeries, falsehoods, and all sorts of delusions," Defoe wrote in his essay "Anatomy of Exchange Alley." One passage, recounting the methods of one of the most successful "stock-jobbers," a future member of Parliament and governor of the East India Company named Sir Josiah Child, offers an early description of the art of spoofing.

> If Sir Josiah had a mind to buy, the first thing he did was to commission his brokers to look sower, shake their heads, suggest bad news from India; and at the bottom it followed, 'I have commission from Sir Josiah to sell out whatever I can,' and perhaps they would actually sell ten, perhaps twenty thousand pound. Immediately the Exchange was full of sellers; nobody would buy a shilling, 'till perhaps the stock would fall six, seven, eight, ten per cent, sometimes more; then the cunning jobber had another set of men employed on purpose to buy, but with privacy and caution, all the stock they could lay their hands on, 'till by selling ten thousand pound, at four or five per cent lost, he would buy a hundred thousand pound stock at ten or twelve per cent under price; and in a few weeks by just the contrary method, set them all a buying, and then sell them their own stock again at ten or twelve per cent profit.

Fast-forward 275 years to the 1990s, and similar antics could be observed over a much shorter time frame on the Liffe floor at the Royal Exchange, which was situated less than a hundred meters from Exchange Alley. "I would get an order to sell two thousand lots and the client, say Goldman Sachs, would tell me to make as much noise as possible," recounts a former broker. "A thousand offered at ninety-nine! A thousand lots at ninety-eight! A thousand at ninety-seven! I'd sell a few, the price falls, and guess who was waiting at ninety-five bid somewhere else in the pit with a different broker? Goldman, who then starts buying everything, pushing the price back up. When the other traders came back to me and said they'd take the contracts, I'd tell them it was all gone."

Spoof was the name of a card game invented in the 1880s by

British comedian and music hall performer Arthur Roberts. The game revolved around trickery, and the verb "to spoof" came to mean to hoax or deceive. Students play a derivation that involves guessing how many coins are concealed in their fists to decide who's buying the next round. In tech circles, it refers to an attempt to imitate someone's identity to gain access to data or money. One of the earliest references to spoofing in relation to financial markets was a 1999 *New York Times* article titled "Chasing Ghosts at Nasdaq," which documented a rise in canceled orders in the stock market.

In the pits, spoofing was to some extent curbed by the fact that traders could see whom they were competing against. Serial offenders were liable to be taken outside and made to understand the error of their ways. But when anonymous, screen-based trading came along, that safeguard disappeared. Another accelerant was the introduction of the ladder. For the first time, market participants could see, not just the current best bid and offer, but where orders were waiting up and down the order book. This provided a valuable insight into supply and demand, but it also created new opportunities for deception. One man who famously capitalized was Paul Rotter, aka "The Flipper." Rotter, a skinny, unassuming German with a rebellious streak, started his career in 1994 in the drab back office of a bank in Munich, where he spent his days punching customer trades into a DTB machine, one of the earliest incarnations of an electronic trading screen. The job was tedious but Rotter found he had a gift for spotting patterns in the way prices moved, and within a year he moved to Frankfurt to take up a position as a junior trader. His arrival coincided with the explosion of electronic trading and by the time the pits closed, he was a lethal online scalper. Making money from Luddite open-outcry traders desperately trying to apply what they'd learned in the pits on a computer was embarrassingly easy. "It was paradise," recalls Rotter. "All these locals were used to seeing JPMorgan and Goldman orders and front-running, but they couldn't do that anymore because it was anonymous and they had no idea what they were doing. There was no algorithmic trading yet and the regulators hadn't brought in all these rules on what you could and couldn't do."

At twenty-four, Rotter moved to Ireland to set up his own fund with some associates. Capitalizing on the herdlike behavior of the locals, he would, according to reports, load up the ladder with buy orders and wait for others to line up alongside him. Then, once the market had gone up by a few ticks, he'd cancel his bids and quickly sell into the unsuspecting traders who'd followed him for a higher price than he paid, closing out his position for a profit. By trading bigger than anyone else, he found he could control the market. However, he encountered a problem: with so much buying and selling, Rotter found he sometimes ended up transacting with himself, a prohibited practice known as wash trading. When he started receiving warning letters from the exchange, he contacted his software provider, Trading Technologies (TT), and said he needed a way to stop hitting his own orders. TT came up with a new function called "avoid orders that cross" that solved the problem but inadvertently helped Rotter take his exploits to another level. Where Rotter had previously had to cancel his orders before swapping direction, now he could do both simultaneously with a single click of his mouse. Traders who had tried to piggyback his orders had no chance of getting out of the way when he switched back on them, instantaneously flipping from buyer to seller and vice versa. At one stage, Rotter was trading two hundred thousand contracts a day and, in a good month, raking in $7 million. Along the way, he made staunch enemies among a community of former locals who, not knowing his identity, christened him "The Flipper" and put pressure on the exchanges to ban him. Rotter's cover was blown on a forum in 2004, and he was confronted in the audience of an industry event in London.

"It was a little bit frightening at that time," he says. "These guys were like, 'You should look behind your shoulder.' I got messages saying, 'We'll come after you.'" Rotter pulled back when HFT arrived and new regulations came in. Today he takes much longer-term positions from his home in the Bahamas, but he's unrepentant. "I've met many people in the market, stockbrokers from the eighties who had all this inside information. I never did anything like that. I was trading the order book and seeing what other guys were doing and reacting. They thought they had a right to wait for orders and front-run them, and I took advantage. But my money was always at risk. It was a fair market."

Inheriting Rotter's mantle as the bogeyman of futures was Igor Oystacher, a Russian day trader who, within a few years of learning to trade, became one of the biggest e-mini traders in the world. Oystacher grew up in a well-off but abstemious family in Moscow where his father, an engineer, introduced him to chess when he was six years old. By age ten, Oystacher could beat his dad, and not long after he was crowned city champion for his age group. He finished high school, an institution for gifted children focused on physics and astronomy, early and moved to Detroit to live with relatives before enrolling in the math program at Northwestern University in Illinois. In his third year, he secured an internship at a prop shop in Chicago called Gelber Group, where he was so successful he quit his degree to trade full-time.

Liberated from the strictures of Russian life and away from the influence of his father, Oystacher devoted himself to making money. By now, he'd abandoned chess for speed chess, a variant of the game that requires players to make decisions in seconds, and with his rapid-fire reactions, pattern recognition skills, and instant recall, he took to the ladder immediately. Dour and inscrutable, Oystacher was known as "Snuggles" among the traders on Gelber's two-hundred-strong trading floor. He approached trading like chess, as a battle with moves and countermoves, and in 2004 he became the focus of unwanted attention when complaints about a mysterious entity with the tag 990 started appearing on the forums. Back then, each firm was given a numeric ID that showed up on post-trade confirmations. Gelber's was 990, and it didn't take long for people to deduce that the perpetrator was the firm's aggressive new Russian whiz kid.

Like Rotter, Oystacher used TT's "avoid orders that cross" function to switch directions rapidly. Buying and selling in huge volumes, he blew through everything in his path. "I know it sounds hard to believe that one person can control a world market but trust me that is what is occurring," wrote a disgruntled e-mini trader on one of the forums. "He started doing this with 300 lots . . . now he has made so much money doing it that he is up to 2000 lots," worth around $120 million. Oystacher ignored the complaints, which he believed to be inaccurate and unfounded, and passed his methods on to a new group of traders, including an unassuming Chinese mathematician named James "Jimmy" Chui whose homework he had copied at Northwestern. In 2007, Chiu was headhunted by Jump Trading, the Chicago high-frequency trading giant, where he would become an even bigger player than Oystacher and pass on his knowledge to a new generation.

Nav, Oystacher, and Chiu were part of an elite cadre of big-ticket human scalpers, and the three sometimes clashed in a market increasingly inhabited by preprogrammed machines. Years later, investigators would talk about the "Spoof Wars" of the late 2000s, an ultra-high-stakes game of brinkmanship in which players would try to wipe each other out by hitting their opponents' spoof orders and getting them to "puke"—close out positions they never intended to consummate for a devastating loss. Nav had read about Oystacher on the boards and throughout his career would complain bitterly to the CME and his peers about "The Russian," who he was convinced was trying to spoof the market higher when he was shorting it. In truth, although the two men did exchange blows, Nav was more often than not duking it out with some other trader who happened to have an MO similar to Oystacher's.

Amid such ferocious competition, Nav looked to other avenues to make money. One tactic was to focus on the "pre-open." During the week, the e-mini traded twenty-four hours a day apart from between 3:15 p.m. and 3:30 p.m. CET, when the market shut down. In that fifteen minutes, traders could place nonbinding orders that the CME used to calculate an "indicative opening price," or IOP, based on the level where the greatest number of buyers and sellers matched. As traders placed, modified, and canceled their orders, they could see the IOP rising and falling until, with thirty seconds to go, it locked up and the opening price was set. Prices fluctuated wildly around the open, and any trader who positioned themselves correctly for the number the CME spat out could make a fast profit. There were rumors that some traders had found a way to affect the outcome by repeatedly placing large orders above or below the prevailing price, inducing other participants to follow suit, then canceling their orders just before the cutoff. It was certainly a lucrative period for Sarao. "I saw him come in for the open, make a hundred thousand dollars, then go home again," recalls one former colleague. But in March 2009, the CME contacted Nav, reminding him that all orders must be "bona fide."

From a hired desk in a small trading arcade in London, it wasn't always clear what bona fide meant. The U.S. Commodity Exchange Act of 1936 made it a felony to "manipulate or attempt to manipulate the price of any commodity in interstate commerce, or for future delivery," but pre-2011, when new legislation was introduced, the policing of futures markets was patchy and ineffectual. Specific rules on spoofing hadn't been brought in yet, and proving manipulation in court was so difficult that the industry's main watchdog, the Commodity Futures Trading Commission, rarely brought cases. Day-to-day oversight of the market was left to exchanges like the CME, which preferred to view market participants as valued customers rather than regulated entities. Anyone suspected of attempting to manipulate prices was given a series of warnings before eventually being hit with a fine that often didn't cover their alleged gains.

As futures markets had evolved, supervision had failed to keep up. Trading was now so fast, and the data it created so voluminous, that the authorities were simply unable to monitor what was happening on their watch. Every time Nav loaded up the ladder he saw spoofing, wash trading, momentum ignition, and other forms of chicanery, with seemingly no consequences. When he complained to the CME about it, which he did frequently, they ignored him or told him he was wrong. If he retaliated and used the same tactics himself, nobody seemed to care. The impression he was left with was that, in the era of the algos, anything went. As he'd commented on the boards back in 2007, "With the volume I do I know the exchange will turn a blind eye."

If Nav had worked at a bank or a hedge fund, there would have been a compliance officer to step in when he strayed into dodgy territory, but as an independent day trader he was on his own. The brokers at GNI were officially supposed to "diligently supervise" his activities, but they were philosophically and financially inclined to stay out of it. When a warning did arrive from the CME, like the one about Nav's trading in the pre-market, they simply passed it along.

Nav believed he was engaged in an existential battle against opponents with superior powers and advantages. If he were to stand any chance, he reasoned, he would have to build a machine of his own. Unlike the HFT firms, he didn't have the resources to create something powerful and rapid from scratch. His approach, instead, would be to take the off-the-shelf software package he already owned and pimp it like a gearhead souping up an old Ford. Despite the gulf in technology, Nav felt confident he could succeed because the robots had an inherent weakness he knew he could exploit. They were *followers*, blindly reacting to signals contained in trading data in preordained, predictable ways. Nav knew he couldn't analyze the order book as efficiently as a machine, and he was always going to be second best in a speed race. But if he could fuck with the signals themselves, he could get the robots to respond to his commands and take back some control. *Oh sheep, come join thy shepherd!*

■

CHAPTER 9

BUILDING THE MACHINE

Ever since Nav started trading at Futex, he'd used a suite of programs provided by the Chicago-based software vendor Trading Technologies. Founded in 1994, TT was run by a futures legend named Harris Brumfield who started using the software after leaving the pits and liked it so much that he bought the company. The software, which was ubiquitous among day traders, gave users the tools they needed to observe the market, place assorted order types, and connect to the exchanges with minimal delays. TT also offered a product called Autotrader that allowed customers with no background in programming to create their own algos in Excel, offering a low-cost way to introduce an element of automation into their trading. On Friday, June 12, 2009, Nav emailed his broker at GNI Touch asking to be put in touch with "a TT technician that will be able to programme for me extra features on TT . . . Obviously I would be prepared to pay for their time / excellence." A few days later, he followed up with a message to TT's London-based sales rep with the subject line "Matrix." It read:

> Hello mate,
> What I need are the following functions

i) The cancel if close function we discussed. I would also like to be able to alternate the closeness ie one price away or three prices away etc etc

ii) Join bid/offer function which will work like the stop market function in that you can hit into orders but you don't get filled. Your order simply joins the bid/offer if it goes bid/offered

iii) A facility to be able to enter multiple orders at different prices using one click

iv) The ability for my orders to rest on a particular size, ie my order will be pulled if there are not x amount of orders beneath it. Of course to make this work we will have to stay at the back of the book, v) this can be done by increasing/decreasing my order by a 1 lot every time a new order is detected where I am resting

vi) To be able to enter an integer and my order will stay working until a clip has entered the order that is of equal or greater value than the integer.

vii) The ability for my orders to only allow 1 clip to go into them. Hence, if I am working 500 lot and a 2 lot trades, the 498 balance is removed immediately.

All of the above shouldn't be difficult to do, since there are people using these matrices in every market I have traded so it is fairly common.

best regards

Nav

Nav's blueprint may seem complicated, but his goal was as straightforward as the Flipper's or Lord Josiah Child's in Exchange Alley: to distort the picture of supply and demand enough to mislead other market participants, allowing him to buy cheap and sell high. The spoofing machine he envisaged would contain a raft of features that could be switched on and off with a mouse as Nav traded in real time, augmenting his natural abilities. Principal among these was what he called the "cancel if close" function, and the U.S. authorities would later describe as a "layering algorithm." When activated, it would allow Nav to place a number of large sell orders a designated number of ticks above the best offer. As the market moved higher and lower, Nav's orders would move in lockstep, always maintaining the specified distance from the current price to minimize the chances of being hit. In the complex world of HFT, it was a surprisingly rudimentary mechanism based around the principle that when algos noticed a jump in the number of sellers relative to buyers, they would also start selling and the market would fall. As the layering algo blew prices lower like an industrial fan, Nav would profit by simultaneously selling some e-minis manually, waiting for the market to fall by a couple of ticks, then exiting his position by buying the same number back and canceling the spoofs. A few minutes later, when conditions had stabilized, he'd start the process again.

The problem with spoofing as a strategy was that it was somewhat akin to picking up nickels in front of a steamroller. To alter the order book sufficiently to have an impact, you had to place big orders. But if a massive hedge fund or bank happened to come along at the wrong moment with a mandate to hoover up a billion dollars of e-minis and lifted all your resting offers, you'd be left watching in horror as the market jumped ten levels, costing you millions. Placing orders several ticks from the prevailing price, as the layering algorithm was designed to do, was pretty safe. But Nav knew if he really wanted to incite the algos, it would be useful to be able to also place some spoofs at or near the best offer, and that was dangerous. The solution he came up with was called "back of the book," and it was designed to take advantage of the CME's First In, First Out (FIFO) queuing system.

Imagine that the e-mini market is a supermarket, and each price level on the ladder represents a different register. Every time a fresh order is placed at a certain price, regardless of its size, it joins the back of the queue for that price and moves steadily further forward as the price fluctuates and the orders in front of it are matched. If, however, a participant adds to their order, like a customer stepping away for a moment to add to their cart, they're judged by the CME to have left the line and sent to the back. Nav's brainwave was to have his algo add a single lot every time a fresh order arrived behind him, thereby constantly sending him to the back of the line and out of harm's way. To keep his order size at the amount he intended, the algo would subtract a solitary contract the next time an order arrived, alternating between plus one and minus one in perpetuity. As a further safeguard, Nav proposed incorporating a feature he called "one clip," which dictated that if any portion of his orders was inadvertently hit, the remainder would immediately be canceled, thereby limiting any potential damage.

Nav's email was forwarded to an engineer in New York named Antonios Hadjigeorgalis, whose job was to help customers get the most out of the Autotrader system. Hadj, as he was known, was a frustrated trader of Greek descent who had taken the job at TT in 2007 when his trading hit a dry patch. In his spare time he was a devotee of self-improvement who practiced yoga and martial arts, followed an ultralow-carb diet, and kept a blog where he reviewed the hundreds of books he speed-read each year. The team Hadj joined was badly overstretched. When he arrived there were four engineers globally, but soon his counterpart in London quit and Hadj was left to pick up the slack. That year he clocked up more than a hundred thousand air miles.

On a summer day in 2009, Hadj touched down in London for a busy schedule of meetings with existing and prospective clients organized by the sales rep. At CFT's offices, Nav talked through the features he wanted. "Cancel if close" was straightforward to set up on the Autotrader system, and Hadj had it up and running within a few minutes. "Back of the book" was more unusual. HFT firms spent millions of dollars to make their systems faster so they could get to the *front* of the queue, but Nav wanted something that did the opposite. Hadj promised to look into it and they parted ways. A couple of months later, in November, Nav emailed again. "The system you set up . . . whereby I turn the Autotrader on or off and when it was turned on it would put offers a specific value and quantity away from the best offer" was proving "really useful," he wrote. "I remember you typing in a code to enable this and was wondering whether you could tell me what it was so I could play around with creating new versions of the same thing." Hadj agreed, but over the next few weeks Nav bombarded him with additional requests until the engineer eventually grew frustrated. All TT customers paid the same monthly fee and any assistance they received was discretionary, but Nav acted as if Hadj was working for him. When Nav pressed him about "back of the book" again, Hadj told him it was beyond Autotrader's functionality and he would need to find an external programmer. Sarao's insistence struck Hadj as odd, but before long TT hired a new engineer in London and it was no longer his problem. He wouldn't give Navinder Sarao another thought until six years later when he saw him on the evening news.

CHAPTER 10

■

THE CRASH

On Thursday, May 6, 2010, Nav awoke in his upstairs bedroom, got up, and switched on the computer that sat at the end of his single bed. He still kept a desk at CFT, but he preferred to trade from his parents' home in Hounslow where there were no distractions or prying eyes. His was a solitary and nocturnal existence. He had few close friends and, beyond the occasional game of snooker or kick-about in the playing fields near his house, he barely left the house. His parents, Nachhattar and Daljit, pressed him to find a wife, but trading was his passion. Every Sunday they headed to the temple with their devout, turban-wearing eldest son Rajvinder and his young family while Nav stayed home and slept.

It's difficult to imagine what it must feel like to invent a machine that prints money and then not tell anyone about it, but that's essentially what Nav had done. The program he'd made using TT software hadn't just worked. It had proven wildly, scarily effective. Following some teething problems, Nav had fine-tuned the system to the point where he could more or less nudge one of the world's biggest markets around at will. The previous day, over a few hours, he'd made $435,185, more than the value of his parents' house. The day before that, his profit was $876,823—

seven times what his hero, Lionel Messi, earned per day at FC Barcelona. Early in his career, Nav made a decision not to talk to his friends and family about his finances because he was worried they would treat him differently. Now, at thirty-one years old, he was outearning the highest paid footballer in the world, and almost nobody aside from his brokers and a couple of financial advisers knew about it.

Nav's activity hadn't gone entirely unnoticed. A few weeks earlier, on March 23, a member of the CME's in-house surveillance unit in Chicago emailed GNI Touch to notify it that, in the space of five minutes, its client had had 1,613 trades rejected with the message "This order is not in the book." Competing market participants had evidently seen Nav's orders resting on the ladder but, when they tried to hit them, were informed that they had disappeared. GNI looked into the issue and determined that Nav was using his software to delete "a huge amount of orders a second." They forwarded him the CME's message and advised him to cut it out.

The following week, Nav emailed the CME, cc'ing his brokers, to "apologise for any inconvenience caused by this." He said he "was just showing a friend of mine what occurs on the bid side of the market almost 24 hours a day, by the high frequency geeks," and asked whether the CME's interest in him meant that "the mass manipulation of the high frequency nerds" was also going to end. Then he went straight back to using the program.

Outside, in the real world, it was a general election day, and residents made their way to polling stations to cast their vote. Britain was in tumult after the financial crisis. Unemployment was up 50 percent, banks like RBS and Lloyds had been nationalized, and the economy remained on life support. The left-leaning Labour Party, which had swept to power on a wave of optimism in 1997, was facing defeat by the center-right Conservatives. Nav didn't care too much either way. As far as he was concerned, all politicians were equally bad. But political uncertainty fed into the markets, which was good for trading.

Nav's trading strategy depended on volatility, and he monitored conditions closely, like a surfer waiting for the perfect swell. When seas were flat, he stayed away. The last couple of weeks had been phenomenal. Between mid-2009 and April 2010, global stock markets had bounced back from their postcrisis lows thanks to interest rate cuts and a glut of central bank money. But the crisis had exposed something rotten in the European Union, and the smell was getting stronger. After bailing out their domestic banks, a number of countries, particularly the so-called PIIGS (Portugal, Italy, Ireland, Greece, and Spain), were saddled with debt and battling recession, unemployment, and social upheaval. The biggest basket case was Greece, where the situation had deteriorated so much it could no longer afford to service its debts. The country was effectively bankrupt, and on May 2 the European Commission, the European Central Bank, and the International Monetary Fund announced they would provide a $145 billion lifeline. In return, Greece's leaders agreed to implement a program of severe public sector cuts. It was the final straw for an already beleaguered population, and on May 4, thousands of protesters stormed the Acropolis in Athens, a stark symbol of how far the country had fallen.

The buzzword in the press was "contagion." If countries started defaulting, the banks that held their debt would require state aid and would be unable to invest in future government bond issuances, leading to a death spiral. And propping up a large economy like Italy or Spain was a different proposition to Greece. With the future of the EU hanging in the balance, institutional investors scurried to safety, pulling assets out of Eurozone sovereign bonds and stocks and piling into gold and Treasury bills. By the morning of May 6, the "fear index," a measure of expected volatility in the S&P 500, was up 16 percent on the start of the week.

Nav bided his time until 3:20 p.m.—9:20 a.m. in Chicago—when, with a click of the mouse, he switched the Autotrader program on. Despite his recent windfall, his home setup was no more complex than the pared-back arrangement at Futex: three monitors containing ladders, charts, a news feed, and a TT interface; a standard keyboard; and a mouse. The only sounds were the planes passing overhead and the thrum of a PC fan straining to combat overheating. Nav activated the "cancel if close" feature and placed four sell orders totaling 2,100 contracts one tick apart, starting three levels above the best offer of 1,163.25. They had a combined value of $120 million. Over the next six minutes, as the e-mini price fluctuated, these orders were automatically canceled and replaced 604 times to ensure they remained in lockstep and therefore unconsummated. With markets already falling, and so much other trading going on, it's almost impossible to know exactly what impact Nav's spoofing had, but by the time he clicked the algo off for the first time that day, the market had tumbled 39 points.

As the day progressed, a pervasive feeling of anxiety took hold of the markets. Apocalyptic news reports from Greece showed black-clad demonstrators hurling Molotov cocktails at armored police, who struggled to keep them at bay with water cannons. In Lisbon, an obdurate Jean-Claude Trichet, head of the European Central Bank, ruled out adopting more drastic measures to curb the crisis, pushing Spanish bond yields to a twelve-year high and forcing the euro lower. By the European close, the EURO STOXX 50 index of blue chips was down 3 percent. The S&P 500 was close behind. If, as Nav had told his acolytes at Futex, the markets were no more than a massive psychological barometer, then the dial was teetering somewhere between fear and panic.

It was on days like this that Nav's approach of focusing his trading on the short side of the market made most sense. When markets rise, they tend to do so in an orderly fashion, climbing steadily over weeks and months. But when they fall, the correction can happen very quickly, and when that occurred, Nav wanted to be positioned to reap the rewards. It explained why, as he would later tell the regulators, he made the bulk of his wealth in no more than twenty days spread across his trading career.

A couple of hours after sitting down to trade, at 5:17 p.m. London time, Nav activated the Autotrader for the last time that day. Usually he liked to use it in five- or ten-minute cycles, per-

haps to evade detection or manage his exposure, but on this occasion he left the orders sitting there for more than two hours. He
also cranked up the size. Nav started the cycle by placing five sell
orders of six hundred lots each, three, four, five, six, and seven
ticks above the best offer. But as the sky grew darker outside,
he added a sixth, bringing the total value of his spoof offers to
$200 million. That barrage sat in an order book that was already
severely imbalanced, helping push the number of sell orders to
twice the volume of resting bids. To ramp up the pressure even
further, Nav used his mouse and keyboard to intermittently flash
scores of *additional* spoofs of 289 and 188 lots. As the market
tumbled, he nimbly carried out his genuine trades, selling chunks
of e-minis at a time, then buying them back for a few ticks less.

Eventually, at 7:40 p.m. in London, 1:40 p.m. in Chicago, Nav
closed the system down and stopped trading for the day. Why he
chose to stop at that exact moment is not clear. Maybe his mother
called him down for dinner. It was, regulators would later calculate, the second-most-frenetic trading session he would ever
have, involving somewhere in the region of 18.5 million orders.
In that final two-hour spell alone, he'd bought and sold 62,077
e-mini contracts with a combined value of $3.4 billion. If, at any
moment, the market had rallied, his entire account could have
been wiped out. Instead, the e-mini fell 361 points, and he made
a profit of $879,018. What happened next, he was only a specta-
tor for.

One minute after Nav shut off the Autotrader program, at
1:41 p.m. CT, the e-mini started to plummet with a velocity and
intensity it never had before. He watched as the S&P 500 shed
5 percent of its value in four minutes, more than it had throughout
the entire day to that point, creating a price chart that resembled
a cliff face. Almost simultaneously, the closely correlated SPDR
exchange-traded fund (known as "the Spider") followed suit on
the New York Stock Exchange. Next, individual shares began to
tumble, igniting a sea of flashing red on traders' screens around the
world. The fear index barreled 20 then 25 then 30 percent higher
as the Dow hurtled below 10,000 points for the first time in six

months. Terrified market participants pulled the plug, draining liquidity and causing the e-mini to cascade lower in gallops of five and ten ticks at a time. At one stage, even crude oil started sinking. From Frankfurt to Shanghai, interconnected financial markets went haywire, an apocalyptic nightmare scenario playing out in fast-forward. Then, at exactly 1:45 and 28 seconds, the e-mini ladder froze. The CME's "stop-logic" function had kicked in after the rate of the fall had breached a set level and, for five long seconds, no trading took place. Around the world, human traders and algorithms paused in unison. The Dow had fallen more in a five-minute period than at any other time in its 114-year history.

When trading resumed, the e-mini started to climb as rapidly and miraculously as it had tanked. The S&P 500 jumped from a low of 1,056 at 1:45 to 1,096 at 1:50 and 1,120 three minutes later, transforming the e-mini chart into a steeply sided V shape. Traders hadn't suddenly woken up from a collective stupor and realized that prices were out of whack. Transactions were occurring automatically at hyperspeed, algorithms interacting with algorithms in frenzied and unpredictable ways. Even as some participants rushed to the exit, the volume of transactions spiked to near-all-time highs, as futures passed back and forth like pinballs.

Away from the CME, the day's most bizarre events were still to come. Between 1:45 and 2:00 p.m. CT, shares in some of America's most familiar corporations changed hands at prices utterly divorced from anything resembling fair value. Proctor & Gamble, Hewlett-Packard, General Electric, and 3M plummeted 10 percent or more, while the iShares Russell 1000 Value Index, a popular exchange-traded fund, fell from $50 to 0.0001 cents. Accenture sold for a solitary cent. At the other end of the spectrum, Apple and auctioneer Sotheby's both transacted at $100,000 a share, momentarily pushing their valuations into the trillions of dollars.

The stock market's twilight zone would also prove short-lived. As the e-mini continued its bounce back, participants tentatively returned to equities markets and individual shares began trading again at levels close to where they'd been before 1:30 p.m. Within half an hour, markets had retraced the bulk of their losses, and by the time NYSE closed, the Dow was back at 10,520.32 points, a sizable but unremarkable 3.2 percent decline on the day. Any trader who happened to leave his desk at 1:30 p.m. on May 6, 2010, and grab a cup of coffee would have missed it, but for twenty minutes or so, the financial world had stared into the abyss. In the end, for reasons nobody quite understood, disaster had been averted, but the repercussions would play out for years to come. As for Nav, he took a couple of days off. Later in the month, when the CME sent him another reminder of the requirement to enter transactions in good faith, he emailed his broker. "Just called" the CME, he wrote, "and told em to kiss my ass."

ACT **TWO**

CHAPTER 11

■

THE AFTERMATH

The U.S. Treasury secretary, Tim Geithner, scheduled an emergency call of the President's Working Group on Financial Markets for 6:30 p.m. Eastern time on May 6, 2010, after the markets had closed. Joining him on the line were Gary Gensler and Mary Schapiro, heads of the Commodity Futures Trading Commission and the Securities and Exchange Commission, respectively; Ben Bernanke from the Federal Reserve; Bill Dudley from the New York Fed; and all the other leaders of the country's major financial authorities. Between them, they were responsible for markets worth hundreds of trillions of dollars. The group had been created by Ronald Reagan in the aftermath of the October 1987 crash to facilitate better coordination between government agencies. Colloquially, it became known as the "Plunge Protection Team" thanks to an unsubstantiated but pervasive rumor that it routinely intervened in markets to serve government ends. The purpose of the call this particular evening was to find an answer to a question being asked by millions of people around the world at that moment: What the fuck just happened?

Geithner asked the participants to talk through what they'd ascertained one by one. The day's events bore some striking similarities to 1987. Amid skittish markets, a sharp fall in S&P index futures had fed through to the stock market, causing a ramp up in trading volume as participants bolted for the exit. This frenzied activity pushed the plumbing underpinning the markets to its breaking point, leading to delays in data feeds and some wildly anomalous trades. The big difference was that, while the '87 crash had played out over a single day ("Black Monday"), the Flash Crash was over in half an hour. And thankfully, this time the markets had bounced back. In terms of who or what had caused it, nobody really had a clue. Rumors ranged from a fat-fingered trader to hackers to terrorists. But the world had moved on from the days when the market's machinations could be observed by the human eye. To get anything approaching a definitive answer, the CFTC, which oversees futures, and the SEC, which is responsible for stocks, would need to obtain and analyze the trading data, microsecond by microsecond, and build a picture of who was doing what and when. It was a gargantuan task of a scale never previously attempted in the electronic era.

One might expect regulators to have real-time oversight of what goes on in their markets, but in fact data is collected by the exchanges and passed along only upon request. In the case of futures, where most products trade on a single exchange, that was relatively straightforward. The CME had already sent a file containing details of the day's e-mini transactions to the CFTC. Stocks were a different story. Since 2005 and the introduction of a set of rules designed to increase competition, the American stock market had become chaotically fragmented. Dozens of exchanges, electronic networks, and obscure trading venues had sprung up from which investors could buy shares, and the SEC would have to wait to hear back from all of them before it could carry out a complete analysis. Geithner proposed that he, Gensler, and Schapiro meet with the heads of the major exchanges the following week and drew the conversation to a close.

Notwithstanding this information black hole, the government was under pressure to reassure the public that it had matters under control. Throughout the next day and into the weekend, the Flash Crash dominated the press, and the consensus was that the rise in algorithmic trading was to blame. "High-Speed Trading Glitch Costs Investors Billions," wrote the *New York Times*. The timing could hardly have been worse. That month, the biggest finance bill since the Great Depression, the Dodd-Frank Wall Street Reform and Consumer Protection bill, was wheedling its way across the floor of the Senate. It was a mammoth piece of legislation that already had staff at the agencies working around the clock. Its focus, however, was on regulating derivatives and making banks more resilient in light of the 2008 financial crisis. There was almost no mention of algorithms or HFT, leading some lawmakers to question whether the authorities were so busy addressing the dangers revealed by the last crisis that they'd failed to spot the iceberg looming up ahead. On May 7, the day after the crash, two Democratic senators, Ted Kaufman and Mark Warner, published a letter demanding that regulators report back to Congress on what happened within sixty days of the ratification of Dodd-Frank. "A temporary $1 trillion drop in market value is an unacceptable consequence of a software glitch," they wrote.

In response to the clamor, the government did what it often does and formed a committee—the Joint CFTC/SEC Advisory Committee on Emerging Regulation—comprising industry leaders, former regulators, and Nobel Prize–winning professors. Its mandate was to consider what, if any, changes should be made to the structure and oversight of the markets in this brave new automated world. It was an illustrious group, but none had any direct experience with high-frequency trading. The youngest member was fifty-five. Meanwhile, staff at the CFTC and the SEC set to work piecing together the events of May 6. Responsibility for the CFTC portion was given to Cyrus Amir-Mokri, an urbane former partner at the elite law firm Skadden, Arps. The goal was to get the Flash Crash investigation wrapped up as quickly as possible while demonstrating that they'd taken the matter seriously.

Amir-Mokri formed a team of around twenty attorneys, investigators, and economists from across the CFTC's nine-story, orange-bricked headquarters in central Washington. Some, from the divisions of Enforcement and Market Oversight, were instructed to interview the most active traders on the day of the crash. Others were tasked with examining the broader macroeconomic conditions. The detailed, trade-by-trade analysis was to be handled by a group of academics led by a young, Ukrainian-born economist named Andrei Kirilenko. Each evening at 7 p.m., the team convened in a conference room on the ninth floor to discuss their progress. For days, they hardly slept. "It was pretty extreme," recalls one staffer. "We'd keep hearing: 'Congress is calling, the White House is calling. They need answers!'"

Adding to the pressure was a constant flow of commentary and speculation in the press. One article in the *Wall Street Journal* suggested, with a hint of irony, that trading by a fund advised by Nassim Nicholas Taleb, author of *Black Swan,* the best-selling treatise on the probability of extreme economic events, may have played a part in the meltdown. Another, on CNBC's website, cited chatter about a mistyped trade in Procter & Gamble shares being the trigger. Then there were the victims' stories. After markets closed on May 6, a broker-dealer industry body called FINRA had struck a deal with the exchanges to cancel any trades that occurred more than 60 percent away from their price before the crash started. Around twenty thousand mostly equities trades were scrapped, but not all transactions met the threshold, resulting in some big losers.

Mike McCarthy, an unemployed father of three from South Carolina, had inherited a modest stock portfolio when his mother died in 2009. As conditions deteriorated on the afternoon of the crash, he called up his broker at Morgan Stanley in a panic and told her to start liquidating his holdings, including 738 shares in Procter & Gamble. Unfortunately for him, the broker executed the order just as the market tanked, and McCarthy ended up receiving $39 per share instead of the roughly $60 he would have got if the trade had gone through either twenty minutes earlier or later. That twist of fate cost him around $17,000. "That's like six-to-eight months of my mortgage payments right there," he told a reporter at *The Street.* Across the country, in Dallas, a small hedge fund called NorCap was burned when, stuck in a losing trade, it was forced to buy some options to cover its position. The order was placed just as the options spiked from around ninety cents to $30, and since FINRA's erroneous trade agreement didn't cover derivatives and the counterparties on the trade, including HFT giant Citadel, refused to rip up the deal, the fund lost more than $3 million.

In a turn of events that would surely have pleased Sarao, Igor Oystacher, his perceived nemesis, lost $3.5 million in a minute after loading up on e-minis after the S&P 500 had fallen 4 percent. Oystacher correctly predicted the market would rebound, but the Russian lost his nerve as the market continued to tumble, and he exited his position for the biggest loss of his career. A few days later he quit Gelber, the firm he'd joined as a student, to start his own outfit. Another casualty was Danny Riley, an experienced pit broker whose operation was almost wiped out when one of his traders accepted a huge order from a hedge fund moments before the market bounced back. "We'd watched the S&P completely fall apart, there was a squawk-box guy screaming . . . (and after it started to rebound) I remember leaning down to look at the other end of the desk," Riley recalls. "Everybody seemed to be cool and I said 'hey is everybody ok?' And everybody nodded their head except one guy at the end who shook his head that he had a problem." Riley pleaded with the counterparty to rip up the trade but it refused, and the firm ended up losing around $8 million. He apportions some of the blame to the regulators for failing to curtail the rise of algorithmic trading. "Who let this stuff in the backdoor and who hasn't controlled it?" he said in an interview on the *Stocktwits* podcast. "I'm a Chicago guy. Things have gotten out of control with this."

A week after the crash, Gensler, Schapiro, and the heads of the major exchanges convened in a large, ornate meeting room near Geithner's office at the Treasury. The atmosphere was tense. On one side, representing the futures industry, was the CME Group's chief executive, Terry Duffy, a bombastic former pit trader of Irish stock who guarded the reputation of "the Merc" like it was his own family. On the other, speaking for the securities markets, were executives from the likes of the New York Stock Exchange and Nasdaq. Tensions had been brewing since the afternoon of the crash. "There was just this big jurisdictional fight to say that the SEC markets were fucked-up and the CFTC markets behaved properly or vice versa," recalls one CFTC official. For two hours, executives took turns explaining how their market had performed exactly as it should when others had failed. It echoed a similar spat between futures and equities in 1987. By the end of the meeting, there was no love lost and little consensus on where to lay the blame.

Back at the CFTC, the investigators' first task was to ascertain who was most active in the e-mini in the period before and immediately after 1:41 p.m. CET, the ground zero of the crash. Trawling through the trade records, they quickly discovered that one entity had sold considerably more e-minis that afternoon than anyone else: Waddell & Reed, a moderately large mutual fund founded in Kansas City in 1937 by a pair of World War I veterans to help families plan for the future "one step at a time . . . regardless of background or level of wealth." Waddell & Reed's flagship investment vehicle was the $27 billion Ivy Asset Strategy Fund, which was comanaged by the firm's president, Michael Avery. For most of 2010, Avery had been bullish, and on the day of the crash, 87 percent of the fund's assets were in shares. But that morning, as the Dow tumbled and bad news from Europe dominated the headlines, his outlook changed and he ordered his staff to hedge their exposure to the stock market by selling seventy-five thousand e-minis worth $4.1 billion. That way, if the market kept falling, the losses the fund took on the shares would be at least partially offset by gains from the e-mini's decline. Normally, the firm's head trader, a man named Jeff Albright, would have overseen such a major transaction, but that day Albright and several of his colleagues were at the bar of the Hilton President hotel at an event hosted by the Kansas City Securities Association. In their absence, the traders in the office utilized an algorithmic platform provided by the British bank Barclays to carry out the trade. In and of itself that wasn't unusual: fund managers invariably use algos to break up large orders and execute them stealthily. It was the specific program they selected that was the problem.

Barclays's platform allowed customers to determine how they executed an order based on variables including market volume, price, and speed. Waddell & Reed's traders opted for a variant that would sell e-minis at a rate of 9 percent of the total trading volume over the previous minute. The idea was that, as trading volumes rose and the market demonstrated greater capacity to absorb the order, selling would increase; and when the market-place slowed down the algo would ease up. However, Waddell & Reed had failed to incorporate any kind of emergency fail-safe, such as a minimum price it was willing to accept per e-mini or a ceiling on how many contracts it was prepared to offload in a given time frame. Under normal conditions, the algo would have served Waddell & Reed's goal of executing a substantial order under the radar, eking out e-minis slowly enough that other par-ticipants wouldn't notice. But when they switched the program on at 1:32 p.m., after a torrid day in Europe, markets were severely out of whack. Within seven minutes, Waddell & Reed's algo had already offloaded around fourteen thousand e-minis. By now, a number of HFTs and hedge funds had become so perturbed by conditions that they'd shut down their machines, and the few buyers who remained disappeared. At 1:41 p.m., with nothing to prop it up, the e-mini started falling like a runaway elevator. If Waddell & Reed's traders had been more responsive, they might have shut the program down. Instead, their volume-sensitive algo actually sped up since—in spite of the exodus—trading activity soared. The CFTC would later conclude that, with no one else to transact with, the automated players that stuck around had gone into a kind of frenzy, firing e-minis back and forth among themselves in what the agency called a "hot potato" effect. By the time the CME's stop-logic function kicked in at 1:45 p.m. and 28 seconds, halting trading for five seconds, Waddell & Reed had sold $1.9 billion worth of e-minis. Over the next six minutes, as the market bounced back, it unloaded the remaining $2.2 billion.

The entire trade, the biggest e-mini transaction of the year, had taken less than twenty minutes and it had occurred during the equivalent of a force 12 hurricane. Gensler described the execution in a speech as like "auto pilot(ing) into a ravine."

The CFTC was in no doubt that Waddell & Reed's mammoth sell order was a major spark for the Flash Crash, but Kirilenko, the economist, wanted to know what role HFT had played. After all, funds and banks had been placing ill-timed and ill-conceived trades forever, and yet markets had never plummeted with such ferocity. Since the preceding year, Kirilenko and his colleagues in a department called the Office of the Chief Economist, many of them PhD students lured to the agency by the prospect of getting access to up-to-the-minute, confidential trade data, had been building a kind of typography of modern electronic futures markets in an effort to understand how pervasive HFT had become, and why it was so profitable. After the crash, that work came to the fore. "HFT was still pretty low on the agenda," recalls Albert "Pete" Kyle, a University of Maryland professor who was at the CFTC at the time, "but we had all these questions, like 'What would happen if one of these algos blew up?' and 'Do they promote or interfere with competitive market-making?'"

On May 6, the researchers found, there were a total of around fifteen thousand participants active in the e-mini, ranging from the smallest one-lot rookies at the likes of Futex to the biggest global pension funds. Of these, they classified sixteen as HFT based on their attributes of trading huge volumes without ever accumulating a large position, and always ending the day close to flat. Despite making up just 0.001 percent of the participants in the trading universe, this group of largely Chicago-based entities was responsible for 29 percent of the trading volume. The HFT lobby liked to talk about how they brought liquidity to the market, making it easier for all participants to buy and sell at reasonable prices whenever they wanted to; but the data suggested that the most profitable of these firms mostly *removed* liquidity by aggressively hitting the resting offers of other participants just as the market was about to move, something academics refer to as "sniping." And on the afternoon of the crash, the majority of HFT firms had either shut down or joined the selling frenzy, pushing prices down further. "During the Flash Crash, the trading behavior of HFTs appears to have exacerbated the downward move in prices," Kirilenko and his colleagues wrote. "We believe that technological innovation is essential for market advancement. As markets advance, however, safeguards must be appropriately adjusted to preserve the integrity of financial markets."

For its part, by late summer the SEC still hadn't managed to corral the nation's equity markets to hand over sufficient trading data to allow it to carry out the kind of analysis for stocks that the CFTC had managed for futures. Absent the numbers, the agency resorted to interviewing traders about their experiences. The conversations suggested there were actually two crashes that afternoon: one in the e-mini between 1:41 p.m. and 1:45 p.m., and a second in individual stocks from 1:45 p.m. until around 2:00 p.m. In a sign of the highly interconnected nature of modern markets, when the e-mini collapsed, it triggered stock traders' systems to shut down automatically. This, in turn, precipitated a bout of selling and, with so few buyers left, shares cascaded. In a few minutes, more than one thousand stocks and exchange-traded funds fell by at least 10 percent. Fueling the exodus was a technical issue at the biggest stock market of all, the New York Stock Exchange, which happened to be upgrading its IT system that day and ended up quoting prices up to twenty seconds old—a virtual lifetime in a marketplace where speed was measured in millionths of a second.

The mystery of why some shares changed hands for less than a cent and others for $100,000 came down to an arcane rule that obliged market makers in a given stock to provide quotes at all times, regardless of conditions. The stipulation was supposed to help prevent events like the Flash Crash by guaranteeing there was always somebody willing to trade, but, as ever on Wall Street, some dealers had found a way around it by leaving extremely high or low quotes in the order book. Before May 6, 2010, it had seemed inconceivable that these so-called "stub quotes" would ever be hit.

On September 30, nearly five months after the crash, the CFTC and the SEC published their joint paper. Determining what caused a market crash is a bit like saying what caused World War I or the rise of Hitler. In a highly complex system, there are always a multitude of factors to which different people will attribute different weights depending on how they view the world. The picture the regulators painted was of a perfect storm in which a huge, clumsy, one-way sell order from an old-school fund arrived at exactly the wrong time, sending an already highly volatile market into meltdown. HFT firms hadn't caused the crash, the authors concluded, but, by either turbocharging the selling or running for the exit, they certainly hadn't helped matters either.

The conclusions inevitably drew criticism, not least from Waddell & Reed, which, backed up by the CME Group, put out a statement saying there was "no evidence to suggest that our trades disrupted the market on May 6" and "trades of the size we initiated normally are absorbed easily by the market." Dave Cummings, an HFT pioneer and the founder of a firm called Tradebot Systems, disagreed. "Who puts in a $4.1bn order without a limit price?" he wrote in a scathing email picked up in the press. "It angers me when people blame technology for what are clearly lapses in human judgment."

Absent from the agencies' 104-page report or the myriad interviews and speeches that CFTC and SEC executives gave on the subject in the months that followed was any mention of spoofing or market manipulation. A preliminary version of the report cited a "significant imbalance of sell orders and buy orders" in the e-mini that "contributed to a sudden liquidity dislocation," but there was no attempt to consider what lay behind the imbalance; nothing, in other words, to tie the maelstrom to a solitary trader with a homemade algorithm on the outskirts of London who would one day become synonymous with it.

■

CHAPTER 12

MILKING MARKETS

On a brisk spring morning in 2010, two men in suits, one in his sixties, the other in his early thirties, waited outside an elegantly understated brick town house in London's historic legal district rubbing their hands to keep warm. They had an appointment inside, in the luxuriant ambience of Pump Court Tax Chambers, but their client was irritatingly, characteristically late. More than an hour after the allotted meeting time, a figure lolloped toward them wearing a beanie and an old pilot-style leather jacket over what appeared to be a Superman T-shirt. In his hand was a brown paper bag from McDonald's. "Nav, great to see you!" the older man, Paul James, said with a smile. Nobody mentioned the time.

James was a partner at a firm of accountants called Advanta based in the English seaside town of Eastbourne that specialized in looking after futures traders, including Nav. He also had a side business introducing clients to investment opportunities and tax schemes for which he received commissions that augmented his accountant's salary. As Nav's assets had soared, the trader had expressed an interest in finding new ways to make money, and James lined him up with his contacts, including his younger companion that day, Miles MacKinnon. Once inside, the three men were taken to a meeting room filled with legal tomes where they were met by Andrew Thornhill, one of the country's preeminent tax barristers, as well as a fifth individual, who specialized in off-shore finance and who had organized the meeting. On the agenda, a subject close to all their hearts: what to do with Nav's large and rapidly expanding fortune.

Since 1969, Thornhill had been advising aristocrats and business magnates on how to structure their affairs to minimize tax without falling foul of the perennial foe, Her Majesty's Revenue & Customs. Not many of them had shown up to his meetings eating a Filet-O-Fish, but Thornhill took an instant liking to his new client. When Nav summed up his trading strategy as "basically in and out, in and out," Thornhill exclaimed: "Splendid!" How, exactly, Nav made his money was less important than what he planned to do with it, and the young trader had already proven receptive to the idea of getting one over on the taxman. In 2005, while renting a desk at Futex, Nav had set up a one-man company, Nav Sarao Futures Limited. (He resisted a colleague's suggestion to name it Chavex Ltd.) When his assets jumped from $330,000 to more than $20 million in 2009, James had introduced him to John Dupont, sales director of a firm called Montpelier Tax Consultants that specialized in close-to-the-line tax avoidance schemes. Nav signed up for a plan that involved his company, NSFL, entering into a series of sham, loss-making derivative transactions that slashed his taxable income. Happy with the result, Nav was now amenable to a more substantive overhaul of his operation.

Thornhill's proposal, contained in documents that he unwrapped from thin pink ribbons, was for Nav to organize his business around two so-called employee benefit trusts registered on the tiny Caribbean island of Nevis. The first would hold the shares in Nav's UK company. To pass muster, it would need to be managed at arm's length by ostensibly independent trustees based in Nevis. The second, established by the company, would house $30 million of accumulated profits, money that would immediately be loaned back to NSFL for Nav to trade with. The structure, Thornhill explained, would allow Nav to use his money without triggering a tax bill. And behind the smoke and mirrors, Nav would be the sole ultimate beneficiary of both entities. To justify an employee benefit scheme of this type, NSFL needed to have more than one employee, so MacKinnon, who was Dupont's business partner, agreed to join the company as a silent director until the structure was up and running, at which point he'd resign.

After signing the documents, Nav caught the Piccadilly Line back to Hounslow. A few weeks later, the offshore specialist convinced him to set up another vehicle, this one in Mauritius, which would be used to invest cash that wasn't tied up in trading. Its name: the "NAV Sarao Milking Markets Fund." Nav paid $2.3 million in professional fees for the work before he'd seen any benefits, 20 percent of which was kicked back to MacKinnon, Dupont, and James for making the connection.

While his advisers took care of his business affairs, Nav was free to focus on trading. The Eurozone crisis continued to roil markets around the world, and by 2011 Nav's system, an amalgamation of a modified TT algo and his own rapid-fire scalping, was working better than ever. His best day, by some margin, came on August 4, when apocalyptic headlines from Italy and Spain collided with weak U.S. employment figures and speculation about a forthcoming downgrade of U.S. government debt, driving the S&P 500 down 4.8 percent, its biggest drop since the collapse of Lehman Brothers. Nav rode the e-mini all the way down. By the time the market closed, he'd made $4.1 million.

With so much money piling in, Nav's biggest problem was knowing what to do with it all. He liked fast cars and expensive watches and trips to fancy night clubs—*in theory*—but nowhere near as much as he liked the feeling of accumulating wealth; and he found it hard not to view any purchases, no matter how small, as eating into his trading capital. When the financiers and lawyers who now courted him inquired about what he planned to do with his growing riches, he gave a host of different answers, like a child who's asked what he wants to be when he grows up: build an animal sanctuary; emigrate to Canada and take up snowboarding; give it away to charity; buy a football team in Spain or South America. For Nav, talk of the future was only ever a fleeting distraction from the immediate and unquenchable goal of accruing more money, something his new advisers assured him they could help with.

SHORT AND stocky, with lightning-fast feet and a low center of gravity, Miles MacKinnon was destined to be a rugby player. He grew up skipping tackles and scoring tries on the playing fields of Kent, then got into the Harlequins squad, one of the country's best, before a heart scare forced him to rethink his future. Privately educated and clubbable if not exactly academic, he bypassed university for a sales job with AXA Sun Life and then Zurich Financial Services, where he was introduced to Dupont, who is five years older and has the blandly reassuring bearing of a Tory politician. MacKinnon lasted less than a month, but the two men stayed in touch.

For the next few years, MacKinnon worked on commission for a firm that, improbably, lined up investors in dives for sunken treasure. Uncovering doubloons was rare, but clients were compensated by the hefty tax breaks they received thanks to a clause in the law designed to promote risky investments. Meanwhile, in 2005, Dupont left Zurich to take up a management position in Montpelier's London office. From a bustling room near Piccadilly Circus, his staff cold-called traders and entrepreneurs and pitched them creative ways to cut their tax bill in exchange for 20 percent of whatever they saved. "Everybody there thought they were Alec Baldwin in *Glengarry Glen Ross*," recalls a former employee, referring to the iconic 1992 movie set in the cutthroat world of sales.

Tax avoidance businesses like Montpelier were engaged in a perpetual game of cat and mouse with the authorities. After identifying a potential loophole in the legislation—around, say, how charitable donations or dividends were treated—they would pay a lawyer to design a scheme and then flog it relentlessly until the Revenue caught up and closed it down. Many of their customers were aware they might eventually be forced to pay the tax but took the view that they were better off having access to the money for a few years. And Montpelier promised to foot the legal bill if it ever came to that. For a while, the going was good. "There was a sense that tax was just another cost to be managed, and that anything you could do to eradicate it without breaking the law was fair game," recalls one tax consultant. But when the financial crisis hit, the government's laissez-faire attitude hardened. In 2010, authorities began investigating Montpelier for propagating tax fraud. Its offices were raided and a senior director on the Isle of Man was arrested. Charges against him were later dropped, but the company was shut down and two thousand customers were ordered to pay back $250 million in unpaid taxes.

Dupont, who was never charged himself, got out before the situation turned ugly. In April 2010, around the time Nav was becoming open to new opportunities, he and MacKinnon started their own company, MacKinnon Dupont LLP (and later MD Capital Partners), a "boutique private equity firm" that connected rich individuals with high-risk, high-reward investment opportunities in exchange for a finder's fee and, maybe, a slice of equity. They rented a basement office on the outskirts of Mayfair, home of hedge funds, private members clubs, and $40 million apartments, and courted introductions from solicitors and independent financial advisers. Finding accountants and IFAs like James, who were willing to send clients their way for a fat fee, was easy. Convincing savvy investors to take a punt on a chain of wine bars, a tech start-up, or a speculative gold mining venture—"expected return over 5 years is 300%"—less so. Dressed in bespoke suits and statement watches, they pitched their prospects in the lobbies of five-star hotels. After hours they networked at charity events and clubs like the Worshipful Company of International Bankers. MacKinnon's style was high energy and relentless. Dupont was a social chameleon who brought a degree of technical knowledge to the table. They built a roster of half a dozen or so clients, of which Nav was by far the largest investor.

It's hard to imagine a more desirable client for a firm like MacKinnon Dupont than Nav. He had a constant flow of money that he seemingly didn't need or spend, and, with the Bank of England base rate of interest lingering at 0.5 percent, he was willing to consider anything that would bolster the paltry returns he was getting on his funds. MacKinnon pitched him on the shipwreck scheme, but Nav rejected it point-blank, saying the returns weren't high enough and he was only interested in projects where he would be the sole or majority investor. While the pair worked up other ideas, they made themselves indispensable. When Nav said he was dissatisfied with his bank, Credit Suisse, MacKinnon organized a meeting with Goldman Sachs. In an office overlooking St Paul's Cathedral, one of Goldman's top private bankers delivered his pitch while Nav slurped an entire cup of coffee with a teaspoon. "Interesting way to drink that coffee, what was that about?" MacKinnon asked when they were outside, to which Nav replied that he didn't normally drink coffee. "Maybe don't get a coffee next time," MacKinnon said.

True to form, in 2011, just a few months after Nav moved his business to Nevis, Her Majesty's Revenue & Customs announced it would be changing the legislation on employee benefit schemes to stamp out what it described as "disguised remuneration." Under the new rules, Nav had two choices: repay the $30 million he'd "borrowed" from one of his trusts, leaving him with no capital to trade; or cough up in excess of $10 million in tax. Meanwhile, the NAV Sarao Milking Markets Fund, pitched as a stepping-stone to Nav never paying tax again, collapsed before it got off the ground. With Nav facing a quandary, MacKinnon and Dupont introduced him to a semiretired tax expert they knew named Brian Harvey who they thought might be able to help. Harvey had spent years as a tax inspector before switching sides and providing advice from his home on the south coast. After listening to Nav and his advisers explain the problem in a hotel lobby off the Strand, he suggested tearing down the entire Nevis edifice and starting again. A few weeks later, in October 2011, he wrote to Nav laying out the proposal in detail.

Harvey's plan, which Nav approved, was even more complicated than Thornhill's. Based around what's known as a "personal portfolio bond," it encapsulates why many people regard the offshore financial system with disdain. First, Harvey appointed a small, friendly offshore insurer named Atlas Insurance Management to establish a new company in Anguilla with the name International Guarantee Corporation, or IGC. Next, Atlas established a bond whose only investment was ownership of IGC. Finally, the roughly $30 million in cash sitting in one of the Nevis trusts was transferred into the entity. Officially, Atlas managed IGC. It appointed its directors from its own staff, opened the post, and signed off on any decisions. But it was a charade. As IGC's sole "investment adviser" and beneficiary, Nav had complete control over the entity. If he wanted to take out any money or make an investment, all he had to do was send a request and it would be done. And, under a so-called guarantee arrangement, Nav's brokers accepted the assets in IGC as collateral, allowing him to continue trading. For this and other assignments, Harvey sent Nav a bill for $510,000. It was a small price to pay for achieving the holy trinity of giving Nav control over his funds, enabling him to trade, and keeping the tax office at bay. There was one issue, though, that even Harvey couldn't eradicate. As a UK citizen, if Nav ever tried to repatriate his money, he'd be hit with an almighty tax bill. The only way to avoid it would be to take up permanent residence elsewhere. But these were concerns for another day.

With Nav's affairs back on track, MacKinnon and Dupont came to him with a new investment idea to catapult him from day trader rich to hedge fund manager rich: wind farms. In Scotland, the incoming government had made a pledge that 100 percent of the country's electricity needs would be met with renewable sources by 2020, and to help it get there it was offering subsidies to anyone with a turbine that pumped juice into the national grid. Scotland is Europe's windiest country, and investors calculated they could make big returns by buying up swaths of uninhabited land and filling it with turbines, all while doing their bit for the environment. Not all residents were happy at the prospect of having their countryside blighted by armies of ninety-foot struc- tures, but MacKinnon and Dupont had a contact in Edinburgh they said was uniquely placed to unlock the country's riches: a quantity surveyor and property developer by the name of Martin Davie, who had founded one of the first businesses to spring up in response to the government's renewable energy pledge. Davie's bedside manner left something to be desired—he'd reportedly brought the inhabitants of Ayrshire to tears during one consulta- tion meeting—but he had struck an exclusivity deal with one of the country's biggest land banks, giving him an in with a long list of farmers and landowners who were potentially amenable to hosting turbines on their property. Davie suggested he and Nav go into business. Nav would provide the capital—an ini- tial $16 million plus a pledge to provide a further $8 million if it was needed—while Davie would run the operation day to day, identifying sites, arranging for surveys, and securing the relevant approvals. When the sites were ready, they would be packaged up and sold to institutional investors. The goal was to develop a portfolio of, to begin with, ten locations capable of producing 500 megawatts. Davie estimated that the enterprise would start mak- ing a profit within three years and, based on the going rate for wind energy, be worth more than $400 million after five, a huge return on investment.

After months of encouragement, Nav warmed to the deal, but he wanted some assurances that his money wouldn't be squan- dered. MacKinnon and Dupont suggested setting up a second company to project manage the venture. The pair would sit on the board, keeping a close eye on any outgoings, and Nav could check the expenses. Nav agreed, and in April 2012, the directors of IGC, his offshore company, and the directors of Eco Projects, a com- pany tied to Davie, established an entity on the tax-friendly Isle of Man that they called Cranwood Holdings Limited. Around the same time, MacKinnon, Dupont, and Davie incorporated Wind Energy Scotland LLP, the management company, in the UK. Nav handed MacKinnon and Dupont an $800,000 finder's fee for lining up the deal and agreed to give them a share of his profits once the seed money had been paid back. To celebrate, they went to a bar in London and drank expensive scotch, Nav's watered down with a coke. Navinder Sarao, business tycoon, was born.

■

CHAPTER 13

THE DUST SETTLES

While Nav mulled what to do with his growing riches, the debate in the United States over high-frequency trading grew louder. CBS's *60 Minutes* aired a segment on the "math wizards" who secretly controlled the market, and scarcely a day passed without reports of another "mini flash crash" involving unexplained blips in stocks like Cisco Systems and the Washington Post Company. On December 8, 2010, two months after the CFTC and SEC published their report, the Senate's Banking Committee held a hearing titled "Stock Market Flash Crash: Causes and Solutions." Kicking off the proceedings, the Democrat Carl Levin said: "Today U.S. capital markets, which traditionally have been the envy of the world, are fractured, they're vulnerable to system failures and trading abuses and they're operating with oversight blind-spots. The very markets that we rely on to jumpstart our economy and invest in America's future are susceptible to market dysfunctions that jeopardize investor confidence."

Shifting uncomfortably before Levin and the other committee members in the Capitol Hill meeting room were Mary Schapiro from the SEC and the CFTC's Gary Gensler. The regulators had already taken some steps to address the public's growing concern. The SEC was introducing circuit breakers to stocks, akin to the CME's stop-logic, which would automatically halt trading if prices rose or fell too abruptly; and stub quotes, which had resulted in shares changing hands for less than a cent, had been outlawed. On the futures side, the CFTC put forth a rule that would make it illegal for the CME or any other exchange to sell select customers faster access to their servers unless the same opportunities were made available to everyone. Still, there was a sense in some quarters that the authorities were rearranging the deck chairs on the *Titanic*. The most glaring issue, as articulated by Levin, remained: "Traders today are equipped with the latest, fastest technology. Our regulators are riding the equivalent of mopeds going 20 miles per hour chasing traders whose cars are going 100."

As the Flash Crash had demonstrated, regulators weren't just unable to monitor in real time what was going on in their markets. Even seven months on, the SEC didn't have the data it would have required to understand what happened to equity markets over a single half-hour period at a granular level. If the umpires couldn't watch the game, how could they hope to referee it? To remedy the issue, Schapiro proposed something called the Consolidated Audit Trail, a vast data repository that would allow regulators to track orders across the market and identify the brokers handling them. It would take at least four years to build and cost an estimated $4 billion. In the meantime, the financial cops would have to continue relying on the private exchanges to alert them to problems.

As financial markets had evolved, the government's ability to oversee them had fallen further and further behind. Fundamentally, it was a question of resources. The SEC's budget in 2010 was just over a billion dollars, while the CFTC got by on less than $200 million. The year before, meanwhile, HFT giant Citadel's founder, Ken Griffin, *personally* took home $900 million. Each year the agencies begged for more money to hire experts and upgrade their aging technology and each year they were knocked back. There was also a glaring skills gap. At the CFTC, where lawyers reigned, investigators and economists with up-to-date computer skills and markets experience were in short supply, and it was easy to understand why. Even the most civic-minded young programmer would struggle to turn down hundreds of thousands of dollars on Wall Street or in Chicago for a $70,000 base salary, no sleep, and bad coffee at one of the agencies. "Resources are a significant concern," said Schapiro with practiced restraint. "We're trying to bring in new skill sets, people with experience in algorithmic trading . . . on trading desks and hedge funds . . . to try to help us have the capability to do the job we've been charged with doing."

About an hour into proceedings, Senator Jack Reed, a former serviceman from Rhode Island, shifted the conversation from the practical to the philosophical: "The presumption of most people who own a few stocks is that the value of stocks, the liquidity of stocks is directly a function of their economic value, the same thing with debt instruments and derivatives. One of the issues we have to deal with is, with the proliferation of these algorithmic, high-frequency traders, some of these algorithms don't take into account the fundamentals of the instrument, the economic value, the dividends, the status of the municipality issuing them. They are simply saying, 'if enough of these are sold then we start selling, and then if we start selling another algorithm kicks in.' To the extent that we get further away from the economic values here, does that not only cause concern, but is that something that's good for the economy? It may be a naïve question but I'll pose it."

"It's not a naïve question at all," Schapiro replied. "It's sort of the fundamental question we're all grappling with."

The Flash Crash had laid bare the regulators' limitations, but more than that, it had awoken the wider population to the fact that the entire structure of the financial markets had shifted under their feet without them noticing. Those few anxious minutes, when it seemed conceivable that the whole edifice would come crashing down, had led to a reckoning. The senators spoke for all Americans when they pondered what the repercussions were of completely automating a system that determined the value of

our companies, our savings, and the food and resources we con-
sumed; in whose interests it was for securities to change hands
thousands of times per minute; who the winners and losers were
from this paradigm shift; and what would happen if the technology were to be abused.

Later in the hearing, after Gensler and Schapiro had left, the
senators asked the owner of an HFT firm named Manoj Narang
what risks high-frequency trading posed to the markets. "It
takes capital to move markets . . . and virtually every HFT out
there controls very little capital . . . so it's entirely implausible,"
he said in a clipped tone. When another panelist suggested that
some HFT firms might deliberately seek to manipulate markets,
Narang was defiant: "I don't know of any HFT strategies currently in use or that can be hypothetically conceived of that are
destabilizing to the market." The exchange was symptomatic of
a growing divide between supporters and critics of HFT that
would play out in universities, cable news studios, trading floors,
and newspaper columns for years to come. Advocates of HFT
argued it brought efficiencies to the marketplace, lowering bid-
ask spreads, a widely accepted measure of value for money; and
adding liquidity, allowing market participants to trade quickly
and easily at stable, transparent prices. They painted their opponents as reactionary has-beens tilting at windmills. The naysayers
portrayed HFTs as leeches who made false claims and brought
instability. By 2011, the debate was no longer just a theoretical
one. For the first time, governments around the world seriously
considered clamping down on high-frequency trading. It wasn't
simply a matter of stability; there was also the question of *fairness*. Was it really appropriate that a small group of lightly regulated firms was creaming more than $10 billion out of the markets
each year, and at what point, if ever, should the government
intervene? With Dodd-Frank still trundling through the system,
agencies mulled whether fresh rules might be incorporated. The
CFTC launched a public consultation and invited two dozen traders, brokers, exchange executives, and professors to Washington
to discuss whether increased regulation was required. The SEC

undertook its own review of equity markets and invited parties to submit their thoughts. Similar inquiries took place in Germany, Italy, and the UK. After years spent hiding in the shadows, HFT was in the spotlight.

Proposals for reform varied widely. One of the more contentious was a transaction tax, or "Tobin Tax," which, depending on its size, would either make it uneconomical for HFT firms to place and cancel so many orders, or at least raise some additional funds for the government. Another was bringing in "speed bumps" to slow down orders, eradicating the HFTs' advantage. Other options included making HFT firms register the code for their strategies, levying fines for canceling too many orders, and forcing market makers to quote prices regardless of how volatile conditions got. "We basically viewed it as a public safety issue," recalls one former CFTC employee. "There are safety measures and speed limits for automobiles. Should there be something similar in financial markets?"

For the most part, the HFT firms and the exchanges where they operated argued that reform was either unwarranted or could be achieved voluntarily. Fifteen of the biggest firms formed a body called the Principal Traders Group, which commissioned professors to write papers espousing the benefits of HFT, gave speeches on the hysteria of the media, and funneled donations to their political allies, including Chicago's mayor, Rahm Emanuel, who visited the CFTC to lobby against one proposed rule. The group appointed an ex-CFTC economist to make its case and, in November 2010, took the agency's chairman, Gensler, out for steaks in Chicago to press their interests en masse in a more informal setting. For once, Gensler, a former senior executive at Goldman Sachs, wasn't the richest one at the table.

While the HFT lobby was slick, well funded, and organized, their opponents were a more motley crew. Within the CFTC itself, one of the regulator's five politically appointed commissioners, the Democrat Bart Chilton, pushed for tighter rules and appeared on business television describing HFT firms as "cheetahs." With cowboy boots and blond locks that gave him the appearance of an aging He-Man, he gamely debated the subject on talk shows, but he represented the minority voice. Also invited to sit on various panels were Joseph Saluzzi and Sal Arnuk, two straight-talking Italian-American brokers from New Jersey, who found it galling to be debating the finer points of regulation when they considered it patently obvious that the whole system was rigged against their clients, the pension, and savings funds. Their influential 2012 book, *Broken Markets,* was among the first to highlight what they saw as the inherent iniquities of HFT in equities markets.

A mysterious commentator writing under the pseudonym R. T. Leuchtkafer—German for "firefly"—captured the attention of the industry with a series of erudite and scathing critiques of the modern market structure that were picked up by the business press. Like Daniel Defoe three hundred years earlier, he painted a picture of a system set up for the benefit of the few. "It is no argument to say the advantages of HFT firms are available to anyone," he wrote in one widely publicized letter to the SEC. "They are not. They are only available to those with the capital and regulatory latitude to pay for those advantages . . . The corruptible but regulated dealer has been replaced by largely unaccountable and unregulated firms. You should not underestimate the widespread and legitimate anger at these firms."

Perhaps the loudest member of the resistance was Eric Hunsader, the founder of a company called Nanex, which analyzed and repackaged oceans of trading data from an office above a barbershop in Winnetka, Illinois. Hunsader detested HFT and built up a cult following on Twitter by posting charts and videos that he said showed spoofing and other forms of cheating. A few weeks after the Flash Crash, Hunsader and his colleagues were scouring data when they noticed that some exchanges were intermittently being bombarded with huge volumes of orders in short bursts, sometimes as many as five thousand in a second. The activity had little impact on prices, but it momentarily slowed the exchanges, leading Nanex to conclude that unscrupulous players were flooding the system with false signals to confound their rivals and gain an advantage. The phenomenon showed up in strange-looking charts that Nanex likened to crop circles and gave names like "crystal triangle" and "chalice." Intriguingly, one occurred as the e-mini collapsed on May 6. Nanex dubbed the practice "quote stuffing" and suggested it was a major, unspoken cause of the crash.

In July 2010, Hunsader was invited to Washington to present his findings to a roomful of people from the CFTC and the SEC, who listened politely and asked questions. But when the report came out, "quote stuffing" barely got a mention. In Hunsader's mind the reason was clear: it was a whitewash. He persuaded Waddell & Reed to send him its trading records and published his own alternative Flash Crash report that vindicated the Kansas City fund manager and said it had been made a scapegoat for the HFT industry. "Why would SEC regulators deny that *Quote Stuffing* exists and that our analyses are 'the stuff of conspiracy theories?'" he asked in one blog post. Maybe "the regulators don't wish to acknowledge that the playground they created has been taken over" and admit "their role as enablers?"

As the debate continued into 2012, two events kept algo-rithmic trading on the agenda. In May, Facebook's long-awaited stock market listing was dogged by technical problems; and, three months later, a bungled software upgrade at Knight Capital Group caused the then-largest intermediary in U.S. equities to fire off erroneous orders for 150 companies. By the time Knight got a handle on the issue, it had lost $460 million, and it was sold soon afterward for a fraction of its valuation before the incident. Yet the more time passed after the Flash Crash, the more the white heat of fervor dissipated. HFT got bigger and migrated to new markets, but there was no repeat of May 6, 2010; no multimarket "Splash Crash," as the doom-mongers had predicted. "There was a lot about HFT that was contested," recalls a senior government official. "For every person that said these algos were bad, others would say, 'No, they're good.' Empirical data was hard to come by. We needed to have a degree of conviction that not only did we understand the phenomenon, but that regulation was a good response to the situation. We weren't going to regulate something just because a bunch of people complained about it."

For every proposed reform, the HFT lobby was ready with a counterargument. A transaction tax was too onerous and likely to damage the U.S. economy; speed bumps were impractical from a technical point of view; forcing market makers to stick around in volatile periods would result only in bankruptcies; making firms send their secret sauce recipes to regulators posed unreasonable security risks. Some small changes crept in. The CME and other exchanges, which already tracked what proportion of their customers' orders were canceled, started penalizing outliers with bigger fines. But the window for a more fundamental overhaul of the market closed. The government's attentions shifted to the rising threat of cybersecurity, the agencies went back to finishing Dodd-Frank, and the assorted committees set up to examine HFT quietly disbanded. "It was strange really, nobody ever said it was finished. We just stopped meeting up," recalls one elderly committee member.

On the fourth floor of the CFTC, one unlikely glimmer of resistance still flickered. After the Flash Crash report, Kirilenko had been promoted to chief economist, and, with little budget at his disposal, he focused on attracting students from the best universities to spend time at the agency. By 2012, there were around forty paid and unpaid researchers devoted to understanding the shifting financial landscape. "The old ways of modeling and understanding financial markets just weren't working anymore, they couldn't capture these new high-speed, high-volume markets," says Steve Yang, a University of Virginia PhD who was among them. "Andrei had this grand ambition to build a research enterprise to address that."

Kirilenko prided himself on being a dispassionate scientist, but there was something about the industry's "nothing to see here" attitude that stuck in his craw. The general public and the press may not have been able to grapple with the finer points of market microstructure, but he sure as hell could; and his work on the crash had shown him that some of the biggest HFT firms weren't just selflessly providing liquidity. It was a convenient illusion. In late 2012, Adam Clark-Joseph, a young Harvard PhD who spent time at the CFTC, issued a paper titled "Exploratory Trading" that posited that HFT firms routinely fired small, loss-making orders into the market like sonar to gather what he described as "private" information about market conditions before placing much larger orders when they knew they were more likely to profit. And in November, Kirilenko and two colleagues put out a paper titled "The Trading Profits of High Frequency Traders." With each publication, the group pulled back the curtain a little further.

Using granular data on trading in the e-mini, Kirilenko et al. were able to substantiate that a vanguard of HFT firms had found a way to make large and extremely consistent profits without taking significant risks. These elite firms, which the professors didn't name, had proven remarkably resistant to competition and made most of their money from retail and institutional market participants—in other words, the pension funds, mutual funds, and day traders they claimed to be making things better for. On December 3, 2012, the *New York Times* ran an article with the headline "High-Speed Traders Profit at Expense of Ordinary Investors, a Study Says," complete with a photograph of a stern-looking Kirilenko. The *Wall Street Journal* published its own account, which quoted the authors asking whether the "arms race for ever-increasing speed and technological sophistication" had any social value. It was incendiary stuff from a government employee, and the following week a letter arrived from the CME's lawyers, Skadden, Arps, accusing the CFTC of breaching data confidentiality laws and putting the exchange's customers' "trade secrets" at risk. As a regulatory agency, the CFTC was permitted—indeed, mandated—to conduct research. But granting outside academics like Kirilenko's recruits access to sensitive data for use in non-CFTC papers was beyond the pale, the CME claimed.

Amid pressure from the HFT lobby, Gensler shut off access to the servers for all noncontracted staff. Two months later, he dismissed twenty-one research economists on temporary contracts. For more than a year, no research was commissioned by the CFTC into high-frequency trading or anything else. Several papers never saw the light of day. "This was fundamental research that was essential to the public's understanding of the way markets worked, and it was flagrantly suppressed," says the University of Maryland's Albert Kyle. The purge took place without the involvement of Kirilenko, who left the CFTC a few days after the *Times* article ran to take up a prearranged position as a professor at MIT. An inquiry into the CFTC's handling of the affair later concluded that while the Office of the Chief Economist's processes for bringing on researchers and keeping data secure were sloppy, there was never actually any breach of the rules on confidentiality. Kirilenko's researchers had always been careful to ensure that no individual firms or strategies could be identified in their work, and the CME's allegations were without foundation. In the end it didn't matter. A sharp jolt of pressure from the HFT lobby was all it took to yank the curtain closed.

■

CHAPTER 14

THOUGHT CRIME

The CFTC did introduce one significant change to the way futures markets were policed, and it was something that both pleased the HFT community and placed Sarao in the agency's crosshairs: an outlaw on spoofing. It was brought in to draw a line under the government's long, woeful record at stamping out cheating.

King Jack Sturges. Mr. Copper. The Boy Plunger. The Hunt Brothers. Crazy Harper. The annals of futures markets are lit up with the names of financial buccaneers who made headlines and fortunes by pushing prices around while the authorities stood helplessly by. In the late nineteenth century, it was gold; in the 1920s, grain; by the fifties and sixties, onions, coffee, and soybeans. The commodities changed, but the methods were consistent: a trader with deep pockets quietly cornered supply and forced prices up; an unscrupulous short-seller spread negative rumors and pushed them lower; supposed competitors formed a nefarious pact. In 1974, after a particularly egregious episode known as the "Great Grain Robbery," President Gerald Ford created the CFTC as a kind of designated cop for futures akin to the SEC. But a few years later, when three brothers from Texas monopolized the silver market and pushed prices up by 713 percent, it was clear little had changed.

Part of the problem was cultural. Since futures markets, unlike stocks, were almost exclusively inhabited by professionals, an ethos of caveat emptor prevailed. Regulation in this clubby world was considered unseemly, and the exchanges, at least nominally, took the lead in keeping everyone in check. Every now and then, after a spike in oil or a collapse in wheat prices, the political pressure to intervene became too much and the CFTC announced a probe. But most of the cases it brought were decidedly small fry. From its inception, the agency was timid, underresourced, and, crucially, hamstrung by the law.

When Congress passed the Commodity Exchange Act in 1936, it banned manipulation but declined to define what manipulation was. That task was left to the courts, which came up with different, often contradictory interpretations. How much and for how long did prices have to move to constitute manipulation? Was it necessary to show a participant meant to impact prices, or would recklessness suffice? What distinguished cheating from legitimate trading based on supply and demand? In a landmark 1982 case involving an entity called the Indiana Farm Bureau, a four-part test was formulated that laid down a heavy precedent. For manipulation to occur, the court said, prosecutors had to prove that a party had the ability to influence prices; that they *specifically* intended to move them; that artificial prices existed; and that the defendant caused them. This turned out to be an almost impossible threshold to meet, and over the next four decades, the CFTC prevailed in just one manipulation case at trial. Proving a price was artificial and determining what caused it was an imprecise, knotty endeavor involving price regressions and statistical analysis that was hard to explain to a jury and easy to refute. The agency had more success prosecuting the lesser charge of "attempted manipulation," which rested on the first two of the four legs, but even then, when it came to intent, traders could usually find some reasonable-sounding explanation for their actions.

As a result, the majority of cases either settled early with a modest fine or collapsed before making it to trial. After one particularly high-profile failure, a group of senators wrote to the agency to say it was "an embarrassment." "The whole purpose of the CFTC was to stop manipulation and it was toothless," says legal scholar Jerry Markham, the author of a paper that characterized commodity manipulation as "The Unprosecutable Crime."

When Gensler was appointed chairman in 2009 following a drawn-out and contentious nomination process, the former banker pledged to plug the gaps in the manipulation rules and bring the CFTC's regime more in line with the SEC. Members of the Enforcement Division came up with something called "Disruptive Trading Practices," which identified acts they saw as antithetical to the fair functioning of markets. These included what's colloquially known as "banging the close," that is, trading heavily during the short window when the settlement price of a commodity is set to benefit another position; and spoofing, which they defined as "bidding or offering with the intent to cancel the bid or offer before execution." By criminalizing specific behaviors, the CFTC hoped to provide its prosecutors with an alternative route to victory at trial, and with little fanfare an amendment was inserted onto page 684 of the draft Dodd-Frank bill in December 2009. The existing manipulation statutes in the Commodity Exchange Act were also tweaked to make it easier for the government to prevail.

At first, few people in the industry seemed to pay much attention, but around a year later, at a roundtable discussion at the CFTC's offices in Washington, several parties, including the exchanges, raised objections. They argued there was no widely understood practice called spoofing in futures and that the CFTC's definition was too vague. They also said that instituting a blanket ban on placing orders you didn't want to consummate risked inadvertently prohibiting legitimate practices like placing stop-losses.

It's part of the dance of rulemaking that industry participants tend to object to new rules regardless of how sensible they might be, but the HFT community got behind the spoofing ban straight-away. Adam Nunes from the New York firm Hudson River Trading said the proposal would "make the market more liquid and more efficient," and "allow legitimate practices to occur without the risk of being manipulated." This, he said, would be "good for end users and good for, you know, firms like those around the table." Nunes's response makes sense when you consider that spoofing in the electronic era specifically targeted firms like his— HFTs that parsed the order book for information that would allow them to predict which way the market was about to move and then traded ahead of it. Their system only worked, though, if the signals the robots were scanning were an accurate representation of their opponents' intentions. If traders disguised their plans by placing sell orders in the ladder when they planned to buy or, like Nav, inputting mammoth orders several ticks from the current price that they had no real desire to consummate, the machines were thrown off-kilter. In a fair and open market, the HFT firms argued, participants had a right to believe that the orders they were seeing were genuine. Not everyone agreed.

"The way regulators think is fundamentally different to the way traders think," says Albert Kyle from the University of Maryland. "Traders think of trading as a game. Many traders have a gaming background: poker, backgammon, computer games. You make moves. I'll bluff and I'll try and maneuver around to get my strategy implemented. Regulators were suddenly talking about it as though it was a bunch of gentlemen trying to accurately communicate what their intentions are."

Markham, who, like Kyle, had worked at the CFTC before entering academia, believes there is a crucial difference between deception, which has been part of trading since markets began, and manipulation, which involves deliberately pushing prices around. "This is not a moral issue," he wrote in a legal filing opposing the spoofing rules. "Trading is a competition and . . . concealment of actual trading strategies is an integral part of that . . . In [American] football, concealment of the actual strategy for each play is critical to success," ergo Statue of Liberty plays and quarterback sneaks. "In volleyball, the setter tries to fool opponents on where the ball will be placed for return. Baseball pitchers disguise their pitches to fool batters. Hockey players try to deceive the goalie as to where the puck will be sent, and on and on. Trading in financial markets is no less a competition."

What's more, says Markham, it's hard to see how an order can be deemed manipulative or "non bona fide" in a world where algos are able to react to fresh information in a matter of microseconds. One option the CFTC briefly considered was to remove any subjectivity from the process and simply limit the proportion of a participant's orders they're allowed to cancel. Anyone who breached the threshold would receive a fine, or worse. Another idea was to mandate that all orders have to remain in the order book for a minimum of, say, three seconds before they can be pulled. Ultimately, though, these approaches were deemed too prescriptive and were discarded in favor of what's known in the legal profession as "scienter," that is, what's going through a trader's mind when he places an order. It was a controversial step. "Prior to this there was no law that said you're not allowed to think certain things while you trade," says Michael Kim, a white-collar defense attorney and former Justice Department prosecutor whose firm, Kobre & Kim, would go on to represent Sarao and several other parties accused of spoofing. "There are no rules on how long you have to leave an order up so the action itself is totally legal. It's only the state of mind that matters. The whole thing has turned into this bizarre thought crime."

After Dodd-Frank was signed into law in July 2010, the Disruptive Trading Practices amendment underwent a process of refinement until, three years later, the CFTC issued a document containing "interpretive guidance" on what was and wasn't allowed. It stated that spoofing included intentionally submitting and canceling orders to give "an appearance of false market depth" or "create artificial price movements." To differentiate between acceptable and unacceptable activity, the agency said it would take into consideration "the market context, the person's pattern of trading activity . . . and other relevant facts and circumstances," giving credence to one commentator's suggestion that spoofing was like pornography—you knew it when you saw it.

There is a common misconception, particularly among day traders, that HFT is responsible for most of the spoofing that goes on in financial markets. While it's true that several HFT employees and firms have been sanctioned for engaging in the practice over the years, for the most part it's actually looked down on by the behemoths at the forefront of the industry. For them, spoofing is a hindrance, and after the introduction of the disruptive trading rules, firms such as Citadel and HTG Capital Partners would go on to work closely with regulators to identify and prosecute parties whose unpredictable trading disrupted the smooth functioning of their moneymaking machines. In a number of cases they appeared as witnesses for the government. "Imagine a system where the biggest, most powerful players get to tell the regulators and the exchanges who to go after based on who is taking money off them," says one prop trader. "Welcome to the futures market."

.

CHAPTER 15

PIMP MY ALGO

In October 2011, Nav was hit with a more immediate threat to his livelihood than a change in the trading rules. MF Global, the firm that gave him access to the markets and provided him with the leverage to trade at such high stakes, declared itself bankrupt. Problems had been swirling around the world's biggest and oldest futures broker for a while, but few realized the matter was terminal, and when MF Global filed for Chapter 11 protection on Halloween, tens of thousands of traders, Nav among them, were left without access to their funds and frantically searching for a new home.

Brokers make their money in two principal ways: from the fees they charge customers per trade and on the returns they make investing the excess funds sitting in client accounts. When the financial crisis struck, both revenue streams dried up as trading volumes plummeted and central banks cut interest rates to the floor. In March 2010, after three years of losses, MF Global's board appointed a new CEO to turn things around. Their pick, Jon Corzine, was a bona fide Wall Street legend who had run Goldman Sachs in the nineties before cashing in his considerable chips and entering politics, first as a senator then as governor of

New Jersey. "It was as if a manager of the New York Yankees was making a comeback in the minor leagues," wrote the *New York Times*.

Corzine, who was a spry sixty-four, had started his career as a bond trader, and he believed the solution to the firm's problems, at least in the short term, lay on the trading floor. It was the middle of the Eurozone crisis, and bonds issued by the likes of Italy, Spain, and Portugal were trading at considerably below their face value, reflecting the heightened probability of default. Convinced the authorities would never let that happen, Corzine quietly bought up $7 billion of the distressed securities, using them as collateral for a complicated so-called "repo" trade that served the dual purpose of keeping the instruments off the firm's balance sheet and allowing it to declare its expected profits straightaway. It was the kind of bold, outside-the-box play that had catapulted Corzine from the family farm in Illinois to the Bilderberg Group. Unfortunately, this time the former high school quarterback had badly misjudged his Hail Mary pass. As the crisis deepened and the value of sovereign debt fell, the counterparties on the repo trades began issuing what are known as margin calls, forcing MF Global to hand over additional cash to cover potential losses. In October 2011, rating agencies downgraded the firm's credit rating to "junk," sparking the equivalent of a bank run, with customers calling up and demanding to withdraw their funds and lenders closing credit lines. In the frenzied final hours, a middle-ranking executive dipped into what should have been sacrosanct, segregated client funds to plug the gaps. It wasn't enough to save the firm, and in the days after MF Global folded, it emerged that $1.6 billion belonging to twenty-six thousand retail traders, farmers, and small businesses was unaccounted for.

While Corzine faced uncomfortable questions about his level of involvement in the scandal, Nav considered a future without his long-standing broker. Financially, thanks to the offshore guarantee arrangements, the blow was manageable. Nav had only a modest sum sitting in an MF Global margin account, most of which he'd eventually get back. Of greater concern was finding a new broker. GNI Touch, the MF Global offshoot, had watched Nav develop; they'd grown comfortable with his trading style and the size of his positions. In exchange for a steady torrent of commissions, the firm's brokers had given Nav the best terms and stayed out of his way even when his methods drew unwanted attention. Finding such a generous and pliant replacement would prove difficult.

The first problem was Nav himself. By any measure, his record was stellar, but few clearers were willing to back someone with millions of pounds without meeting them first, and the eccentric trader didn't always make the best impression. After calling one City brokerage and requesting an after-hours appointment so no one would see him, Nav turned up wearing sweatpants and carrying his trading statements in an old Tesco plastic bag. "He was in the office for about an hour. He wouldn't look you in the eye. You had to pull information out of him. I was about as unimpressed as it's possible to be," recalls one of the executives who interviewed him. Still, day traders are an odd bunch and, recognizing there was money to be made, the firm offered Nav a contract on less attractive terms and lower leverage than he was looking for. "We talked about it and figured he would probably carry on making good money, but if he really hammered it at the levels he wanted and the market jumped back and he got caught, he could have wiped us out," says the executive. Nav declined and walked away. "He wanted to be worshiped," the firm's owner says. "Not only did he want outsized risk at frankly uneconomical terms, but he wanted us to ruffle him, which we weren't prepared to do."

The monumental size of Nav's positions was another issue. As he later recounted to a friend: "I tried to get a broker's deal with RCG," the Rosenthal Collins Group, one of the biggest clearers in the United States. "They said, 'How much do you make?' and I said, 'On a good day, nine hundred grand.' They said, 'That's crazy.'" A week later, after Nav sent them his statements, RCG turned him down. When he asked why, they told him they didn't think it was possible for a trader in his bedroom to make that much money. "They said they believe that it's a Ponzi scheme,"

Nav recounted. "They thought I was Bernie Madoff!" Nav hoped he'd found an alternative when Knight Capital agreed to take him on, but then the firm lost $460 million and he was left brokerless once again.

Unable to trade and with few other interests, Nav returned to the proverbial garage to work on his trading machine. The layering algorithm he'd created in 2009 with help from Hadj at Trading Technologies had worked exactly as planned, firing blocks of sell orders into the market to drive prices lower that stayed far enough from the prevailing price to almost never be hit. But it was a blunt instrument, and Nav's competitors—principally the big HFT firms and a handful of gifted manual scalpers like him— were getting stronger and more sophisticated by the day. To bait the latest algos, he needed to be able to place his spoofs nearer the action, either at or close to the best offer, and that was risky. Nav knew he had to evolve. So on a Monday evening in October 2011, he left a voicemail with a software developer in Chicago who specialized in pimping TT systems.

AROUND THE time Jitesh Thakkar listened to Nav's message, he was engrossed in a book called *Secrets of the Millionaire Mind* by T. Harv Eker, a mullet-sporting fitness store owner turned motivational speaker. Thakkar had his own business and was a sucker for a self-help book. "Rich people believe: 'I create my life.' Poor people believe: 'Life happens to me,'" he wrote in a fifteen-point summary of Eker's bestseller that he posted on social media. "Rich people think big. Poor people think small." Thakkar had already devoured *The Secret*, Rhonda Byrne's touchstone on the law of attraction. "Ask. Believe. Receive," he repeated to himself on the commute from suburban Naperville to his office downtown.

Thakkar's family had moved from India to Chicago when Jitesh was thirteen years old, and his path in life was set a few months later when he came across an Apple model IIe in the computer lab at school. Beige and boxy, with a green and black screen, it allowed users to write programs and play rudimentary games. Thakkar was smitten and taught himself to code. He studied computer engineering at the University of Illinois, where, in his spare time, he designed chess and puzzle games in his bedroom. One of Thakkar's first jobs was at the investment bank UBS, where he created applications to price options. In 2001, he took a role at a market maker called Stafford Trading, building systems that cut down any lag between a customer placing an order and its hitting the exchange. It was a much sought-after skill, and two years later he was hired by Trading Technologies to oversee a department. Away from work, Thakkar and his wife were adherents of The Art of Living, a spiritual program based around the teachings of a guru named Ravi Shankar. The couple gave classes on meditation and deep breathing, and went to "Yoga Raves," where sober crowds danced and whooped to Indian-tinged electro music.

In 2007, with the HFT industry exploding, Thakkar left TT to start his own firm, Edge Financial Technologies. As well as helping customers minimize latency, Edge introduced old-school point-and-click traders to automation by working with them on designing and developing their own algorithms. He rented an office near the CME and assembled a small team of developers. There weren't a lot of other consultants targeting TT users—most sizable HFT firms built their own software systems from scratch—and business flowed in via referrals from his former employer. "Jitesh was the guy," says a former TT employee. "If a customer wanted anything a little bit complex, anything beyond what we could do ourselves, we sent them his way."

"HELLO NAD," Thakkar wrote to Sarao on October 3, 2011, after mishearing his voicemail. "I received your message regarding TT related programming. This is what we specialize in. How can I help you?" A little over a week later, after they'd spoken on the phone, Nav sent Thakkar an email laying out the functions of the system he wanted Edge to build for him. It read:

1) *JOIN*—This function will put pending orders along either the bid or offer which will become active once the market has flipped price. So if I placed a 300 lot JOIN on the bid at 51 and it is trading 53-54. If either the 53 Bid or the 54 Offer is traded out then my 300 will appear at the same time at 51 Bid.

2) *JOIN SIDE*—The same as above but the pending order is only activated if the side it is on is flipped. So, in the above example the 300 lot will only join the 51 Bid if the 54 offer is traded and the price goes 54 Bid. If the price simply goes offered down to 51 Bid then the order is automatically pulled and never activated.

3) *Back of the Book*—For both of the above order types we need to have the option to keep the order at the back of the book. We achieved this by increasing/decreasing the order by 1 lot after it was activated every time a new order was placed on my JOIN activated order. This started to look a little strange with 1 lots changing all the time, so we will have to make it that the order is increased by 1 every time an order greater than say 20 lots is placed. This value may be subject to change.

. . .

5) *SNAP*—This is a pending order ready to trade as soon as the price is available. For example if the price is trading 47-48 and I want to sell 300 at 49 I place the pending order to do so. As soon as it is bid at 49 my 300 lot to sell will become active, whilst it was hidden up to that point. Vital to this is a box with a volume quantity . . . the minimum amount that needs to be on the bid for the SNAP order to become active . . .

6) *MY ICE—*Similar to SNAP, the difference here being that you are instructing this order to maintain constant snapping of the bid/order until the full order is complete . . . This order needs to be quick enough to be able to catch all flash orders and spoofers that flash on the bid/offer for a millisecond . . .

He signed off:

Please get back in touch with your thoughts as soon as possible. I have decided to stop trading until I have this application since I am so far behind my competitors so time really is of the essence.

Regards,

Nav.

Nav wanted Edge to make him a program that he could control through an interface that would sit next to the ladder on his screen. It would contain a series of buttons which he could turn on and off with his mouse. The top two order types, JOIN and JOIN SIDE, would be used for spoofs. The idea was that Nav would select how many orders he wished to place, click JOIN or JOIN SIDE, then activate them at a given level. They would remain pending until the next time the e-mini price changed, so as to slip into the book amid the commotion of a price move. To minimize the chances the orders would ever be executed, they would be loaded with the "back of the book" feature that TT had declined to make for Nav two years earlier. When "back of the book" was switched on, it would automatically modify orders by alternately adding and then subtracting a single lot every time a new order arrived, constantly sending them to the back of the queue—like the shopper who leaves their line at the supermarket. On the rare occasions a portion of a spoof order was hit, the remainder would immediately be canceled.

While the spoof orders were working their magic, Nav would simultaneously be selling e-minis, building a genuine short position. Seeing all this activity, other participants would also start selling, driving the e-mini lower. Once the price had fallen by a couple of ticks, Nav would surreptitiously start buying back e-minis using the order types he called SNAP and MY ICE, which were designed to remain pending but invisible to other market participants until the requisite number of orders became available, at which point they would strike, viper-like. The goal, as ever, was to give off as little information as possible. Once Nav was flat—after he'd bought back the same number of e-minis he'd sold—he would cancel the spoof orders and wait a few minutes before starting the sequence again.

As the rest of the industry migrated to fully automated systems, Nav chose to remain in the cockpit, directing all buying and selling himself, only with an enhanced set of weaponry. By the time he approached Edge, his plan was fully developed and he sought no advice on the mechanics of the system or the market. He simply needed someone to help him realize his vision. The language Nav used to describe the program was somewhat idiosyncratic, which made sense; he was an autodidact. Everything he knew, he'd learned by sitting and watching the ladder. With no friends at any HFT firms to guide him and no master's degree in financial engineering, he'd gotten to a point where he was able to reverse-engineer the strategies of the "nerds" he renounced and create his own system to beat them. Questions of legality aside, it was a remarkable feat. "I would have employed him in a heartbeat," says the owner of one HFT firm.

Thakkar took Nav's plans and instructed his developers to build a prototype that he sent back on November 11, 2011. He named the file "NAVTrader." Over the next two months, Edge fine-tuned the program and Nav tested it. By late January, they'd made sufficient progress that Nav was willing to sign a contract. Thakkar originally offered to do the work for a fixed price of $12,500, stating that "this is sort of below cost for us, but we would do it in hopes to make money by selling it to other customers." After spending many additional hours getting the program to Nav's satisfaction, he increased that to $24,200—still a modest sum considering how much money Nav was making. Before the program was completed, Nav had one request. He didn't feel comfortable having such a controversial system named after himself, so he asked Thakkar to change the filename from NAVTrader to MASTERCHIEF, the name of the protagonist in the popular video game series *Halo*. In the games, Master Chief is a soldier who uses state-of-the-art battle armor and sophisticated artificial intelligence to lead humanity to victory in an epic battle against a technologically advanced alien race. Thakkar didn't honor the request, and the NAV Trader moniker stuck.

With the government's clampdown on spoofing, Nav was careful never to explicitly talk about how he planned to use the program, and Thakkar never asked. The programmer made a point not to pry into his clients' trading strategies, and he would later tell investigators there were potentially legitimate uses for all the functions Edge built. He was certainly well positioned to understand the issues at hand. In spring 2012, Thakkar was one of two dozen or so experts from across the futures industry invited to join a new committee set up by the CFTC to examine how regulators might better understand and oversee high-frequency trading. The subcommittee Thakkar was a part of, Market Microstructure, was tasked with exploring the negative and positive ways automated trading impacted markets, and its members talked about spoofing during their regular conference calls and meetings. (Thakkar would remain on the committee for two years, during which Edge continued working on different iterations of NAV Trader.)

In summer 2012, with his new weapon ready to unleash, Nav finally found a new broker to replace MF Global, an independent Chicago firm with Irish roots called R. J. O'Brien. His contact there was a forty-two-year-old former MF Global employee named James Prince, who lived in a grand house in the English countryside and would prove as incurious about his client's tactics as the brokers at GNI. R. J. O'Brien wasn't prepared to extend Nav the same level of credit as MF Global, though, and the size of his positions came down. The heady days of bulldozing the market around with $200 million spoofs were over. But the loss of firepower was balanced out to some degree by the heightened precision and efficiency that NAV Trader introduced. One day a few months later, Nav used his new weapon for a little over a minute to make $55,000. Another time, he made $23,000 in one hundred seconds. For the Master Chief, milking markets had never been quicker or easier.

CHAPTER 16

■

JESUS ENTERS

Nav may have been preternaturally gifted at making money, but he had little expertise in how to invest or manage it. Nav erected an impenetrable wall between his home life and his business affairs, and when Daljit, his mother, left the house each morning to work behind the till at a local chemist, or Nachhattar, his father, walked to the doctor's office to pick up a prescription, they did so with no inkling that their son was a multimillionaire. Money for Nav was an abstraction, and the more of it that flooded in, the more he turned to MacKinnon and Dupont for guidance. By now the pair had taken to describing themselves as Nav's "family office"—a kind of one-stop shop that handles every aspect of a high-net-worth individual's financial and investment affairs—and not long after the wind deal was finalized, they introduced him to another opportunity, this one involving a mysterious young Mexican businessman named Jesus.

Jesus Alejandro Garcia Alvarez was the owner and CEO of a Zurich-based company called IXE, an Aztec word apparently meaning "one who shows their face and keeps their word." Dupont first encountered him in the summer of 2011 when he was in the audience of a presentation Garcia was giving to a roomful of financial advisers, solicitors, and accountants in Mayfair. On its website, IXE described itself as a kind of broad-based advisory business, offering everything from asset management and legal advice to "ultra sumptuous travel." That day, though, Garcia was touting a different opportunity. Garcia had moved to Europe five years earlier at the age of thirty, he told the attendees, to grow the family business. The Garcias had high-level relationships around the globe, he said, and had identified an opportunity to capitalize by providing short-term credit to facilitate the trading of "physical" commodities such as coal and cooking oil. The mechanics were somewhat opaque, but the idea was that IXE would act as a middleman between buyers and sellers in exchange for a fee. Rather than waiting months to receive payment for a shipment of coal, for example, a supplier in China would accept a reduced sum from Garcia's firm to get the money now. IXE would deal only with governments and companies with the best reputations; and it would protect itself by making sure the transacting parties signed legally binding "letters of credit" in which they pledged to abide by the terms of the deal. IXE was already making big profits, Garcia said, but there was so much demand for capital it had decided to open up the opportunity to outside investors, which is where the introducers came in.

"We are offering alternative investment vehicles that provide constant returns to investors," Garcia explained in an accent so thick it left the audience straining to understand him. "The investment in real economy makes the advantages obvious—investors are benefitting from constant returns generated from actual transactions with zero speculation and zero volatility."

Garcia didn't exude gravitas. He was small and stocky and thickset with jet-black eyes that blinked perpetually and a mouth that turned downward when he spoke, like a ventriloquist dummy. He delivered his presentation in a monotone that veered in and out of coherence. Bizarrely, he was accompanied at the meeting by a smartly dressed British couple in their sixties named Lynn Adamson and Chris Sawicki, who had agreed to be IXE's UK agents despite meeting Garcia themselves only a short while earlier.

Adamson, who sported a cravat and drove a sports car, had spent most of her career advising middle managers on how to reduce stress, but she wound up writing IXE's pitch documents because Garcia's English wasn't up to snuff.

Garcia's words may have been faltering, but his pitch was undeniably enticing. IXE was offering "participants" (it eschewed the word "investors") who made a minimum deposit of $1 million a *guaranteed* return of 8 percent per year. The money would be held in their own personal accounts with a Swiss bank called Hinduja and could be accessed only with their sign-off. Since the cash would exclusively be used as a "backstop" in pre-agreed trades, it would never actually be put at risk. Introducers, such as MacKinnon and Dupont, would get a meaty 4.5 percent a year on everything their clients invested. Asked about IXE's pedigree, Garcia told the attendees it was a "sister company" of a $300 billion Dubai-based entity called ETA Star, "the largest conglomerate in the Middle East." IXE also claimed to be regulated by FINMA, the Swiss financial regulator.

MacKinnon and Dupont weren't legally licensed to offer financial advice to their clients, but in the weeks that followed they gently nudged Nav toward the IXE opportunity, and in July 2012 they accompanied him to Zurich to meet Garcia in person. It was Nav's first trip out of the country since visiting relatives in India as a boy, and when Dupont picked him up on the way to Heathrow in an Aston Martin—Nav asked him not to park on his street in case anyone saw them—the mood was jubilant. Their guide in Switzerland was Adamson's partner, Sawicki, who drove them to a nondescript building with a creaky lift on a residential street where they were surprised to discover the Swiss bank Hinduja was based. After obtaining written confirmation from one of the bank's directors that Nav's money couldn't be touched without his approval, the party proceeded to IXE's headquarters in the center of town.

IXE's office was small but tastefully decorated, with wood paneling and a door thick enough for a bank vault, creating a sense of theater. In a boardroom overlooking the Limmat River,

Garcia talked Nav through what he called his "Physical Commodity Participation" opportunity one more time. The meeting was something of a slog, as Garcia's impenetrable accent butted up against Nav's inner-city English, but Nav was enthusiastic about the concept and excited about the returns on offer. Afterward, they went for lunch by the river, where Garcia and Nav bonded over football while MacKinnon and Dupont gritted their teeth and Sawicki sweated through his suit. By the time the bill arrived, Nav had made up his mind to participate.

Around the same time, however, a development back in London threatened to derail the deal before it got off the ground. One of the introducers at Garcia's Mayfair presentation had convinced a sovereign wealth fund to invest hundreds of millions of pounds in the venture. Before signing contracts, the fund had hired a corporate investigator to carry out some due diligence, and, based on what it discovered, it had decided to walk away. The investigator had found a 2010 legal complaint filed in Florida in which both Garcia and IXE were accused by Mongolia's central bank of participating in an elaborate scheme to rob it of more than $20 million. The alleged scam, which was based around letters of credit, was the brainchild of a Florida native named Burton Greenberg, who would later serve an eight-year stretch for an unrelated fraud.

When Garcia discovered that an introducer was spreading potentially damaging information about him, he instructed a lawyer to draft a rebuttal vigorously denying the allegations and pointing out that neither he nor IXE was ever a defendant in the case.* Unlike MacKinnon and Dupont, Nav was never told about the Mongolian suit, and after negotiating with Garcia to bump up his interest to 9 percent a year, he signed off on the transfer of $17 million from his offshore company to a new account in his name at Hinduja Bank. Three months later, the first statement

---

* IXE and Alejandro Garcia declined to answer questions or be interviewed for this book. The company said in a statement it considered the information presented in this account "tendentious" and it "did not agree with the publishing context."

arrived. Where previously Nav had been lucky to receive a couple of thousand dollars a quarter in interest, he was now banking in the region of $380,000. Via the power of compounding interest alone, his funds stood to double within eight years. Nav was so intoxicated with the influx that he suggested transferring the $15 million or so sitting in Cranwood, the wind holding company he co-owned, into Hinduja as well, so it could generate some decent returns until it was required.

IXE posed something of a quandary for MacKinnon and Dupont. Thanks to Nav's initial deposit, they were now receiving a residual $500,000 a year in commissions, and they didn't have to do a thing. Privately, they had reservations about Garcia and the people he surrounded himself with; but they reasoned it was ultimately up to Nav what he did with his money. Cranwood was a different matter. As directors in Wind Energy Scotland, many of their day-to-day expenses were covered by the Isle of Man entity; and if Martin Davie, its head, achieved half of what he said he could, they were set to become very wealthy. Preserving that capital was paramount. On the other hand, Hinduja seemed to be a respectable, independent entity, and if they did deposit the additional $15 million with IXE, the pair would receive an extra $450,000 a year in commissions. In the end, they agreed: Cranwood's money would be transferred to a second account at Hinduja, from which Wind Energy Scotland's costs would be doled out on a rolling quarterly basis, as needed.

Shortly after Nav made his first deposit, Western governments announced sanctions against Iran, and IXE wrote to investors telling them they would need to move their money out of Hinduja, which had Iranian connections, to Morgan Stanley, where IXE also held an account. It was an unwelcome development, but IXE provided written assurances that no money could be accessed without account holders' approval. Comforted by Morgan Stanley's involvement, Nav approved the transfer.

By the following summer, Nav had made two further deposits into his IXE accounts, bringing his total investment to around $50 million. Like the George Eliot character Silas Marner hoarding his gold coins, Nav watched the numbers in his bank accounts grow, never withdrawing a penny for himself or his family. He liked to boast he could buy a Big Mac every minute with the interest he was making. Meanwhile, those around him enjoyed the spoils of their success. MacKinnon and Dupont, who were now receiving commissions of around $750,000 a year each from IXE alone, moved from the outskirts of Mayfair to its epicenter, Berkeley Square, renting an office in a plush town house, which they decorated with a giant map of Scotland and an antique rifle. Away from work, MacKinnon remodeled his farmhouse, which had a tennis court, a swimming pool, and a wine cellar. Dupont bought an elegant apartment in the country and a Ferrari California. Every quarter, money rolled in via a company set up by the husband-and-wife duo of Adamson and Sawicki, who, after a lifetime of near misses and failed ventures themselves, had finally struck gold.

Meanwhile, over in Zurich, Garcia's star was rising. After promising to raise substantial funds, Garcia was invited to join the board of the Swiss arm of Robert F. Kennedy Human Rights, a philanthropic group where he mingled with the city's business elites. Cruising around town in an eye-catching BMW electric sports car, a Maserati, or a chauffeur-driven limousine, his Russian wife, Ekaterina, in tow, the young entrepreneur cut a striking figure. In November 2013, he was profiled in the prestigious Sunday newspaper *Neue Zurcher Zeitung am Sonntag*. "Switzerland's most important farmer has an urban workplace: Jesus Alejandro Garcia Alvarez performs his daily work in an office at Zurich central within the sight of the railway station," the piece began. "In his mid thirties in a dark suit, he differs from the usual Swiss professionals in many respects. While farms in Switzerland have an average size of 22.8 hectares, Mr. Garcia and his family have more than 50,000 hectares on which 60,000 cattle graze."

In twelve months, IXE had apparently morphed from an advisory and trading business into an agricultural powerhouse with holdings in potatoes, avocados, and livestock, and a client roster that included Walmart and US Foods. The article and accompanying photograph painted Garcia in an almost mythic light: the pioneering young heir of a great Latin American dynasty, forced out of Mexico by the constant threat of kidnapping, and now driven to build an empire that would make the father he shadowed as a child proud. Reflecting this shift, the company's website was completely overhauled. Gone were the references to advisory services for rich people. IXE now described itself as "a group of companies worldwide . . . clustered around our core competencies in agribusiness, commodity trading and venture capital." An org chart showed nineteen IXE subsidiaries spanning Europe, Asia, and the Americas.

With his newfound status, Garcia was invited onto Al Jazeera, CNBC, and Bloomberg TV, where he opined monotonously on subjects ranging from food standards to the wonders of quinoa to his latest obsession, Bolivian lithium, which he described as "white gold." IXE didn't publish any financial accounts, but one publication estimated Garcia's worth at $280 million, placing him firmly in its list of Switzerland's three hundred richest people. Another suggested he was a billionaire. "Our fathers' businesses and deals were based on a handshake," Garcia said in an interview. "This spirit lives on in IXE. Our business relationships are built on trust and a word still counts."

CHAPTER 17

■

MR. X

Navinder Sarao's arrest would ultimately involve an army of people from agencies including the CFTC, the FBI, the Metropolitan Police, and the Department of Justice, but the investigation started with a lone individual with no affiliation to the government. He was a day trader, like Sarao, grinding out a living in a small prop firm in Chicago who, in 2012, happened to be back-testing his system using data from the day of the Flash Crash when he spotted something the whole world had missed. His identity has never been made public. We'll call him Mr. X.

Mr. X is a few years older than Sarao and started his career as part of a pit trading firm's first forays into electronic trading. For a long time he was at the bottom rung; he struggled to cover the rent. He contemplated whether to pursue a career in his primary love, design. Money was never his major priority, but he was good with computers and over time he got sucked into trading. "I liked the problem-solving aspect, looking at markets like a puzzle," he says. Eventually, he struck out on his own, renting a desk at various firms before teaming up with a handful of traders and programmers he'd met along the way to start their own outfit. In the beginning, Mr. X was a "point-and-click" trader like Sarao, placing every order with his mouse and keyboard. But as algorithms proliferated, he realized he would need to adapt. Working with a programmer from Europe he'd been recommended, he started to develop his own algos—basic ones at first, intended to cut down on keystrokes; then more complex iterations that capitalized on the patterns and relationships he'd observed. "I'd describe it as gray box now," he says. "There's a lot of automation, but it still takes manual inputs and interaction."

Mr. X, who speaks quickly and continuously, as though he's worried if he stops he might not get another chance, describes himself as a market maker, a timeworn strategy that involves constantly posting orders on both sides of the market and making money on the bid-ask spread. By providing liquidity, he believes he is offering a service to the wider financial ecosystem as well as earning a decent living. At its core, market making is straightforward—you post a bid to buy an e-mini for, say, $1 and an offer to sell one for $1.02 and, when both orders have been lifted, you pocket two cents. Do that hundreds of thousands of times a day and you have a business. But markets move around quickly, and providing two-way prices can be risky. Making consistent profits irrespective of market conditions is a specialized and complex undertaking. To maximize his returns, Mr. X asked his programmer to develop a program that would help him identify his competitors based on the footprints participants leave behind when they trade. The ladder is full of potential clues: the size of one's orders, how long they're left for, how far away they are from the current price, and so on. Using his design background, Mr. X created tools that allowed him to visualize what was happening in the markets more clearly using things like color-coding, flashing, and charting. "You're trying to figure out what kind of drives the markets, and hopefully, get a sense of other people's strategies," he explains. "It can be difficult and speculative, but sometimes patterns emerge."

In August 2012, at the tail end of a heat wave, Mr. X and his developer were updating their detection software to incorporate some new features. With little forethought, they decided to test the upgrade on the most eventful day in recent market history: May 6, 2010. Like everyone else in his industry, Mr. X had taken a keen interest in the Flash Crash. He was at his desk when the bottom fell out of the market, and, while he escaped without losses, he was left with a residual feeling of disquiet about the precariousness of the system. In the months that followed, he'd read and reread the SEC/CFTC report, and he was familiar with the work of Kirilenko and his peers. He had some theories of his own, but the decision to run his software over the day of the crash was, at least consciously, the result of blind luck.

When the results came in, two things struck Mr. X. The first was the glaring imbalance between resting buy and sell orders in the e-mini order book that day—anomalous even after factoring in all the negative economic sentiment. The second, driving the first, was the monolithic slabs of sell orders beginning three levels above the best offer that started appearing in the ladder at 9:20 a.m. Chicago time and moved in lockstep with the e-mini as it made its descent. For the first couple of hours, the blocks showed up for a few minutes at a time before disappearing again, but from a little after 11 a.m. until 1:40 p.m.—a minute before the market tanked—they were left to stand there like an unassailable wall.

Two years had passed since the government's inquiry into the causes of the crash, and Mr. X had watched as spoofing had risen to the forefront of the trading fraternity's collective consciousness. He'd read about how nine stock traders and their bosses from New York brokerage Trillium were fined $2.3 million for systematically entering "layered, non bona fide" orders to "create the false appearance of market activity." Trading forums were suddenly awash with, on the one hand, complaints about the preponderance of spoofing, and on the one other, fretful discussions about what was and wasn't allowed under the new regime. As Mr. X examined the e-mini data from May 6, 2010, he was unequivocal: "I was immediately sure what I discovered was massive manipulation."

Mr. X checked and rechecked the data, and had drawn-out

conversations with his colleagues about conceivable alternative explanations. In the end, though, nothing aside from spoofing made sense. One of the factors that convinced him was the way the seller's orders reacted when fresh information entered the marketplace. "This entity designed some questionable behaviors into its strategy," he explains. Many legitimate strategies involve loading the book with orders at multiple price levels, which are then canceled and reposted frequently with the goal of improving the odds of getting to the front of the queue. This algo did the opposite. The orders all moved to the back of the line every time the price moved, greatly reducing the chances they'd ever actually be hit. "If this was a valid strategy, the participant would have immediately overhauled the design because he wasn't getting any fills," Mr. X says.

Mr. X spent the next couple of days in a state of confusion. Was it really possible that one of the biggest intraday crashes in the history of financial markets was at least partially the result of a single entity's manipulation? And if so, why had nobody else noticed it? It was surreal. Mr. X went back to the CFTC/SEC's findings and read them line by line. A preliminary version of the report states: "At or about 1.30 p.m. CET, the electronic limit order book in the e-mini S&P 500 futures market exhibited a significant imbalance of sell orders and buy orders. In the backdrop of declining prices, this imbalance appears to have contributed to a sudden liquidity dislocation despite increased trading volume." The agencies, then, had identified the massive preponderance of resting sell orders but had seemingly not probed what—or who—lay behind it. They focused instead on consummated trades, which led them to Waddell & Reed's door. "It's unfortunate that regulators did not use a more expansive data set," says Mr. X diplomatically. More perplexing to him is the failure of the CME, whose $2 billion of profits in 2011 could have funded the CFTC for a decade, to identify what was happening in its market. "There is no way this behavior could escape exchange oversight, simply because it was so large," he says.

As Mr. X considered his next move, he recalled a recent

article in the *Wall Street Journal* by Scott Patterson and Jenny Strasburg titled "For Superfast Stock Traders, a Way to Jump Ahead in Line." The piece told the story of Haim Bodek, the forty-one-year-old founder of an electronic trading firm who had inadvertently stumbled upon what he perceived as evidence of collusive practices between the exchanges and their HFT clients. In December 2009, Bodek was standing at the bar at an industry party when he complained to an executive from one of the newer stock exchanges, Direct Edge, about a recent dip in profitability. The executive quickly diagnosed the problem. Bodek was still placing trades using standard limit orders instead of one of the newfangled order types his exchange and others had quietly created at the request of the HFTs. The executive walked through one particular order type called "Hide Not Slide" that allowed users to conceal their bids and offers until they were consummated and, under certain circumstances, to jump to the front of the queue—the holy grail of many HFT strategies. Bodek was blown away. He scrawled the words "HIDE NOT SLIDE" on a napkin and left the party. "Man I feel like an idiot," he wrote in a follow-up email a few days later. "Never grasped the full negative alpha in a normal day limit."

But Bodek wasn't an idiot. He was a wunderkind in the world of electronic trading, the son of a renowned particle physicist who, when he was in his mid-twenties, worked for a firm called Hull Trading that was acquired by Goldman Sachs for half a billion dollars. Bodek had held senior positions at Goldman and UBS, reaching the top of the Wall Street totem pole before packing it in and starting his own firm, Trading Machines, in 2007. He prided himself on his knowledge of the inner workings of the markets, yet he'd only stumbled upon the order-type trick by buying the right guy a drink. What hope did anyone else have? Bodek started using Hide Not Slide orders and his profits improved, but he was still perturbed. Part of what appealed to him about trading in the first place was its Darwinian nature. Sure, some participants were faster or better informed than others, but there was nothing to stop people from investing in better technology. This was something else. By developing enhanced functions and then letting only a small proportion of their customers in on the secret—those who traded the highest volumes, who generated the most commissions, and whose executives sat on their committees—the exchanges were stacking the deck. It was as though they had created a cheat code for a computer game and only passed it along to their friends.

Bodek could have kept the code to himself, but instead he chose to take his findings to the SEC, which launched an investigation. Blowing the whistle can be hazardous for one's career, but Bodek took the view that if nobody came forward, nothing would ever change. The photograph accompanying the *Journal* article showed him staring into the camera, hands clasped on the hilt of a sword, the sun casting a bright light on his perfectly bald head. While alerting the authorities was a brave move, Bodek's motives weren't solely altruistic. A few months earlier, as part of Dodd-Frank, the government had introduced a new whistle-blower program that provided monetary awards to anyone who came forward with original information that resulted in a successful enforcement action. Bodek, who eschewed his right to anonymity, now stood to receive between 10 percent and 30 percent of any penalties the SEC collected.

The article included a quote from Bodek's lawyer, Shayne Stevenson, from the Seattle-based firm Hagens Berman Sobol Shapiro. Sensing an opportunity, Mr. X gave him a call. Stevenson was an idealistic young attorney who'd grown up in a trailer park and set up a workers' rights organization at Yale Law School before landing a coveted spot clerking at the U.S. District Court for the Southern District of New York. Smooth talking, with a shaved head and goatee, he could have walked into any white-shoe firm but instead returned to his native state of Washington. "Anyone who knows me knows that world isn't me," he says. "I grew up in the Pacific Northwest and I love it here. I was never going to be a corporate lawyer. My dad is an environmental biologist. From my office I can see three bodies of water; there's snow-capped mountains."

Stevenson worked as a state prosecutor for a few years before leaving to join Hagens Berman as a plaintiff lawyer. A big part of his new job was helping individuals and groups bring actions under the False Claims Act, a piece of legislation that allows for members of the public to blow the whistle against entities that are defrauding the government in exchange for a financial reward. So when the SEC and CFTC whistle-blower programs were drafted using the same language, he positioned himself as a go-to lawyer in the emerging space. Bodek was his first Dodd-Frank whistle-blower client. "Me and Haim actually bonded over our love of straight-edge, punk, thrash, and hard-core music, specifically the sweet spot of 1984 to 1989," he says. "Metallica, Slayer, Anthrax, Dead Kennedys, Minor Threat. We both played in punk bands, and if we weren't talking about the case we'd be discussing some new Viking metal band."

When Mr. X called and told Stevenson that he'd uncovered evidence of manipulation on the day of the Flash Crash, the lawyer was skeptical. For one thing, he estimates he takes on about one case for every fifty inquiries he receives. "You don't know how many times I've been told the S&P 500 is rigged," he laughs. For another, most whistle-blowers have some kind of *inside* information; they're employees or contractors who have witnessed malfeasance firsthand. What Mr. X claimed to have done was more remarkable. If what he was saying was true, he'd taken publicly available data from one of the most closely studied days in the history of the markets and seen something everyone else had overlooked. He might as well be claiming to have spotted a second shooter on the grassy knoll in the grainy footage of John F. Kennedy's assassination. Yet everything else about Mr. X engendered confidence: his two decades of trading experience, his technical expertise, the logical, exacting way he spoke. By the time Mr. X had walked Stevenson through the data broken down into charts, images, and slow-motion videos, the lawyer was sold. "When you see it all laid out in that format with that level of sophistication, there really is no other explanation," he says.

With Stevenson's help, Mr. X filled out the CFTC's whistle-blowing documentation and, in November 2012, sent it to Washington along with some supporting data. While he waited to hear back, he daydreamed about who the mystery entity might be and what a huge controversy it would cause if Goldman Sachs or Citadel were found to have caused the Flash Crash. "I got pretty obsessed," he says. "Based on the data I guessed it had to be the work of a large prop trading firm, maybe with an internal clearing arm to shield it from the authorities. The scale and the audacity of the behavior were so massive I couldn't imagine it was one individual. As it turned out I was very wrong."

■

CHAPTER 18

NAVSAR

The CFTC's Division of Enforcement is made up of prosecutors, who gather evidence and make cases, and investigators, who usually come from the finance industry and have a greater degree of technical expertise. Historically, the lawyers, who are better paid and come from fancy law schools, ruled the roost, but as markets grew in complexity, they increasingly came to rely on investigators with a grounding in data analysis, trading, and math to make sense of the world. In early 2013, Jessica Harris, a thirty-three-year-old investigator, was bashing out code in her small, dimly lit office in Washington, DC, skate shoes up on the desk, keyboard resting on her knees, when she received a call drafting her onto what would turn out to be the biggest case of her career.

Mr. X's tip-off had landed at the agency a couple of months earlier, and the head of the division handed the assignment to a small satellite office in Kansas City that, coincidentally, was walking distance from the headquarters of Waddell & Reed. The investigation there was being run by a team of Midwestern attorneys—Jo Mettenburg, Jenny Chapin, and senior prosecutor Charles "Chuck" Marvine—who had distinguished themselves over the past couple of years by busting a string of small-time

Ponzi schemers and scam artists. They were experienced prosecutors, but they had scant knowledge of the high tech world of
electronic trading and, since the initial tip-off, the case had only
grown in complexity. Within a few weeks, Mr. X had passed
along a second batch of data tying the as-yet-unidentified trader
to suspected spoofing in the days before and after May 6, 2010.
After that, he produced evidence that suggested the same entity
was augmenting its layering of the order book by manually placing and canceling orders in clips of 287 and 189 lots. This spigot
of new material wouldn't stop pumping for over a year.

The CFTC's job was threefold: to substantiate Mr. X's findings; to establish what, if any, offenses had been committed; and to
build a case that would stand up in court. Marvine and the other
attorneys could handle parts two and three. Part one was more
challenging. Mr. X's information looked compelling, but it was
incumbent upon the agency to independently verify the allegations, which was more difficult than it sounds. Simply re-creating
the e-mini order book in the age of HFT, when billions of orders
are placed, modified, and canceled each day, was a feat of computing power and human endeavor that had never been attempted
on this scale by the agency before. Assuming it was possible, the
team would then need to piece together the target's trading strategy and demonstrate intent. The specter of failed manipulation
cases loomed large.

The Kansas City attorneys needed an investigator well versed
in wrangling data, and when they heard Harris was available,
they drafted her onto the team from afar. Since joining the CFTC
in 2009, Harris had tried her best to keep up with the evolving
markets. She'd worked on one of its first spoofing cases, meticu-
lously piecing together wheat trader Eric Moncada's manipulative
trading on an Excel spreadsheet with ten million columns that
slowed her PC to a crawl; and when the division invested in a new
program called SAS (Statistical Analysis System) that allowed it
to store, interrogate, and visualize large quantities of data more
effectively, she'd been among the first adopters. She enjoyed the
field so much she'd signed up for an accelerated master's program

in systems engineering at the University of Virginia, and she was now spending her nights and weekends taking pre-req classes in scientific programming, linear algebra, and statistics.

"To be honest, training at the CFTC was pretty minimal, and there weren't a lot of people in the division who had experience in any kind of advanced statistics and who actually understood how to get data sources and analyze them," Harris says. Previously, Kirilenko and his fellow academics in the Office of the Chief Economist might have been able to offer some technical assistance, but the unit had just been decimated following the data breach complaint. "It was difficult to do the job without the right foundation. So I took it upon myself to get it."

GROWING UP in Ann Arbor, Michigan, Harris always had a lot of questions. Her father, Charles, was a former Navy officer of Welsh descent from a long line of military men. He worked at the sprawling General Motors factory in Romulus, Michigan, and inspected the kids' rooms before they went to bed. Her mother, Guerda, a nurse and, later, the owner of a catering business, was born in Haiti. As a child, Guerda had escaped François "Papa Doc" Duvalier's brutal regime under dramatic circumstances that were never openly discussed. The secrecy drove Jessica and her two siblings mad.

With their tract house, soccer practice, and Friday night football, the Harrises blended in with the neighborhood kids. "We dressed kind of preppy and it was hard to know where we were from," says her elder brother Chris. But on weekends, they were taken to get-togethers in Detroit and South Michigan where the adults drank rum and talked Port-au-Prince politics, and the smell of rice djon-djon and fried griot filled the air. Guerda came from a prominent family in Haiti before it was ripped apart by Duvalier—one of her brothers, Pierre François Benoit, would go on to become the country's ambassador to the United States— and it was at these parties that the children first caught snippets about their mother's life on the Caribbean island. "There were always unanswered questions, a lot of mystery," says Chris.

The children knew better than to pry, but Jess was a natural investigator. When she was twelve, a stranger arrived at the family home in a BMW claiming to be one of Charles's cousins. "Jess just looked him up and down and pegged straightaway he was a mooch," says Chris. To the kids' irritation, the distant relative hung around for weeks, eating and sleeping for free, talking up his latest plans, and inviting himself to gatherings. "The only thing he cared about was his car," says Chris. "Then one day he comes in shouting because someone had snapped the antenna." Jess was tight-lipped about the incident, but a few days later the interloper left, defeated.

Harris studied business administration at Western Michigan University and then landed a job as an assistant to a commodities broker at MF Global in Chicago. It was her first exposure to the world of trading and, while she got a kick out of the pace of the markets, she found the work soulless. So when she read about an opening at the National Futures Association, she decided to apply. The NFA is a quasi-regulatory body that oversees futures brokerages and trading firms, investigating misdemeanors that either aren't serious enough for or haven't yet been referred to the CFTC. Harris felt instantly at home there and rose rapidly from auditor to investigator, then to senior investigator, and then to supervisor. She walked into firms with a name badge, sat down with company directors twice her age, and asked them whatever she wanted. "She wasn't just good. She was stellar," says Dan Driscoll, who is now chief operating officer of the NFA. "Really, one of the most determined people I've ever met. A complete bulldog." In 2009, Harris was working on a fraud case that involved liaising with the CFTC, and when the case wrapped up, a manager at the agency asked her if she'd be interested in joining. "It's a real Cinderella story, I know, right?" she laughs.

. . .

HARRIS'S OFFICE was sparse and functional: a couple of whiteboards scrawled with charts and formulae, some big stacks of paperwork, a bike helmet hanging on the door handle. Outside the floor was buzzy, but Harris spent most of her days alone, staring at her screens, immersed in data. Every once in a while, a colleague popped their head around the door to ask a question or say hello. "Truth be told, I might as well have been in my mom's basement drinking Mountain Dew in my sweatpants or something," she says. After landing the Sarao case, Harris's first task was to pull in trading data from various sources. Historically, the CFTC's first port of call on manipulation cases was something called the "Trade Capture Report," or TCR, which listed every completed or partially filled trade. Kirilenko and his colleagues had relied on TCR to identify Waddell & Reed's errant algo in the days after the Flash Crash, and had used it as the foundation of their joint report with the SEC. But modern trading was as much about canceled orders as consummated ones, and the patterns Mr. X had identified—the rapid-fire placing and modifying of blocks of orders several ticks away from the prevailing price—didn't show up since, by design, the orders were almost never hit. To isolate the spoof orders, Harris had to use two additional data sets provided by the CME called Rapid and Armada. Rapid logged every order placed by an entity, regardless of whether it was filled, partially filled, modified, or canceled, allowing Harris and her colleagues to view their target's activity in all its complexity. Armada enabled her to rebuild the ladder, nine levels above and nine below the best bid, and offer at any given moment, helping her place the trader's actions in the context of what was going on around them.

Rather than identifying traders by name, the CME allocated each entity an ID code, and for the first few weeks of the investigation, the target was known only as NAVSAR. Based on the size of the orders and the scope of the activity, the team speculated as to whether they were dealing with a large HFT firm or a bigshot trader at a Wall Street bank. They could see the participant traded through MF Global, and under normal circumstances they would have been able to get the entity's details from the broker quickly. However, since MF Global was in bankruptcy proceedings, all they could do was write to the liquidator and wait. In the meantime, Harris continued to work the data.

NAVSAR's activity in the e-mini was consistent with spoofing, but many trading strategies involve placing bets across multiple markets, and it was entirely possible the e-mini trades were part of some cross-asset approach she wasn't aware of. Harris ruled that out quickly when she ascertained that her subject was usually active only in the e-mini. Next, she pulled together a series of distributions to determine how the entity's trading compared with the rest of the market. "You want to find out what's normal," she explains. "What's the average trade size in the e-mini? What proportion of orders is canceled? How long do orders usually rest in the order book? What is an outlier?" NAVSAR may have been trying to manipulate the market, but if everyone else was doing the same thing or worse, it would be hard to justify bringing a case.

By any measure, NAVSAR was an outlier. In the twelve days the CFTC ended up selecting to illustrate the entity's activity, its layering algorithm canceled or modified orders 182,000 times, corresponding to $35 trillion in notional trades—double the size of America's gross domestic product. On eight of those days, not a single one of those orders was hit. The size of the orders was also immense: an average of 504 contracts, where the average across the market was seven. On the day of the crash, the layering algo accounted for close to a third of *all* canceled trades in the e-mini, the second-biggest futures market in the world. "Undoubtedly, we were looking at the biggest spoofer that has ever traded," says Mr. X.

In March 2013, the account documents came back from MF Global's trustee. They showed that NAVSAR represented an entity called Nav Sarao Futures Limited, a British company with a single director. Nobody at the agency had heard of the firm, but new prop shops sprouted up all the time. It was only when the team looked up the address on Google Maps that eyebrows were raised. Did one of the five biggest S&P traders in the world really operate from a semidetached house in suburbia? While Harris was busy with the data, the attorneys in Chicago started interviewing Sarao's brokers and others from across the market. Kernels about the trader's eccentricities came in slowly: how demanding he was, his abstemiousness. One broker relayed how Sarao had gotten lost on the way to their offices and needed to be guided in, step-by-step, on the phone. Others painted a more sinister picture. A straitlaced surveillance employee at the CME told the story of how Sarao threatened to fly to the United States and "cut your fucking thumbs off" if he didn't sort out an issue he was having. Harris and her colleagues couldn't tell if they were dealing with Forrest Gump or a character from a Guy Ritchie movie.

As work on the case progressed, the team encountered another roadblock, this time internal. Ultimate responsibility for overseeing the case resided with a manager who had been with the division since trading was still carried out in the pits. He had never been convinced of the case's merits, and in tense meetings, he pooh-poohed the idea that Sarao could have had such an impact on the market. The debate was ostensibly focused on the technicalities of proving that injecting so-called false liquidity actually moved markets; but all conversations around Sarao had an unspoken subtext: How would it look if the CFTC turned around and suggested that spoofing had helped cause the Flash Crash, when three years earlier it published a report that didn't even mention it as a factor?

By fall 2013, the team had verified and built on much of Mr. X's evidence, identified Sarao, and pulled together some of his interactions, including the warnings he'd received from the CME about his trading during the pre-market. It was a promising haul, but they knew it wasn't sufficient to nail him. Spoofing was a brand-new offense, completely untested in court. And meeting the standard for manipulation required them to prove that Sarao *intended* to cheat, an ominous cliff face to climb. There were also aspects of the case that gave them pause. If what they were seeing was as clear-cut and persistent as it appeared, why hadn't the surveillance people at the CME taken any substantive action? And how had MF Global allowed a day trader in his bedroom to trade with such insanely high stakes?

Unlike the criminal authorities, the CFTC had no power to subpoena or exercise a search warrant on Sarao, a non–U.S. citizen. Faced with an impasse, they made a decision to reach across the void and make contact with their quarry. Harris and one of the attorneys drafted a letter containing open-ended questions designed to yield information without alerting Sarao to the existence of a full-blown investigation: tell us about your trading career; what software do you use; what is your strategy. Beneath the gentle language was an unmistakable message: *We're on to you.*

■

CHAPTER 19

CORNBREAD AND THE CME

Nav's first instinct upon receiving the CFTC's letter was to ignore it. Every once in a while he got a missive from one of the exchanges asking him about his trading practices, but nothing ever came of it, and he was inclined to view any contact from the regulators as worthy of disdain. A few weeks earlier, R. J. O'Brien had forwarded him the CFTC's "Interpretive Guidance . . . on Disruptive Trading" document, which detailed exactly what was and wasn't allowed under the spoofing rules. Rather than reflecting on his own tactics, Nav wrote back to his broker: "Lol, guarantee if I switch on my computer I'll see the same people breaking all those rules, day in, day out." When he told MacKinnon and Dupont about the letter, though, they implored him to take the matter seriously, and in December 2013, MacKinnon took Nav to meet three lawyers in London, who all told him the same thing: ignore this at your peril. Nav nodded along when they offered to engage with the CFTC on his behalf, but after discussing fees he opted not to take them on. Shortly afterward, a group of traders in Chicago filed a lawsuit against the CME Group that resonated deeply with Nav and played a part in how he chose to respond to the authorities' inquiries.

. . .

AT THE Chicago Board of Trade, where it was an unwritten law that everyone had to have a nickname, they used to call Bill Braman "White Cornbread," then just Cornbread, a riff on his polite "aw, shucks" demeanor and the WCB initials on his name badge. Braman, who is tall and lean with a shaved head, joined the Treasury pit from college just before Black Monday in 1987, and stayed there until the summer before 9/11, when he started trading on a screen. The transition was tough, and many of his friends fell by the wayside, but Braman was a quick, determined learner and before long he was earning more money than he ever had. "I had the best years of my life because I knew how to trade and the banks and the smart people hadn't figured out the electronic side of it yet," he recalls. "I loved to go to work every morning at five a.m. and be done by lunchtime, have a workout, and come home to pick up the kids from school. It was a nice life."

Sometime around 2007, things started to change. As high-frequency trading proliferated, the strategy Braman had honed, which involved betting on relative movements between bonds with different time horizons, became less and less effective. He tried to adapt, incorporating algorithms and investing in technology that allowed him to execute trades more quickly. He even taught himself some code. But the HFTs were too fast, gobbling up opportunities before anyone else could react. Eventually, in 2012, Braman gave up and left the industry that had come to define him. Within a few years, he was divorced and working as a barista at Starbucks. In his spare time, he developed a bicycle dog leash called the DoggerJogger. "Going from millionaire to broke doesn't help your family life very much," he says. "I know people who have killed themselves. They go from driving fancy cars and owning big houses, and they can't face their family and friends."

Braman says there are thousands of dispossessed traders like him, the diaspora from the once-heaving amphitheaters of the Chicago Board of Trade, LIFFE, and the CME. He is philosophical about the evolution to screen-based trading, viewing it as part of the march toward mechanization that touches all industries. But the ascendancy of HFT has been harder to take. "Imagine we're in the pits and I have a really good spot next to the broker and I can hear all the trades coming in, and then one day two six-foot-eight guys come along and stand in front of me and crowd me out and I can't see the trades like I used to," says Braman. "It used to be a meritocracy. If you traded big and took big trades and could service the brokers, they'd make room for you. HFTs aren't big guys. They're just weasels who were able to sneak in, listen to what's about to happen, and jump in front of it while taking no risk themselves."

Worse than the HFT firms, to Braman's mind, is the CME Group, the $75 billion corporation that owns the formerly member-owned exchanges and whose directors got rich by letting in the vampires to bleed them all dry. So when an old pit buddy known as "Missile" called and asked if he was interested in joining a class-action suit against the CME, Braman was receptive. The suit was the brainchild of a former pit inhabitant named R. Tamara de Silva who had parked her own dreams of making it as a trader in order to train as a lawyer. De Silva believed that, by giving preferential treatment to select customers, the CME Group was perpetrating fraud on a massive scale. But convincing her buddies from the market to sign up as plaintiffs wasn't easy. "You've got to understand, Chicago is a trading town and the Merc is very powerful," says Braman. "People are genuinely afraid of it, like the mafia or something." Cornbread figured he had nothing to lose and agreed to add his name to the complaint.

De Silva had been admitted to the Northern Illinois federal trial bar only fairly recently, in 2007, and she had limited experience with cases relating to the Commodities Exchange Act. What she did possess was a sense of righteous self-confidence that pervaded all aspects of her life. On her website, which featured a logo of her name with the scales of justice jutting out of the R, de Silva described herself as "an aggressive and fearless advocate" who would "not take no for an answer" and who specialized in bringing "cases that other lawyers will not take." She also kept a blog, "Timely Objections," containing heated takes on the issues of the day. Outside work she ran a kennel called Mythmaker that bred spaniels whose exploits she chronicled on Instagram. Braman likened taking on the world's biggest commodity's exchange to the movie *Erin Brockovich* and, with her shock of golden curls, de Silva made a fitting lead.

The first iteration of *Braman et al. v. The CME Group Inc.* was filed on April 11, 2014. In it, de Silva alleged that the CME had entered into "clandestine contracts" with HFT firms, allowing them "to see price data and unexecuted order information before anyone else in the financial world" while publicly claiming everyone got it in "real time." In doing so, she wrote, the CME was guilty of manipulation, fraud, and providing false information. The filing was a sparse seventeen pages and offered no evidence to substantiate its claims. It also contained some questionable assertions, such as that HFTs generally entered very large orders: in reality, most traded little and very often.

Two days later, the CME issued a withering response: "The suit is devoid of any facts supporting the allegations and, even worse, demonstrates a fundamental misunderstanding of how our markets operate. It is sad when plaintiffs' lawyers bring a suit based on a desire for publicity, and in the rush to file a suit fail to undertake even the most basic effort to determine if there is a basis for their allegations."

One thing de Silva's suit did have going for it was timing. The previous month, Michael Lewis, celebrated author of *The Big Short* and *Moneyball,* had published *Flash Boys: A Wall Street Revolt,* a devastating exposé of the stock market and high-frequency trading. Through the character of Brad Katsuyama, an archetypal outsider determined to change the system, Lewis described how markets had devolved into a monstrously complex and fragmented realm in which speed was everything and legalized front-running was the norm. "The U.S. stock market was now a class system of haves and have-nots, only what was had was not money but speed (which led to money)," he wrote. "The haves paid for nanoseconds; the have-nots had no idea that a nanosecond had value. The haves enjoyed a perfect view of the market; the have-nots never saw the market at all."

Lewis wasn't the first to question the fairness or utility of modern markets, but he had an audience, and by stating the case so starkly, he brought the debate about HFT—a debate that had flickered and then fizzled out in the aftermath of the Flash Crash—back into the mainstream with a bang. *Flash Boys* was an instant bestseller, and within a week the DOJ and the SEC both announced they were opening investigations into the HFT arena. Launching his own probe, New York attorney general Eric Schneiderman dubbed HFT "insider trading 2.0." The exchanges and trading firms pushed back, decrying Lewis's book as sensationalist and willfully misleading, but many financial insiders sided with the author. Joseph Stiglitz, the Nobel prize–winning economist, described HFT as a form of rent-stealing that distorted markets and discouraged investment. Charlie Munger, Warren Buffett's right-hand man, said it was "the functional equivalent of letting rats into a granary."

Arriving in the middle of this groundswell, de Silva's suit against the CME attracted widespread media attention. However, futures markets and stock markets are built on fundamentally different architecture, and, as the CME and others were quick to point out, many of the structural issues laid bare in Lewis's book simply didn't apply. For one thing, while the shares of major U.S. companies could be bought and sold on dozens of different venues, most futures, including the e-mini, were traded on a single exchange. As a result, many of the scenarios Lewis described, involving predatory algorithms waiting for an order to hit one exchange, then racing over to the next, could never happen in futures.

Still, as loudly as CME chief Terry Duffy insisted his markets were immune to the kind of systematic front-running that beset equities, the fact remained that between 2006 and 2013 high-frequency trading had gone from representing 30 percent of U.S. futures market volume to more than 60 percent. It begged the question: If HFT didn't have an edge, then what were they doing there?

Under something called the Federal Rule of Civil Procedure 9(b), plaintiffs alleging fraud in the United States are required to lay out the basis of their case "with particularity," a higher bar than for other offenses, and in May the CME filed a motion to dismiss the case for essentially being too vague. Before the judge could rule, de Silva asked for a chance to refile and started contacting other attorneys who might help strengthen her claim. Among them was Lovell Stewart, a firm founded by a pioneering commodities lawyer named Chris Lovell, who had built a practice helping parties affected by manipulation and price-fixing bring civil claims for damages. Lovell and his colleagues had successfully sued a number of exchanges and, while they perceived de Silva's filing as flimsy, they could see the merits in suing the CME. After speaking to the plaintiffs and carrying out their own research, they agreed to help redraft the complaint.

Cornbread, Missile, and their peers contended that HFT firms benefited from a host of disclosed and undisclosed advantages gifted to them by the CME Group, which had an interest in keeping volumes as high as possible. The problem the plaintiffs had was that any data that might help illuminate the issue was closely guarded by the CME itself. If they could convince a judge that there was a case to answer, they could force the exchange to hand over evidence as part of a pretrial discovery process. Their best chance, the lawyers at Lovell Stewart advised, would be to consolidate everything already in the public domain and mold it into something compelling.

The bedrock of the amended complaint was a May 2013 article in the *Wall Street Journal* titled "High-Speed Traders Exploit Loophole," which revealed how firms that paid to connect directly to the CME's servers were able to profit by receiving confirmation of their own trades a few milliseconds before it reached the so-called "public tape" and using it to ascertain which way the market was about to move. "If crude oil is selling for $90 on the CME, a firm might post an order to sell one contract for $90.03 and a buy order for $89.97," the *Journal* wrote, citing one of several potential uses of the loophole. "If the sell order suddenly hits, the firm's computers detect that oil prices have swung higher. Those computers can instantly buy more of the same contract before other traders are even aware of the first move." This "latency loophole" was an open secret within the HFT industry, the *Journal* reported, with Jump Trading and DRW Trading both acknowledging they utilized it, and "a person familiar with the thinking" of Virtu Financial suggesting it was actually good for the market because it increased liquidity. It certainly seemed to be good for Virtu, which disclosed in its 2014 IPO prospectus that it had just one losing day out of 1,238 in the five years to February 2014.

CME Group promised to try to minimize the lag and pointed out that anyone could pay the $75,000 a month it charged for direct access to its servers, but the plaintiffs insisted the HFTs' advantages went beyond just speed. Citing confidential witnesses, they alleged that the CME had entered into "clandestine" fee deals with select firms that slashed their cost of trading relative to the majority of participants, resulting in a "two-tiered marketplace." The CME published details of its clearing fees on its website, but it also negotiated private "incentive" programs that were highly valuable and, according to the complaint, susceptible to conflicts of interest, given that some of the exchange's biggest customers were firms operated by its own board members. The CME maintained that the deals were essential to bringing liquidity to the markets, but, as a *Bloomberg* article cited in the complaint pointed out, they were in place in some of the busiest markets in the world. It was akin to suggesting tourists needed to be paid to visit Times Square.

Last, Braman et al. alleged that the CME Group was turning a blind eye to manipulative and disruptive trading practices that were "integral" to HFT, such as wash trading and spoofing.

Wash trading is when an entity buys or sells securities from itself to push the market around or hit volume targets so it qualifies for rebates, and by 2013 it had become widespread enough that the CFTC began an investigation. Publicly, the exchanges supported the clampdown, but they made so much money from all the additional buying and selling that they had little motivation to enforce it. And since most HFT firms had dozens of accounts, there was nothing to prevent them from transacting with each other and then claiming they were running unrelated strategies. With regard to spoofing, there was little evidence, despite the change in the law, that the practice was on the wane. By now, an estimated ninety-five out of every one hundred e-mini orders was canceled, creating, in the plaintiffs' words, a "false impression to other traders about supply and demand." Sanctions remained rare, and even serial offenders escaped with fines in the tens of thousands of dollars.

The revised complaint was lodged on July 22, and it significantly upped the stakes. This time the plaintiffs claimed to represent a class that included anyone who had ever bought or sold a future or paid for data from the CME between 2005 and 2014, a group that included virtually every financial institution, farmer, and food producer in America; and they demanded not only restitution for everything they'd ever lost, but the effective dismantling of the entire HFT industry. The opening paragraph was a call to arms:

> Over the past decade, the Chicago derivatives markets have engaged in agreements with certain high frequency trading firms to erode the integrity of the marketplace and manipulate prices. These exchanges, together with a sophisticated class of technology-driven entities known commonly as "high frequency traders" have provided and utilized information asymmetry along with clandestine incentive agreements and illegal trading practices to create a two-tiered marketplace that disadvantages the American public and all other futures marketplace participants, all

the while continuing to represent to the public and their regulators that they continue to provide transparent and fair trading markets to the global market. In reality, the advantages given to HFTs by the Exchange Defendants effectively create a "zero sum" trading scenario where the HFTs gain what the Class Members lose by effectively providing HFTs with the opportunity to skim an improper profit on every futures transaction.

FOUR THOUSAND miles away, Nav read the complaint and was filled with a sense of vindication. There, over fifty-nine pages, was everything he'd suspected but never been able to prove: the secret deals, the front-running of orders, the race for speed, the industrial-scale manipulation. The CFTC had recently sent him another letter, this time via the UK regulator, asking if he'd be willing to come in for a voluntary interview. But how could anyone criticize *him* when the whole show was a racket from top to bottom? Over the years, Nav had made videos of the markets in an effort to capture evidence of cheating by his competitors. Now he cranked up the recording, filling hard drives with footage accompanied by an expletive-strewn running commentary. He talked to his advisers about sending the material to the plaintiffs, and even considered joining the class action himself. In the end, he decided it would be wiser to keep a low profile. But the criticism surrounding the HFT industry gave him a renewed sense of confidence about his own situation, and on May 29, in lieu of an interview, he finally emailed the regulators back.

NAV WROTE:

Below is the answers to your questions as well as a general overview of my trading and how I would advise the market could become more fair and efficient.

I am an old school point and click prop trader. To this day I am still using the mouse to trade. That is how I trade, that is how I always have traded, admittedly very very fast because I have always been good with reflexes and doing things quick . . . I am a trader who changes his mind very very quickly, one second I am prepared to buy the limit of 2,000, the next second I may change my mind and get out . . . This is what is unique about my trading . . . What makes me change my mind? Well it could be anything, a move in one of the other markets that I look at, a chart set up that I suddenly remember from my 11 years of trading, or simply the WAY I was filled made me doubt my position, or for the large part it is just my INTUITION.

Nav went on to describe himself as

a guy . . . who is trading from the UK and whose system is miles too slow compared [to the HFTs, and whose] orders have to travel further than everyone else's who are trading in USA. No wonder they can manipulative [sic] on top of my orders without any risk . . . I don't like the HFT arena and have complained to the exchange numerous times about their manipulative practices, please BAN IT.

Asked about his setup, Nav wrote:

I have traded using a basic TT for numerous years. Due to the fact that there were some individuals in the emini SP who quite remarkably seemed to know WHERE 100% OF MY ORDERS WERE RESTING . . . I decided to pay Edge Financial to build a program for me that would help disguise my orders more effectively . . . I do not know if this can be described as HFT, to me it is just giving me the ability to have some extra functions . . . It is called Navtrader, but it could be called anything and I was the only one who helped design it, albeit my design ideas were 100% generated from what I had already seen other traders using . . .

Nav went on to describe the JOIN, ICE, and SNAP order types, the last of which he said had

> worked rather beautifully when the mass manipulator of the e-mini sp was doing his normal manipulative activity at price 1800.00 on Friday 24th January circa 12.23pm.

Describing the layering algo, the tool that placed big blocks of orders several ticks from the prevailing price, Nav wrote:

> This is to catch any blips up/down in the market so that I can make a small profit as the market comes back into line (almost immediately). These orders are placed rarely and only when I believe the market is excessively weak or strong.

All told, it was a fairly accurate description of Nav's trading setup, albeit with some serious omissions. There was no mention of NAVTrader's all-important "back of the book" feature, which pushed orders to the back of the queue every time another order arrived; and his suggestion that he *occasionally* layered the ladder with orders several prices from the best bid to catch "blips" was hard to square with the reality that he used the layering algo most days, and the orders it posted were consummated less than 1 percent of the time. The "mass manipulator" he referenced was Igor Oystacher: even when trying to placate the authorities, Nav couldn't resist crowing about getting one over on his rival. The overriding message was that any dubious-looking trading on his part was really just a reflection of his indecision and lightning-fast reactions. Oblivious to the forces mounting across the Atlantic, he optimistically signed off:

> I hope this is helpful and sufficient for you.
> All the best,
> Nav.

■

CHAPTER 20

MINDGAMES

The clock was ticking for Jessica Harris and her colleagues at the CFTC. More than four years had passed since the Flash Crash, and the agency was subject to a five-year statute of limitations, meaning if they were going to charge Sarao for his actions that day, they needed to act fast. Sarao had continued to trade, of course, but it was his activities on May 6, 2010, that caught the attention of Mr. X, and the agency was keenly aware it was Sarao's association with the crash that elevated just another manipulation case into a blockbuster. The team had pulled together everything they could, but the reality was that the evidence still looked light. Beyond the trading records Harris had prepared, there were some dubious messages between Sarao and his brokers, as well as a handful of testy exchanges with the CME on the need for bona fide orders. They painted a compelling picture, but nobody felt confident it would be enough to meet the "by a preponderance of the evidence" standard applicable in civil cases. When Chuck Marvine, Harris's boss, was promoted in spring 2014, he was relieved to hand responsibility for the case to a senior prosecutor in Kansas City named Jeff Le Riche.

Le Riche had grown up obsessed with science and space in a

small town in rural Missouri, devouring Carl Sagan and Stephen Hawking books. At university, he majored in chemistry, but he came to the conclusion he wasn't going to cut it as a scientist, so he went to law school instead. He worked in private practice for a while, then, after his kids were born, joined the CFTC so he could spend more time at home. When electronic trading exploded and markets grew bigger and more complex, his grounding in statistical analysis and data came to the fore and, like Harris, he found himself in demand.

One of the CFTC's abiding concerns was that Sarao's methods, and the high-frequency trading arena in general, were too complex for a layperson to comprehend. It was easy to imagine a jury being unwilling to condemn someone for a crime they didn't fully understand. To help cut through the noise, Le Riche hired a University of California, Berkeley finance professor named Terry Hendershott as an expert witness. Hendershott's main job was to analyze the most blunt and readily understandable weapon in Sarao's arsenal—the layering algorithm he'd developed with Hadj at Trading Technologies. The professor examined Sarao's use of the algo over a sample of twelve days between 2010 and 2014 and concluded it was consistent with spoofing. The orders the algo placed were comparatively huge, rarely if ever hit, and were likely to have had a "statistically significant" impact on prices—around 0.3 basis points on a thousand-lot order. And while Hendershott noted there were legitimate reasons to layer an order book, such as market making or hedging another position, he said Sarao's trading bore none of their characteristics. "Based on the above analyses and my experience the Layering Algorithm's massive volume of orders were designed not to execute and there is no clear business motivation for wanting those orders to execute," he concluded in a report. On the subject of the Flash Crash, he was more circumspect. Resisting pressure from the CFTC to tie the day's events to Sarao, Hendershott would only note, somewhat tortuously, that "the layering algorithm *contributed* to the overall Order Book imbalances and market conditions that the *regulators say* led to the liquidity deterioration *prior to* the Flash Crash."

Having a renowned finance professor testify that Sarao's trading was consistent with spoofing was helpful, but there were still some big holes in the investigation, not least a lack of tangible evidence of Sarao's intent. The team's efforts to get Nav to sit down for a voluntary interview in the UK had gone nowhere, and the CFTC lacked the legal powers to access his communications. A breakthrough came in June 2014, with the arrival of a new head of enforcement. Aitan Goelman was a spiky former prosecutor from the Southern District of New York who made his name as a member of the team that prosecuted Timothy McVeigh, the Oklahoma City bomber. After hearing about the case in Kansas City, Goelman suggested they see if the Justice Department was interested in coming on board. The CFTC had recently partnered with the DOJ on the Libor scandal, a sprawling, multiyear investigation into interest-rate rigging across Wall Street, and Goelman was aware just how useful the criminal authorities' powers could be. At this point, Commodity Exchange Act violations were rarely charged as felonies, but the reverberations of the Flash Crash were felt around the world. "I wanted the deterrent effect of putting an actual human being in jail," says Goelman. "It's much more effective than taking some money or getting a cease-and-desist order," the sanctions at the CFTC's disposal.

The American criminal justice system is divided into ninety-three local U.S. Attorney's Offices, plus "Main Justice," the head office in Washington, and Goelman had a decision about whom to refer the case to. There was his old stomping ground, the Southern District in downtown Manhattan, setting for the HBO show *Billions,* where the biggest white-collar cases tended to reside. There was the Northern District of Illinois in Chicago, heartland of futures, where at that moment the first-ever criminal spoofing case, involving a former pit trader from New Jersey named Michael Coscia, was taking shape. In the end, Goelman reached out to an old buddy from law school and the Southern District who had taken up a senior role in the Fraud Section at Main Justice. The two had worked a gang case together early in their careers, and when Goelman told him about Sarao, the supervisor agreed to assign some of his best people to take a look.

Picking up the baton at the DOJ were the prosecutors who would be there at McDonald's in Hounslow for Sarao's arrest, Brent Wible and Mike O'Neill. Wible, another Southern District alumnus, was raised in Kentucky and had a penchant for country music, particularly Johnny Cash. He wore Buddy Holly glasses, moved slowly and methodically, and brought a welcome air of unflappability to the investigation when pressure to file charges was mounting. His partner, O'Neill, was a rookie in the Fraud Section with a perfect faux-hawk haircut, a magna cum laude degree from Harvard law, and the dedication of an Eagle Scout. After a couple of telephone briefings, the pair flew to Chicago with their CFTC counterparts to watch a presentation from Mr. X. Manning the software was the whistle-blower's European programmer, who didn't say much but picked up the nickname "Crazy Eyes" thanks to his intense expression. By the end of the trip, the DOJ was convinced that Sarao was a massive manipulator but concerned about the lack of evidence of intent—an even bigger consideration for the criminal authorities, since they would have to prove their case beyond a reasonable doubt. Fortunately, they had some levers to pull that the CFTC didn't. The Justice Department's investigative arm is the FBI, and Wible recruited an agent in Chicago to pull together a search warrant request that would give them access to Sarao's private emails. When the judge signed off, they waited for the results to come back with one eye on the calendar.

NAV CALLED Brian Harvey, the tax guru, in an uncharacteristically glum mood. On paper, he was a very rich man, but the empire he'd spawned had become so byzantine and unwieldy it was causing him anxiety, and he was concerned that some of his advisers might be, in his words, "taking the piss." Two years had passed since Cranwood Holdings Limited had been set up with $15 million of Nav's money, and so far not a single plot of land to house wind farms had been secured. During that time, he complained, the business had eaten through more than $3 million. Martin Davie, the irascible Scotsman running things, had been paying himself a six-figure salary despite having a second CEO job with his other wind company. At first, Nav had kept his distance, rarely attending the monthly get-togethers or going through the budgets. However, recently he'd started to examine the expenditures and he was incensed. Not only was Nav funding the Edinburgh office, but MacKinnon and Dupont were charging Cranwood $3,000 a month to help cover their rent in Berkeley Square, on the grounds that they were spending time there on Wind Energy Scotland. Cranwood also footed the bill for a corporate membership at Archerfield, a spectacularly picturesque Scottish golf club, because Davie said it was essential for building relationships.

Unlike many of the people in Nav's orbit, Harvey was paid a fixed sum for his services and so had no vested interest in how the trader invested his money. After helping Nav avoid a $10 million tax bill in 2011 by establishing a complex ownership structure in the Cayman Islands, he'd come to the rescue again a couple of years later, relocating the operation to Guernsey when the Caribbean administrators got cold feet. Lately, Nav had taken to calling Harvey up regularly to seek his advice or just for a chat. Harvey had four children not much older than Nav, and he had grown to feel protective of his impressionable young client. On several occasions, he'd warned Nav away from proposals, telling him that if something seemed too good to be true, it probably was. Whenever Nav felt out of his depth, he asked Harvey if he would be willing to take over the day-to-day running of his business empire. Nav was a trader at heart, and all these distractions were throwing him off his game. Harvey always politely declined, saying it went beyond his skill set. He was approaching retirement and looking to slow down. Before hanging up, he urged Nav to raise his grievances with MacKinnon and Dupont and try to simplify his affairs.

When Nav eventually stumped up the courage to confront MacKinnon and Dupont, they told him that the forthcoming referendum on Scottish independence was making it difficult to secure commitments, and assured him that things would pick up when it was out of the way. They agreed to pay back $60,000 for the disputed rent and flew him to Edinburgh to spend some time with Davie and the team. Nav had rarely visited the countryside and, peering out the window during one drive, he exclaimed: "What the fuck is that . . . It's a fucking sheep!" The visit culminated on a golf course, where, for nine interminable holes, Nav whiffed a ball around while his companions looked on through strained smiles. Later that year, with relations repaired, MacKinnon and Dupont introduced Nav to a new opportunity they'd heard about on a networking trip to the French Riviera. Rather than cutting ties with the financiers, Sarao ended up plunging headfirst into another venture.

DAMIEN O'BRIEN is six feet four and wears a ponytail that gives him the air of a young Steven Seagal. On the day he met MacKinnon and Dupont, he arrived at a beachside restaurant wearing white trousers with an oversize Hermès belt buckle, a pink shirt, and Gucci loafers, and immediately ordered a dozen bottles of champagne for the busy table. O'Brien hailed from an Irish family and made his first fortune subleasing vacant rooftops to telecom companies, before moving to Manchester, where he got in with a professional football crowd. It was there that he came up with the idea that would make him rich: *X Factor* for soccer. The show, named *Football Icon* and later *Football's Next Star,* offered talented underachievers one last shot at joining the academies of some of the world's biggest clubs. It was picked up by Fox, which replicated the format around the world, providing O'Brien with a stream of income that he splashed around with a generosity that bordered on the pathological. He moved into a mansion previously owned by Cristiano Ronaldo that was plastered with the footballer's trademark "CR7" crests, and was now looking for investors for a new business he was launching in the online gaming space.

O'Brien's latest venture combined two of Nav's passions: markets and gambling. The Irishman had established a company called Iconic Worldwide Gaming that would allow punters to bet on movements in currencies and securities using an interface that looked like an online casino, with a roulette wheel and buttons for higher and lower instead of red and black. "Financial markets are on the news and in the paper daily, part of modern daily life," ran a pitching document. "But participating in that market is seen as daunting and targeted at experienced, number-crunching wizards, involves countless spreadsheets, brokers, expenses and commissions, and huge potential downsides. Wouldn't it be great to just put a 'bet' on gold to rise next or where the FTSE will land?" The patented software was called MINDGames, short for Market Influenced Number Determination Games. It may not have pleased Gamblers Anonymous, but the projections were mouthwatering. O'Brien predicted the company would go from a standing start to a cash balance of $175 million by the end of its third year. He had also attracted some big names to the board, including the former CEO of betting giant Ladbrokes and a High Court judge.

Nav was immediately taken with O'Brien, who was gregarious, upbeat, and larger-than-life. Like Nav, he had come from humble beginnings and lived by his own rules. Unlike Nav, he was the center of any party, and he took the young trader for a couple of nights out in London with his high-rolling friends. Shortly after they met, the soccer World Cup was taking place in Brazil, and Nav took some time off to immerse himself in the tournament, which he feverishly looked forward to every four years, going as far as to buy himself a replica of the trophy. O'Brien rented a boardroom with a giant television screen at 45 Park Lane, a five-star hotel overlooking Hyde Park, and the Iconic team would watch the matches there after business meetings. Later, when O'Brien found out how much Nav loved Lionel Messi, he gave him a framed pair of boots signed with what he claimed was a personal message by the Argentinian superstar. Midway through the tournament, on July 1, 2014, Nav invested $3.8 million in Iconic Worldwide Gaming in exchange for a stake in the low double figures. O'Brien talked hungrily about how they were going to conquer America. That week, Nav won a long-shot bet on the football and chuckled at his good fortune.

SARAO'S EMAILS landed at the Justice Department shortly after Christmas 2014, and they bolstered the case significantly. The material fell into two broad categories: "trading" and "money." The first bucket included Sarao's messages to Hadj at TT in 2009 laying out the modifications he wanted to make to his off-the-shelf software and, later, thanking the engineer for helping him build the layering algo. Then there was his ongoing correspondence with Jitesh Thakkar at Edge regarding the creation and development of the more sophisticated NAVTrader program. Bucket two was made up of documents and interactions relating to Sarao's business outside trading, including records of multimillion-dollar deposits into IXE and Iconic, and invoices from Harvey for tax advice. They helped show how much money Sarao had made, and his use of havens like the Cayman Islands to squirrel it away. The DOJ shared the material with Le Riche, Harris, and their colleagues at the CFTC, and staff from the two agencies trawled through the evidence late into the evenings. In their downtime, they joked about who was going to play them in the inevitable movie.

From a prosecutor's point of view, having Sarao describe his algorithms in his own words was desirable because it made it harder for the trader to lie about his intentions on the stand. There were also the kind of nuggets that tend to resonate with a jury, like Sarao's boast about telling the CME to "kiss my ass." His recent response to the CFTC's questions contained demonstrable falsehoods and omissions, and there were several examples of Sarao complaining to the CME about what he perceived as cheating by his rivals, which, while highlighting broader issues in the markets, suggested that he understood what was and wasn't allowed.

Taken together, the evidence was about as strong as any prosecutor could realistically hope for in a white-collar case. Still, there was nothing to blow the whole thing open; no clumsy acknowledgment buried in the email archives that showed he was deliberately seeking to manipulate the market and that he knew what he was doing was against the law. Maybe that was too much to hope for, but the Fraud Section instructed the FBI to start preparing a search warrant so that, when they arrested Sarao in the UK, they could simultaneously take possession of his computer and other effects. They also began the process of securing the expedited backing of the British regulator and the Metropolitan Police for an overseas raid, a delicate process that would normally take several months.

In the meantime, the prosecutors debated what laws to charge Sarao with breaking. It was a complex decision that could have serious ramifications for their prospects of success down the line. A major consideration was the fact that, before Sarao could even stand trial in the United States, they would need to secure his extradition from the UK. In international law there is something called the "Doctrine of Specialty" that states that an individual can be tried only for the offenses for which they were extradited. Since the prosecutors couldn't add charges at a later date, only subtract them, it was in their interests to cast the net wide. Eventually, Wible, O'Neill, and their colleagues settled on twenty-two counts encompassing an array of statutes with different criteria. The first was garden-variety wire fraud, a kind of catchall offense that involves knowingly operating a scheme to obtain money by making false representations or promises using electronic communications—in this case the orders Sarao placed on the CME over a five-year period. Counts two to eleven related to individual instances of alleged commodities fraud. Twelve through twenty-one were examples of alleged manipulation and attempted manipulation, that slippery offense that had historically proven so difficult to land. The final count was for a solitary instance of alleged spoofing in March 2014, after the CFTC's disruptive trading guidelines had been published, which would give the government an opportunity to test the new statute in a courtroom without staking the entire case on it. Cumulatively, the maximum sentences for the charges added up to 380 years.

As they raced to beat the statute-of-limitations deadline, the authorities discovered that Sarao was trading again. By now, most of his money was locked up in investments, but in October 2014 he'd opened a second brokerage account with R. J. O'Brien, depositing $8 million. He'd also contacted Thakkar at Edge about making further refinements to NAVTrader. The agencies knew they had to move quickly, and the CFTC started pulling together a motion for a restraining order.

Compiling the dossier of evidence, Harris was once again struck by just how unusual a target Sarao was. At the time, the enforcement division was working on a fairly typical case involving a serial fraudster named Anthony Klatch who lied about his investing prowess to misappropriate funds that he squandered on fast cars and cocaine. Sarao was the exact opposite, concealing his talents from the people around him and never spending the money he made. The emails the DOJ had seized offered some glimpses into the man behind the screens. There were laments about how his parents were pressuring him to get married, and boasts about his success with women that came off like teenage braggadocio; references to his father's diabetes and declining health; social invitations that he accepted and then backed out of at the last minute. "It happens a lot in these cases," says Harris. "You have a perception of someone and then, as you look through their bank statements and interview their associates and read their emails, a real person emerges. Sometimes that weighs heavy."

Meanwhile, Goelman, the new head of enforcement, was navigating more political waters. Throughout the investigation, the CFTC had been aware that linking Sarao to the Flash Crash might leave the agency open to criticism, and with Nav's arrest looming, such considerations came to the fore. "You're faced with a choice," says Goelman. "You're concerned about protecting the reputation of the agencies and you don't want to admit that you missed something, so do you just practice willful blindness or do you investigate and go wherever the facts lead even if it's going to be embarrassing?" The CFTC held its course, but there were drawn-out discussions between the team and senior management about how to describe Sarao's involvement in a way that was justified by the evidence while minimizing the appearance of a conflict with the earlier findings. They also had the SEC, their coauthors on the 2010 report, to consider. In early 2015, Goelman and the CFTC's new chairman, Tim Massad, hosted a conference call with SEC head Mary Jo White and her head of enforcement, Andrew Ceresney, to talk through what was coming. When Goelman finished laying out the evidence, their counterparts thanked him for the heads-up and asked jokingly what the hell the CFTC was thinking reopening a matter that had already been laid to rest.

On February 11, 2015, four years, nine months, and five days after the Flash Crash, Wible flew to Chicago and made his way to the federal courthouse with the agent he'd drafted from the FBI. Inside, they presented a judge with a copy of the freshly completed complaint against Sarao as well as a warrant for his arrest. The judge signed the documents and sealed them from public view until the authorities were ready to pounce. Nav's life was already over—he just didn't know it yet.

EVER SINCE Jesus Alejandro Garcia Alvarez appeared in Zurich out of nowhere in 2006, he'd talked about wanting to buy a bank. Swiss secrecy laws are among the strongest in the world and, for the very wealthy, owning your own lender can be more efficient than parking your money elsewhere, which explains why there are around four hundred bank branches in a city of four hundred thousand people. After a couple of false starts, Garcia was introduced to the owners of Banca Arner, a small private bank founded in 1984 in Lugano. Arner had been struck low after it emerged that Italian prime minister Silvio Berlusconi, on trial for tax fraud, had hidden tens of millions of dollars there. So, in 2014, Garcia purchased a 9.8 percent stake for a few million euros and convinced the board to let him acquire the rest. Citing his experience at IXE, Garcia said he wanted to transform Arner from a discreet bank into a powerhouse that would help facilitate the trading of commodities and agricultural goods around the globe. In June, Arner opened an office in Zurich, and Garcia began recruiting executives, including his wife, Ekaterina, whom he named head of media relations. He also found a new chairman, a big player in Swiss banking circles named Michael Baer, part of the Julius Baer family, who he hoped would help smooth the takeover with the regulator.

Over the course of that summer, Garcia came to London to see Nav and IXE's half dozen or so other British investors at IXE's newly rented offices, which overlooked the Royal Exchange, where the Liffe pits once roared. Exchange Alley (since renamed "Change Alley"), the swindler's paradise Defoe described, was a hundred meters away. Garcia told the investors that, because Morgan Stanley was selling its Swiss unit and the acquirer had no interest in the trade finance space, it was going to be necessary for them to transfer their funds to Arner. This time, though, he explained, the deal would be structured slightly differently. Rather than everyone having their own individual accounts, all the money, around $90 million, would be consolidated into a single account in the name of "IXE Trading AG," which would distribute the returns. Also, instead of simply being used as a "backstop" for the "riskless" trades of third parties, the funds would also now be utilized to make "direct" investments into agricultural markets. Garcia assured participants their money would be as secure as ever and presented them with a stark choice: Anyone who transferred the money would receive even more interest. Those who didn't could no longer participate at all.

For three years, IXE's investors and their introducers had

received their payments every quarter without fail. Against a backdrop of rock-bottom interest rates and pitiful returns, they'd seen their wealth climb and climb. Back in 2012, when Hinduja Bank was hit with sanctions, they'd transferred their money to Morgan Stanley with no problems. So when Garcia told them they needed to move the money again, nobody blinked. Nav filled out the paperwork agreeing to transfer his $65 million to Arner Bank in September. After finding out he could add yet more millions to the pile he had been assiduously building since the first day he placed a trade, he didn't hesitate for a microsecond.

In little more than a decade, Nav had gone from a standing start to the point where signing off on such multimillion-dollar deals seemed perfectly reasonable to him. He'd forged his own path to get there, eschewing the traditional routes to success in the financial world, and still bringing in the kinds of numbers that the highest earning big-bank traders and hedge fund managers a few miles away in the City of London aspired to. But the intensity of his focus and the strength of his obsession had rendered Nav blind to virtually everything else, including the perils that now swirled all around him. It was only a few weeks later, when he was abruptly awoken by the sound of his father's voice telling him the police were on the doorstep, that the reverie was finally broken.

ACT **THREE**

■

CHAPTER 21

WHERE'S THE MONEY, NAV?

When the U.S. government finally descended on Hounslow to arrest Nav on April 21, 2015, one of his overriding emotions, he would later tell investigators, was relief. Twelve years had passed since he'd arrived at Futex with not much more than the money in his pocket, boasting about how he was going to make a billion pounds. No one could accuse him of not giving it a good go, but lately, the pressures he was facing were weighing him down: the regulators' letters; the ceaseless demands of his business associates; the six-figure losses that seemed to come more frequently now. Nav was adamant he'd done nothing wrong, but he'd grown morose, that steel-box mind, normally so resistant to unnecessary feeling, buckling under the strain. As he was driven from his parents' house, handcuffed, in the back of an unmarked police car, he could at least console himself in the knowledge that, no matter what came next, the running was over.

After a night in the cells, Nav was taken to Westminster Magistrates' Court, a modern, clinical building in an otherwise touristy stretch of north London between Baker Street and Edgware Road. The story of how a young British trader came to be blamed by the American government for helping cause a trillion-dollar market crash from his childhood bedroom had dominated the news cycle, and by 9:30 a.m. a queue had formed outside Court One. When the clerk unlocked the doors, reporters hurried to the forty or so seats in the gallery at the back. Seated among them, in a beige jacket and a baseball cap pulled low over his eyes, was Nachhattar Sarao, Nav's father. Shortly after 10 a.m. the judge motioned for a guard to fetch the defendant. The room fell silent as Nav shuffled into the dock, his fading canary-yellow sweatshirt providing a rare splash of color. Slumped behind a reinforced glass wall, he looked as fragile as a bird.

Nav listened to the charges, rejected the DOJ's extradition request, and confirmed his personal details so quietly the judge had to tell him to speak up. He was represented by a solicitor named Richard Egan whose firm, Tuckers, had chanced into the assignment by being the next name on the duty roster. In the afternoon, the parties agreed on a date for the extradition hearing in mid-August, four months hence. "I suspect the last twenty-four hours or less have been somewhat traumatic for you," said the judge, before granting Nav bail on the condition he stay off the Internet, report to a police station three times a week, and hand over £5.05 million—everything in his R. J. O'Brien trading account plus £50,000 surety from his parents—to deter him from fleeing. As soon as the money arrived, he would be allowed to go home.

News of Nav's arrest had spread quickly among those who knew him. Lynn Adamson was at home listening to Radio 4. Miles MacKinnon got a call from a journalist as he was boarding a train. In Chicago, Jitesh Thakkar was forwarded an article by a friend who recognized Sarao's name. Futex alumni shared anecdotes on WhatsApp, and a Bloomberg Television crew traveled to Woking to interview Paolo Rossi on the trading floor where Nav cut his teeth. "Nav was always going to be the kind of person that I believed would be legendary, potentially legendary in some way," said Rossi. (CVs flooded into Futex for days.) For their part, Wible, O'Neill, and the FBI agents avoided the glare of the courtroom, flying back to the United States after a night out with the team from Scotland Yard.

While Nav waited to be released, he was held in Wandsworth Prison, a vast Dickensian fortress south of the Thames. He expected to be there a matter of hours, but the following day one of the solicitors visited to explain there was a snag. Before Nav was arrested, the CFTC had secured a freezing order on his assets, prohibiting U.S. broker R. J. O'Brien from releasing his funds and requesting any non-U.S. entities to do the same. Tuckers was working to resolve the situation, the solicitor said, but for now, Nav would remain incarcerated. Wandsworth houses roughly 1,700 inmates across eight wings, ranging from serial shoplifters to violent sexual offenders. Many, like Nav, are in a kind of limbo, either on remand or waiting to be moved on to another jail. Built in 1851, its foreboding gray stone facade was featured in *A Clockwork Orange*. In 1965, the train robber Ronnie Biggs escaped from the yard. Nav's cell, where he was locked up for twenty-three hours a day, was six by ten feet and contained a toilet, a bunk with a plastic sheet, and a barred window. Highly sensitive to light and noise and unsure how long he'd be there, he found it impossible to sleep. After a week, he was taken back to court in a gray, prison-issue tracksuit, where a judge declined a request to alter the terms of his bail. When the same thing happened a week later, he shouted toward the gallery as he was led away: "What am I in jail for? I didn't do anything wrong apart from being good at my job!" It was the five-year anniversary of the Flash Crash.

In early May, Nav was taken to a prison meeting room, where he was greeted by Roger Burlingame, a former high-ranking DOJ prosecutor turned defense attorney who'd carved a niche in London representing European targets of U.S. criminal investigations. Burlingame, who was forty-five and had a low-key, disarming manner, was a partner at Kobre & Kim and had been drafted in by the British lawyers to deal with the U.S. side of the defense. His first job was to get Nav out of jail. The problem, he explained, was that the American government considered Sarao a flight risk. Nav had no ties to the U.S. and, according to the CFTC's calculations, had made $40 million trading the e-mini since 2009 alone, most of which was sitting offshore and out of their grasp. If the money was unfrozen and he was released, what was to stop him from disappearing? Other than emulating Ronnie Biggs, Nav had three possible routes out of Wandsworth: convince the CFTC to unblock his assets, persuade the British judge to lower the bail, or come up with the £5 million from somewhere else.

Before settling on a course of action, Burlingame needed a better understanding of Nav's finances. He listened while his client described a sprawling empire that stretched from the Isle of Man to Switzerland to the Cayman Islands, and included investments in renewable energy, gambling, trade finance, and insurance. Once he'd gleaned everything he could, the lawyer began contacting Nav's associates, who told him that all the money set aside for the wind venture was stuck in a bank account they couldn't access; that Iconic, the online gambling company in which Nav owned a stake, was hemorrhaging money so fast it had borrowed an additional £1 million from Nav a few weeks before the arrest; and that, while there was some cash sitting in IGC, Nav's offshore corporation, liquidating it abruptly would spark a tax bill in excess of $30 million. The only chance of getting funds quickly, then, was IXE, which, according to the statements it produced, now held around $65 million of Nav's money at the Swiss bank Arner.

When Garcia eventually called Nav's lawyers back, he said he was sorry to hear about Nav's predicament, but there wasn't much he could do. Nav's funds were subject to strict lock-up clauses, the earliest of which expired in January 2016. What's more, even though the CFTC's freezing order was for all intents and purposes unenforceable outside the United States, IXE's directors had taken the decision not to make any payments to Nav or his introducers until the situation was resolved. Eventually, Garcia said he thought it *might* be possible to release a chunk of Nav's cash a bit earlier, in November. But that was six months away, and Nav's lawyers were starting to worry he might not survive that long.

After eight weeks in Wandsworth, Nav was unraveling. Severely sleep-deprived, he'd taken to draping his blanket over the window to try to block out the light, but the cacophony of prison life was incessant and terrifying. A few days earlier, another inmate had been moved in. Their bunks, divided by a plastic screen, lay less than two meters apart. When his new cellmate tried to hang himself, Nav held up his thrashing legs until a guard arrived. Outside on the wing, the atmosphere was feral. Inmates smoked drugs until they passed out and protested at their treatment by flinging feces. Nav's only reprieve was the weekly bail hearing at Westminster, which always ended in crushing disappointment. To occupy himself, he read philosophy books. One of his favorites was *The Celestine Prophecy* by James Redfield, a kind of modern-day fable in which the protagonist embarks on a perilous journey to Peru, where he learns important life lessons, such as the futility of accumulating material wealth.

Across the river, back at the courthouse, the battle for Nav's release was escalating. By now, it was clear that there were no liquid funds to pay bail, so the focus turned to persuading the British judiciary to show mercy. To handle the forthcoming extradition hearing, Tuckers had appointed an eminent barrister named James Lewis who, on May 20, took the matter to the High Court. Lewis asked that the bond be cut to just his parents' £50,000, arguing that Nav was from a "tight-knit family" and would never do anything to jeopardize what amounted to their life savings. The judge was unmoved, saying £50,000 was "no assurance at all" on profits of $40 million, particularly since Nav had no partner or children. All the confusion around Nav's finances brought to the fore another delicate issue. By now there were half a dozen lawyers working on various aspects of the case. If the money was tied up or worse, how were they going to get paid?

The defense team hired a psychiatrist who, after meeting with Nav, determined he scored highly on the scale for Asperger's syndrome, a condition on the autism spectrum marked by social difficulties, obsessive interests, and a heightened sensitivity to stimuli. Nav had never visited a psychiatrist before, and, although he'd spent his life being told he was odd or weird, it was the first time anyone had suggested he had a specific condition. A 2015 study by the University of Cambridge found autistic traits, such as attention to detail and difficulty taking another person's point of view, are more common among those working in mathematics and science-based professions.

The CFTC's restraining order was due to expire in June, at which point there would be an injunction hearing where a judge would decide whether to extend the freeze until the case was wrapped up. Aware that could potentially lock up Nav's funds for years, Burlingame called the CFTC to try to hammer out a deal. The agency's priority was restitution. Nav had accumulated tens of millions of dollars, and the regulators wanted to make sure that, if he was found guilty, he paid back every cent of it that came from cheating the market. After listening to their concerns, Burlingame made a novel proposal. Chasing foreign assets is a frustrating, arduous process, but Kobre & Kim had some expertise in the field. If the CFTC agreed to modify its restraining order to unblock Sarao's global assets, the firm would act as a kind of bounty hunter, tracking down the loot on the government's behalf and placing it in an escrow account. The first deposit would be the £5 million at R. J. O'Brien. Of the money Burlingame and his team retrieved after that, $2.5 million would be set aside for legal fees plus whatever was required for bail. If the total pot reached more than $30 million, the excess funds would be used to cover any additional fees as well as Nav's living expenses. The CFTC agreed, and on June 29 the restraining order was amended.

Nav's prospects of release may have improved, but his business empire continued to disintegrate. Iconic Worldwide Gaming, into which he'd now plowed $5 million, was supposed to go live later in the year, but the project was behind schedule, and when the payment processing company heard about the controversy surrounding Nav, one of its chief investors walked away. Members of Iconic's board quickly followed. By now, Damien O'Brien, its ponytailed founder, had already commissioned a sixty-second action-movie-style advertisement starring mixed martial arts superstar Conor McGregor, and was preparing for a splashy launch at the MGM Grand in Las Vegas at McGregor's next fight. A month after the bout, the company was placed into liquidation.

"Iconic was a business with great potential, but after the arrest it all fell apart," says O'Brien. "Partners, banks, and executives walked away. I did everything to keep it afloat, but no one wanted to be associated with the guy blamed for causing the Flash Crash. I personally lost around twenty million dollars. But I liked Nav and I wish him all the best."

Meanwhile, IXE decided it was now going to halt *all* outgoings, which had a devastating impact on those who had come to rely on the money. Lynn Adamson and her partner were bombarded with calls from angry investors and introducers who couldn't understand what Sarao's legal problems had to do with them. Cranwood, the wind project, was shuttered before a single turbine had been erected. An increasingly desperate MacKinnon and Dupont hired lawyers to try to force Garcia to release some funds, and reluctantly handed back the keys to the office in Berkeley Square. For five years, they had clung to Nav's coattails and been rewarded with money and success. Now they were tarnished by association.

Nav was finally released on August 14, 2015. The judge agreed to cut bail to £50,000 because still none of the assets had been retrieved. In a few weeks, he'd be back for the extradition battle. Until then, he was a free man, provided he remain within London's M25 ring road and wear an electronic tag. It was a drizzly afternoon, and photographers jostled to capture the infamous Hound of Hounslow as he made his way to a taxi, his hair grown long under the pointed hood of a black coat pulled, wizard-like, over his head.

■

CHAPTER 22

#FREENAV

No sooner had Nav's arrest been made public than the backlash began. The antipathy toward high-frequency trading was at its post–*Flash Boys* zenith, and every element of Sarao's story, from his humble beginnings to his criticism of HFT to the heavy press of the American government to the outlandish nature of the allegations, seemed precision tooled to provoke a sense of indignation. Before the details of the complaint had been absorbed, commentators had lined up behind the underdog. "The simple idea that a chap in West London, playing around at home with an off-the-shelf algo programme on his PC while his parents are off at the gurdwara, can up-end the entire U.S. equity market is comical," wrote one *Financial Times* journalist, adding that "you know, instinctively," the case is "nonsense." A few days later, the *New York Times* published an op-ed titled "The Trader as Scapegoat" by Columbia professor Rajiv Sethi, who suggested Sarao's tactics were understandable, even laudable, in a world dominated by front-running algos. "If regulators and prosecutors are serious about enforcement of securities laws, they should focus on the largest players in the fragmented markets for stocks and not on an individual, acting alone, who managed to fool an algorithm," he wrote. In *Bloomberg,* Michael Lewis questioned why it had taken the regulators five years to bring charges.

For members of the case team, the fallout was predictable but irritating. A lot of the coverage seemed lazy and misleading. Yes, it was true that Sarao lived in his parents' house, wore a tracksuit, and drove a moped. But he was also worth $70 million, and could have bought every house on Clairvale Road if he'd wanted to. And, yes, he traded from his bedroom with a comparatively slow connection, but he had also been, for long periods, among the five largest e-mini traders in the world, consistently trading higher volumes than most of the world's biggest banks and hedge funds. The authorities knew better than anyone how bizarre the facts of the case were, but that didn't make them untrue, and it was galling to see the fruits of their labor rejected because it didn't *feel* right. A common complaint was that the regulators were "scapegoating" Sarao for an easy win, which struck them as ironic given how hard they'd had to work to convince their managers to reopen a case that had already been put to bed.

Still, the agencies had also made life unnecessarily difficult for themselves. In the lead-up to Sarao's arrest, there had been extensive discussions at both the CFTC and the DOJ about how much emphasis to place on the Flash Crash. Some argued that pinning the events of May 6, 2010, on Sarao was unnecessary and risked weakening the whole case, particularly since the "disruptive trading" provision didn't come into force until 2011. Others wanted to make the connection as strong as possible for maximum impact. In the end, the agencies took the view that it would be intellectually dishonest not to highlight Sarao's prodigious spoofing that day. Even so, they agonized over the right set of words. The DOJ's indictment stated Sarao's trading "contributed to the order-book imbalance that the CFTC and the SEC have concluded, in a published report, was a cause, among other factors, of the Flash Crash," a formulation that was hard to refute. However, all those layers of nuance were lost after the press office sent out a release with the headline "Futures Trader Charged with Illegally Manipulating Stock Market, Contributing to the May 2010 Market

'Flash Crash.'" Sarao was duly dubbed the "Flash Crash Trader," and much of the subsequent debate about his innocence or guilt disregarded the hundreds of other days he was trading.

The prosecutors, busy preparing for trial, discounted the media's fixation with the Flash Crash as an unfortunate sideshow, but the truth was, for Nav, it was profoundly important. Historically, spoofers and manipulators were handled civilly, with fines or temporary bans; so the government's decision to charge Sarao criminally marked an escalation. He was the first alleged market manipulator ever to be extradited, and some of the counts against him carried sentences of up to twenty years in prison. If the principal reason for this difference in treatment was that Sarao had contributed to a market collapse, then it was essential to determine whether that was valid. One ex–CFTC employee who worked on the original investigation believes the decision to link Sarao to the crash was ill-advised. "It's perplexing to me and others I've spoken to why they would make that assertion," he says. "They should have recognized that it introduces risk into the case, because it's something they would never have been able to prove. It looks like grandstanding." His comments reflect a schism that opened up in the days after the arrest between the authors of the original Flash Crash report and those involved in Nav's case. Andrei Kirilenko, one of the leaders of the 2010 probe, rejected the notion that Sarao had any bearing on the Flash Crash at all. Speaking to the *Wall Street Journal,* the economist described the impact of Sarao's layering orders as "statistically insignificant" and pointed out that the trader's program was switched off when the e-mini tanked. Others conceded there had been an oversight. We "should have seen this," said Cornell University's Maureen O'Hara, who sat on the committee set up by CFTC chairman Gary Gensler to oversee the first inquiry. "Nowadays, market manipulation doesn't just involve the trades. It's about the orders."

For academics interested in market microstructure, Sarao's case reignited a long-running debate about the extent to which unconsummated orders, including spoofs, really impact prices. The University of Houston's Craig Pirrong, who blogs under the name "The Streetwise Professor," suggested that Terry Hendershott, the UC Berkeley finance professor and expert witness for the government, had shown that Sarao's trading had such a small bearing on prices that it served only to undermine the CFTC's case. "Yes, Sarao's conduct was dodgy, clearly, and there is a colorable case that he did engage in spoofing and layering," he wrote. "But the disparity between the impact of his conduct as estimated by the government's own expert and the legal consequences that could arise from his prosecution is so huge as to be outrageous." It was a view shared by the authors of a paper titled "The Flash Crash: A New Deconstruction," an early version of which was picked up by the press in January 2016, on the eve of Sarao's extradition hearing. After analyzing e-mini and SPY trading data for the first time at a millisecond-by-millisecond level, Eric Aldrich, Joseph Grundfest, and Gregory Laughlin concluded that the events of May 6, 2010, were caused by "prevailing market conditions combined with the introduction of a large equity sell order [Waddell & Reed's] implemented in a particularly dislocating manner," a perspective in keeping with Kirilenko's. On the subject of Sarao, they calculated that his away-from-the-market spoof orders contributed to a decline in the e-mini of, at most, 0.324 basis points over two minutes compared to the total 500 basis points it actually fell in the five minutes before 1:45 p.m. CET. As a result, they said, it was "highly unlikely that, as alleged by the United States Government, Navinder Sarao's spoofing orders, even if illegal, could have caused the Flash Crash or that the crash was a foreseeable consequence of his spoofing activity."

Four years after the spoofing rules came into force, questions were once again asked about whether the practice was as heinous as the government suggested. John Arnold, a renowned energy trader and hedge fund manager worth an estimated $4 billion, wrote a piece in *Bloomberg* arguing that spoofing in the electronic era was actually a necessary counterbalance to the "front-running" perpetrated by many HFT firms. "A front-runner profits by gleaning the intentions of legitimate market participants and jumping in front of their orders, thereby causing the original traders to buy and sell at a less favorable price," he wrote. "But with spoofers in the mix, the picture looks quite different: When the front-running HFT algorithm jumps ahead of a spoof order, the front-runner gets fooled and loses money . . . Suddenly the front-runner faces real market risk and makes the rational choice to do less front-running." The only losers from spoofing, Arnold surmised, were front-running HFTs whose "strategies are harmful to every other market participant." Others disagreed. Kipp Rogers, the owner of an algorithmic trading firm, pointed out on his blog "Mechanical Markets" that all trading, regardless of the time horizon, is ultimately about using data to predict the future, so to describe entities that were particularly adept at it as front-runners was, to his mind, a "gross misuse of the term." Rogers also rejected Arnold's contention that only HFT firms were impacted by spoofing, arguing that all participants had an interest in the integrity of the marketplace.

Among the independent trading community, Nav's reputation didn't turn on whether he caused the Flash Crash or the ethical merits of spoofing. To the dwindling army of day traders, Nav was nothing short of a god, the lone trader who took on the machines and won. For years, human scalpers had been squeezed out by the "HFT geeks" and Wall Street traders, with their innate advantages and connections. Now somebody on a home PC had found a way to fight back, all while sticking two fingers up at the establishment. Who cares if what he was doing was legal; Nav Sarao was a rock star. "To be honest I think the guy involved in this story is a trading hero and an inspiration to everyone out there," wrote one forum poster. "To think he started trading 1 lots 10 years or so ago and is now one of the biggest S&P traders in the world using . . . software and brokers any one of you can get access to . . . thats what we all dream of."

"There's always been a strong feeling in this industry of us versus them," says Tom Dante, an ex–Futex recruit who now coaches trading under the moniker Trader Dante. "So when they went after a guy for taking the fight to the HFTs, it seemed completely unfair." The day after Sarao's arrest, the hash tag #freenav started appearing on Twitter. That week, an online petition was launched to protest against his extradition. "He is like Galileo," remarked one of its signatories. "Succeeding to that level is such a rarity, it takes so much work and talent, and when an individual who actually makes it has everything taken away from him it makes me question the integrity of the industry," says Alex Haywood, another Futex alumnus who now runs his own arcade, Axia Futures. "As traders we were upset because it showed that there is a clear hierarchy and prop traders are at the bottom."

For the prosecutors, the hammering they received in sections of the press offered a useful insight into the kinds of arguments they might face at trial. In meetings, they read from blog posts and strategized about how to parry various critiques. Still, none of them were immune to the moral complexities of the case, and hearing about Sarao's difficulties in jail and his psychiatric diagnosis gave them pause. Searching for potential victims of the trader's alleged crimes, the CFTC and DOJ visited the owners of some of the biggest and most profitable HFT firms. After meeting one particularly obnoxious young multimillionaire, who greeted them in his palatial high-rise office wearing flip-flops and a Hawaiian shirt, they joked to themselves: "So, these are our victims?"

One individual whose perspective never faltered was Mr. X, who watched the circus that grew up around Sarao with a sense of bewilderment. "The main problem in understanding the event in my view has always been the odd obsession with finding a single cause," he says. "People either believed he caused the crash or that he didn't. It has been somewhat comical from my perspective. The markets are very complex systems. Instead of focusing on agent interactions, everyone wanted to find out who pulled the plug." Asked whether, after learning of Sarao's identity, there was any part of him that respected what he'd pulled off, Mr. X replied: "I think it is rather odd that you ask if I 'grudgingly respect' someone for committing massive fraud. No, I don't. I don't respect anyone who steals money from other market participants. No matter how clever they are or how justified they feel. Sarao did not target high-frequency traders. He was not a victim of the markets.

He stole money from *all* participants without a specific focus. He tried to make the most money he could by using common cheating techniques. His 'genius' was his lack of fear and belief that he would never face the consequences. This allowed him to cheat massively with enormous size over a long period of time. The size and volume was a large ingredient to his success. And I'm not aware that he gave his money away like Robin Hood. There's nothing admirable about stealing money for your own personal gain."

CHAPTER 23

■

ALL IS LOST

After his release from Wandsworth, Nav eased back into a familiar routine. Having no access to money barely impacted his life, and he filled his days playing badminton in the garden with his brother's kids, visiting the local shopping center, and going to McDonald's. When he could, he joined his old schoolmates in their weekly game of football. Three times a week, he cycled to a nearby police station to sign the register. He'd bought himself a bright yellow, Lamborghini-branded bicycle for £200, and it amused him to ask people, "Do you like my Lambo?" One day his barrister, James Lewis, a man who had once helped the Spanish government secure the extradition of General Pinochet, came over to the house to observe him trading on a demo. By now, Nav was convinced that the anonymous whistle-blower who had reported him was one of the big American HFT firms acting in cahoots with the Justice Department, and he was optimistic that when all the facts were known he'd be exonerated. That faith was tested on September 2 when the DOJ published its indictment, which contained a raft of damning new evidence.

Four months earlier, shortly after Nav was arrested, the CFTC was contacted by Shayne Stevenson, Mr. X's attorney, with news of a strange development. After seeing Sarao's name in the press, Mr. X's developer—the quiet one who had operated the software during the whistle-blower's presentation, and who had been dubbed "Crazy Eyes"—recalled that he *himself* had previously exchanged emails with Sarao that he thought the agency should see. When the printouts arrived they showed that, in January 2009, before Sarao contacted Trading Technologies for the first time, he had hired Crazy Eyes to build his spoofing program for him. It was a twist that was hard to fathom: the same coder whose software Mr. X would go on to use to *identify* Sarao's spoofing had previously worked on a prototype of the program that would become NAV Trader. He'd never actually succeeded in building a system to Nav's satisfaction, and the project was abandoned after a few months before any money changed hands. But Nav was considerably more candid in his correspondence with Crazy Eyes than he would be with the later developers. "If I am short I want to spoof it down," Sarao wrote in one email from February 1, 2009. "If I keep entering the same clip sizes, people will become aware of what I am doing, rendering my spoofing useless," he remarked on February 24. "I've tried phoning you and e-mailing you . . . I need to know whether you can do what I need, because at the moment I'm getting hit on my spoofs all the time and it's costing me a lot of money," he wrote three days later.

The CFTC quickly called the DOJ to share the news. There was something uncanny about the way the evidence had materialized. None of the messages had shown up in the email search warrant, presumably because Sarao had taken pains to delete them, and the language was so explicit, so *on the nose*, it seemed almost too good to be true. Alive to a potential conflict of interest, the prosecutors made sure the developer didn't stand to benefit financially from any reward Mr. X might receive, and ordered the programmer to preserve his hard drive in case the authenticity of the emails was ever called into dispute. When questioned, Crazy Eyes said he'd simply never linked the two episodes in his mind. By now, more than five years had passed since the emails were exchanged, meaning the statute of limitations had elapsed, and the authorities, grateful for the developer's assistance, didn't look to pursue charges against him for his role in developing Sarao's prototype.

For Nav's camp, seeing the emails in the indictment was a devastating blow: hard, irrefutable evidence of Sarao's intent. To give them time to respond, the judge agreed to push back the extradition hearing until February 2016. There were still potential legal challenges they could raise, not least the argument that the rules governing spoofing were so vague, so unevenly enforced, and so widely misunderstood as to be unconstitutional. However, the question of when and how the lawyers were going to get paid remained unresolved. IXE had reneged on its promise to release some of Sarao's money early. Over the course of the winter, the outlook only grew bleaker.

On October 19, Igor Oystacher, Sarao's long-standing rival and one of the last surviving point-and-click behemoths, was charged by the CFTC with spoofing and "employment of a manipulative and deceptive device" in the e-mini, as well as in copper, crude oil, natural gas, and volatility futures—allegations he strenuously denied. Part of the narrative Sarao's lawyers were looking to spin was that the U.S. authorities had arbitrarily targeted a solitary British trader while others got a free pass. Now, in the case of Oystacher at least, that was no longer true. Oystacher's MO—like the legendary Flipper's before him—was to place mammoth orders on one side of the market, wait for other entities to follow suit, and then, once the market had moved a few ticks, use TT's "avoid orders that cross" function to switch direction and hit into them with a single click of the mouse. He'd used the tactic for years and maintained it didn't constitute spoofing, because he never knew which orders he planned to execute or cancel in advance. An affidavit written by the CFTC showed that the agency had started investigating Oystacher after HFT firms, including industry giant Citadel, complained. The Russian's sleight-of-hand, carried out in real time with a mouse, apparently made it impossible for Citadel's sophisticated algos to predict which way the market was about to move with the level of certainty they were accustomed to. Oystacher was indignant at the idea that the enforcement agenda was being set by the world's most powerful HFT firm, and he chose to fight. Like Nav, he hired Kobre & Kim to defend him.

A month later, the whole futures industry looked on as the first-ever criminal trial for spoofing took place in Chicago. The defendant, who was also charged with commodities fraud, was a barrel-chested, fifty-three-year-old former pit trader from Brooklyn named Michael Coscia who paid his way through college delivering mail and was the antithesis of the new breed of computer whiz kids. When the pits closed, Coscia had started his own screen-based trading firm, and in 2011 he asked a programmer to build an algo that would allow him to, according to an email preserved by the coder, "pump the market." It was a landmark case, and Coscia hired a Murderers' Row of New York attorneys from Sullivan & Cromwell, including a future head of enforcement at the SEC, a former general counsel at the CFTC, and the lead prosecutor in Martha Stewart's insider trading trial. Over the course of a week, the polished defenders took turns explaining to a sometimes befuddled-looking jury that canceling orders was standard practice, algorithmic trading was the norm, and the nascent spoofing rules were ambiguous and ill conceived. They painted Coscia as a humble family man, a "stand-up guy" struggling to compete in a world of machines, and emphasized that he'd only used his algo for two months in 2010 when the disruptive trading rules were still being debated. Coscia had already agreed to pay fines of more than $3 million to various civil authorities in 2013, and he'd been under the impression that the matter was closed until the DOJ knocked on his door a year later, reigniting the trauma.

The government was represented by a hyperactive young prosecutor named Renato Mariotti, whose approach was to cut through the industry-speak and statistics and bring the discussion to a level that the jury—men and women from the same Chicago streets as him—could engage with. He called a chicken company executive as a witness to explain how ordinary businesses relied on commodity markets, and treated cross-examination like a performance, chuckling to himself, rolling his eyes, and goading Coscia until the trader bellowed from the stand: "I'm not dealing hot dogs, I'm dealing futures!" At the end of the trial, Mariotti turned to the jurors and, with the poise of an actor delivering a soliloquy, said: "You know, it reminds me of something that I used to see on the playground at school when I was a boy. There was a kid who would put his hand out like this, like he was trying to shake your hand, and he'd pull it away right when you were about to shake his hand, or he'd put his hand up like this like he was going to give you a high-five, and he'd pull it down like that. He thought that was very funny. I didn't. But, it was a trick, right? . . . And ladies and gentlemen, that's the exact same thing that happened in this case."

It took the jury less than an hour to find Coscia guilty. He was later sentenced to three years in prison, earning him the unfortunate accolade of being the first individual in the history of financial markets to serve time for spoofing. The case shattered the perception, built up over decades, that manipulation-type cases were nearly impossible for the government to win, and represented a disastrous omen for Sarao, who had used his program for five years next to Coscia's ten weeks, and earned $40 million versus Coscia's $1.4 million.

Rounding out a season of bad news, just before Christmas, an Illinois judge dismissed Bill "Cornbread" Braman's suit against the CME, the class action Nav had considered joining and that had imbued him with a sense of misplaced confidence regarding his own predicament. Braman et al. had accused the CME of granting HFT firms special privileges, creating a two-tiered marketplace that allowed predatory strategies to thrive. But the judge concluded that the plaintiffs lacked any specific evidence and questioned why they had sued the exchange rather than the firms themselves. "This Court's task is not to adjudicate the fairness or appropriateness of high frequency trading," he wrote, providing little solace to Cornbread and his pals, who wondered how they were supposed to get hold of any hard evidence without access to the CME's trade data.

With no money, and evidence mounting up against him, Nav's last remaining hope was to convince the British courts to block his extradition. The two-day hearing was held in the first week of February 2016, in the by now painfully familiar environs of Westminster Magistrates' Court. Nav arrived flanked by lawyers and looking respectable in a dark suit and tie. Only sharp-eyed observers would have noticed his trousers and jacket were a different shade. Extradition between Britain and the United States is governed by a treaty that dictates that both countries will hand over criminal targets in all but the most exceptional circumstances. There is a list of possible objections, or "bars," that an individual can raise, but the barrier to success in each is so high that extradition is almost considered a formality. For the United States to prevail, it does not have to prove its case, only that there is a case to answer. Britain's readiness to give up its citizens has been the subject of considerable controversy, and in 2010 the government ordered an inquiry into whether the regime was fair. Lord Baker, who led the review, concluded it was, but the issue refused to die thanks to a string of high-profile cases, including that of Gary McKinnon, a Glaswegian IT worker who hacked into various U.S. military and NASA computers, leaving messages like "Your security is crap." McKinnon, who was diagnosed with Asperger's and suffered from psychotic episodes, said he was looking for evidence of UFOs. His plight became a cause célèbre among MPs and public figures such as David Gilmour, Chrissie Hynde, and Bob Geldof, who recorded a song to drum up awareness. The campaign failed to sway the High Court, but on the eve of McKinnon's departure, then–home secretary Theresa May intervened to block the extradition on human rights grounds. The case might have provided a useful precedent for Sarao except for the fact that, uncomfortable with the pressure she'd been placed under, May had permanently rescinded the power of the home secretary to consider last-minute representations, removing another possible avenue for appeal.

As Sarao took his seat in the dock, the atmosphere was as charged as when he'd first sat there, blinking and befuddled in a yellow sweatshirt, the morning after his arrest. Over the past ten months, his celebrity had grown, and journalists had traveled from as far as India and the United States to attend. Unlike in a standard trial, there is no presumption of innocence in a UK extradition hearing. The onus is on the accused to demonstrate to the judge why they *shouldn't* be extradited. Arguing on Nav's behalf was Lewis, one of the few barristers with any pedigree blocking U.S. extradition requests. When Lewis and his junior, Joel Smith, took on Sarao's case, they planned to attack the DOJ's assertion that the trader had anything to do with the Flash Crash, arguing in a pretrial hearing that the association was unsubstantiated and would make it impossible to get a fair trial. Since then, the Americans had barely mentioned the events of May 6, 2010, in court. As it stood, Lewis's best argument was that, while Nav's antics might have constituted an offense in the United States, they wouldn't have in Britain, and the case therefore failed the Extradition Act's requirement for "dual criminality." "The key question for this court is whether the conduct of Mr. Sarao amounts to a crime if it were to happen in the U.K.," said Lewis, pointing out: "There is no English crime of spoofing."

Literally speaking, he was right. Neither the Financial Services and Markets Act nor the Financial Services Act that succeeded it makes any reference to spoofing, or the act of placing orders you don't intend to execute. The U.S. government claimed, however, that Sarao's behavior was caught by sections of the legislation prohibiting "misleading statements," as well as by the Fraud Act, which says it is an offense for a person to make a "false representation and in doing so" makes a "gain for himself or a loss for another." That contention raised the novel legal question of whether a trader's orders can, in and of themselves, be classified as statements or representations. Lewis argued no, pointing out that more than 90 percent of all e-mini orders are canceled. To help make the case, he relied on the testimony of a professor named Larry Harris from the University of Southern California, who was patched into the courtroom via video link. Harris, an ex-SEC economist who wrote a book called *Trading and Exchanges:*

Market Microstructure for Practitioners, had worked with Burl-ingame on a prior case, and agreed to take the job in part because he was so affronted by the DOJ's decision to link Sarao to the crash.

Harris's job as an expert witness was to explain how elec-tronic trading worked, and he emphasized repeatedly that any orders that enter the book are at risk of being hit, particularly those of someone like Sarao, whose connection to the exchange was many times slower than most HFTs. The United States "char-acterizes these orders as being bogus, but they were real orders that exposed the defendant to the real possibility of trading at the prices at which he posted his orders," Sarao's lawyers wrote in a summary argument. Harris also suggested that layering orders away from the best offer was a legitimate tactic used by partici-pants to capitalize on the rare occasions when a large, aggressive buyer comes along and sweeps up several levels of the ladder at once. By placing such orders, Harris suggested, Sarao was actu-ally providing valuable liquidity to the market, unlike the class of "parasitic" high-speed entities he called "quote-matchers," who were in the habit of waiting for large sell orders to show up in the ladder, then placing orders of their own one level lower, a practice known as "leaning." It was an interesting insight into the tactics of some HFT firms and the ethical arguments around spoofing, but, as the judge pointed out, Sarao wasn't on trial yet and the legal issues at hand were narrower than that. Under cross-examination, Harris's credibility as a witness was called into question when he was forced to disclose that, unlike Hendershott, he'd never actually seen Sarao's trading records. Sarao had run out of money after Harris was taken on, and the professor agreed to complete the assignment for a fraction of his normal rate. His conclusions, as a result, were entirely theoretical.

Perhaps the biggest hit to the "dual criminality" argument came from the revelation that, just a few months before the hear-ing, Britain's financial regulator had fined a Swiss hedge fund called Da Vinci Invest Ltd. £7 million for spoofing and layering. It was a civil rather than criminal action, but the facts were strikingly similar, undermining the assertion that Sarao's actions wouldn't constitute an offense in the UK. As the discussion swirled around him, Nav sat slumped forward with his head bowed, prompting the judge to ask after his well-being. Lewis said his client was fine but revealed that, as well as having Asperger's, Sarao was now being treated for post-traumatic stress disorder following his time in jail. In the past, such a diagnosis might have offered up another argument against extradition, but recent case history made it clear that a target's mental health was rarely considered sufficient grounds to block a request.

The defense's second argument related to jurisdiction. According to the Extradition Act, an individual should not be extradited if the judge decides it is not in the "interests of justice," taking into consideration such factors as where the bulk of the offending took place, where the victims were, access to evidence, and whether the British authorities intended to carry out their own proceedings. Sarao traded exclusively from the UK and, as Lewis pointed out, had never even visited the United States on holiday. Plus, the e-mini was a global marketplace whose participants came from all over the world. The stumbling block to this argument was that no British powers had expressed any interest in pursuing Sarao, raising the likelihood that, if his extradition were to be blocked, the trader would escape prosecution altogether. "It was American individuals, American companies and the American market integrity as a whole that suffered," said U.S. government barrister Mark Summers.

SEVEN WEEKS after the hearing, on March 23, 2016, the judge approved Sarao's extradition. "I note this case has attracted much publicity under the banner headlines of involvement in the Flash Crash," he wrote, but "complaint of involvement in this emotively named event is but a small part of the conduct alleged here." On the subject of dual criminality, he found that " 'representations' *are* made by making orders/contracts," and said that "the prosecution can show the motivation for this fact given the heavily modified software." He also said there were good grounds to conclude that the United States was "both the desirable and practicable venue" for a trial, adding: "Navinder Sarao self-evidently and understandably does not wish or desire to be extradited. Few do." Nav's lawyers waited a few days before lodging an appeal with the High Court, the last remaining shot at a reprieve.

Despite the gravity of his situation, Nav seemed constitutionally unwilling or unable to be laid low by the passage of events. When some trading pals bumped into him that summer, he told them: "At the minute they're winning everything. But once I go to trial and start putting out the real statistics it's going to look different." Asked how he stayed so upbeat, Nav replied: "You don't know what's going to happen tomorrow. I could win my case, walk out the court, and get hit by a car." This Zen-like attitude extended to how he was perceived by others. "You cannot control what people think about you," he said. "That's something I learned in prison. They tried to make the whole world hate me, but if your happiness is dependent on what other people think then you'll always be unhappy."

Nav seemed to relish the opportunity to unburden himself, and the conversation ended up lasting more than two hours. As they prepared to part ways, he reflected on his journey and the decisions he'd made. "All I wanted is to be the best I could be," he said, unlocking his Lambo from a lamppost. "As long as I reach my own potential, why does it matter what everyone else is doing? That's how I broke the barriers. But I was on the hamster wheel for too long." Nav said he'd always planned on giving money away to charity, and felt annoyed at himself for having "delusions of grandeur." "When I went to prison that was the one thing I was upset about," he said. "All this money I had and I basically haven't helped anyone out. But I loved doing it too much and it was difficult to get away from it."

■

CHAPTER 24

COME TO JESUS

In August 2016, the German business magazine *Brand Eins* published an article with the headline "Bezahlt wurde noch nicht," or "It hasn't been paid yet." Its author was an investigative reporter named Ingo Malcher who had noticed the hype in Zurich surrounding Alejandro Garcia and decided to do some digging.

Malcher's piece began in a lawyer's office in 2007, where a then-thirty-year-old Garcia had shown up with a few sheets of paper and a translator, looking for help setting up his own bank. His partners at the time, according to the paperwork, included an Iranian entity and a businessman from Florida named Burton Greenberg. The details were vague—when asked for a name, Garcia said he wanted to call it "My Bank"—and the discussion didn't go anywhere, but six years later the lawyer was flicking through the Swiss newspaper *Neue Zürcher Zeitung am Sonntag* and was surprised to see a picture of Garcia atop a profile describing him as the heir to one of Latin America's biggest agricultural families. After that, Malcher noted, Garcia was all over the press, taking about lithium and gold one minute, cattle and quinoa the next and, in December 2014, announcing his plan to acquire Arner Bank. Like IXE's investors, journalists seemed intoxicated by this swashbuckling magnate from faraway climes, and, with every article, estimates of his family's worth climbed higher. Garcia maintained that IXE was a multibillion-dollar company, but there were no public accounts, and Malcher set about holding his claims up to the light.

One of the first things the journalist discovered was that Garcia's partner in "My Bank," Greenberg, was a convicted felon who, along with his wife and son, was implicated in a string of audacious investment frauds. Greenberg, who was seventy-five, had been imprisoned just that year, in February 2016, for scamming pensioners out of $10 million. But it was an earlier con involving the Central Bank of Mongolia that really caught Malcher's eye. In 2005, the government of Mongolia, an impoverished country where temperatures routinely fall below minus-forty degrees Celsius, was struggling to raise $1 billion for badly needed public housing when its officials were introduced to some Western financiers who said they could assist, according to a complaint filed in Florida in 2010 by the central bank. Greenberg and his associates boasted of connections to the world's foremost banks and asset managers, and they told the Mongolians that, if the government could issue $200 million of "letters of credit" as collateral— essentially legally binding IOUs—they would be able to come up with the funds. The gang promised to return the instruments, untouched, at maturity; but as soon as they had the documents in their possession, records show, they began trying to find financial institutions willing to cash them out early for a heavy discount. By the time the Mongolian officials cottoned on to what was happening, the offenders had managed to extract $23 million. They had attempted similar schemes in Laos, Burundi, and Guinea.

Malcher had found the same legal filing that emerged around the time Nav was first considering investing in IXE, and which the company had worked hard to downplay. As IXE emphasized at the time, Garcia was never a defendant himself. Unlike the other parties, he resided outside the United States. However, the complaint alleged that Garcia "unlawfully, knowingly and intentionally" participated in the enterprise, attending meetings with the Mongolians in Zurich, using his contacts and entities in the Middle East to liquidate the letters of credit, and "lining his pockets" with at least $3 million. Garcia declined to comment to *Brand Eins* on his ties to Greenburg or the other details contained within the complaint, but in September 2010, Greenberg and the rest of the defendants were found guilty and ordered to pay $67 million to the Mongolian central bank, triple the alleged damages.

Spurred on by these findings, Malcher started looking into some of Garcia's other purported business interests. In media interviews and correspondence with potential investors, Garcia claimed he had secured the exclusive right to grow quinoa on 2.1 million hectares of prime land in Bolivia. However, when Malcher contacted the country's Ministry of Agriculture about the deal, he was told they knew nothing about it. Malcher also spoke to Edgar Soliz, head of the International Quinoa Center in La Paz, who informed him that 95 percent of the country's quinoa acreage was in the hands of communities and cooperatives. Bolivia is a socialist country, and it would be virtually impossible for a private foreign entity to come along and buy that much land, Soliz said. The idea that IXE could produce 2.1 million hectares of quinoa was "crazy," he added, considering the country's entire output in 2013 was 170,000 hectares.

Malcher found the same story when he asked around about lithium. Garcia had recently started telling reporters and investors that IXE had set up a joint venture with the Bolivian state to extract lithium from the vast salt plains of the Uyuni region. In one article, he appeared dressed in a poncho with his arm cast out across the saline wilderness he claimed to control. But the country has strict laws prohibiting foreigners from extracting or exporting the element, and the head of the National Board of Salt Rocks described Garcia's claims as "impossible." Another anecdote Garcia liked to tell was how he'd grown up tending to the family's extensive farmlands in Mexico by his father's side. Yet Mexico's Association of Agricultural Producers told Malcher it had no record of any Garcia Alvarezes owning notable holdings. In fact, the only plot belonging to the family that the reporter did manage to track down was 113 acres of mostly potato fields in Florida. Even Garcia's CV didn't check out. In 2007, he'd told the Zurich lawyer that he had an MBA from the University of Texas, but on IXE's website it said his master's was from the Federico Villarreal National University in Peru. When Malcher asked Garcia about this and the other discrepancies he'd discovered, Garcia declined to comment.

As *Brand Eins* was preparing to publish its exposé, the *Wall Street Journal* ran a piece reporting that IXE's acquisition of Arner Bank had fallen through amid "finger-wagging and confusion." Garcia was quoted claiming he got cold feet after discovering the true extent of the bank's problems, but internal correspondence cited by the *Journal* indicated he'd been unwilling or unable to come up with the $28 million in capital required by the regulator or produce the necessary documentation, including his tax returns. The bank's owners had been left out of pocket after funding Garcia's expenses during the protracted courtship. Michael Baer, the storied banker drafted in as chairman, walked away bemused and embarrassed. "Businesses that need money often don't look hard enough at potential partners, a mistake that can be expensive and damage their reputation," Malcher wrote in his piece. "Not enough executives stop and ask who it is that's making an offer and what their background is."

For the IXE investors who read it, Malcher's article served only to confirm their worst suspicions. Sixteen months had now elapsed since Sarao's arrest, and Garcia still hadn't released any of the $75 million entrusted to him by the eight or so UK participants, including the $55 million belonging to Nav. For a long time Garcia had blamed Sarao's legal woes for his intransigence, but when MacKinnon and Dupont persuaded the U.S. government to insert an amendment into Nav's restraining order authorizing IXE to unblock the circa $10 million sitting in the Cranwood account, he moved the goalposts again, saying he now needed sign-off from the authorities in South America. In truth, there was no clear legitimate legal reason why IXE couldn't release the money, and when Garcia stopped returning calls or answering emails, investors wondered if the Sarao situation had been a convenient fig leaf all along.

ON OCTOBER 14, 2016, Nav's barristers arrived at the Royal Courts of Justice in London for one final attempt to halt the extradition. Again, they pressed their case that spoofing wasn't a crime in the UK, and that, even if it were, the trial should happen in the country Sarao resided. But it was a desperate plea, and shortly after lunchtime the High Court rejected the appeal. Nav was given twenty-eight days to hand himself over to the FBI. Before that he had to make a decision: keep fighting and take the case to trial in the United States, or try to strike a plea deal. His lawyers laid out the situation in stark terms. A trial might take two years to schedule, during which Nav would be incarcerated in a Chicago prison that would make him pine for Wandsworth. And, realistically, his chances of success had nosedived with the emergence of the Crazy Eyes emails, particularly since, with no money, he'd be represented by a public defender. If Nav pleaded not guilty and lost, he could be locked up in the United States for decades. Even for him, it was a gamble too far. Later that month, Burlingame caught a flight to Washington to sound out the DOJ about a deal.

The mood in the United States was buoyant. That summer, members of the various investigating authorities had gotten together at the DOJ's cyber lab in Washington for what felt like a reunion. The material seized from Sarao's parents' house had been extracted and logged and was finally ready to be viewed. Over the course of a week, Jessica Harris and Jeff Le Riche from the CFTC, Mike O'Neill from the DOJ, and one of the FBI agents went through Nav's files one by one with a detective from Scotland Yard. Also in the room was a Fraud Section manager named Rob Zink, who had inherited responsibility for the case after Brent Wible left to take a job at the White House. After obsessing over Sarao for so long, it felt both thrilling and slightly voyeuristic to be trawling through his hard drive. Early on in the process, the investigators were relieved to discover that the NAV Trader program was intact, complete with logs detailing each time Nav had used it, the trading equivalent of a murder weapon.

If the software program was all the team got that week, they would have been happy, but at some point somebody clicked on a file and a video popped up showing footage of Sarao's monitor as he traded. It seemed to have been recorded by a camcorder positioned just behind Sarao's head. The group watched, transfixed, as the trader bought and sold millions of dollars of e-minis, his cursor flying around the screen, placing trades and activating the bespoke functions created for him by Edge and TT. Every once in a while, Sarao's voice could be heard commenting angrily on the action, or a shock of his black hair appeared at the bottom of the screen. When the clip was over, they clicked on another file, which contained footage from a couple of days later, then another, and another. The team had heard rumors there might be videos. Now they saw he'd been taping himself for years, archiving the clips as evidence of what he perceived as cheating by other market participants. In doing so, he'd captured himself breaking the law again and again.

Watching Sarao in full flow after months spent trawling through lifeless reams of data was miraculous, the speed of his decision making and the way he reacted to the ladder unlike anything any of them had seen before. What had possessed him to document his exploits this way was a mystery, like a robber who takes selfies outside the banks he has hit and leaves them on his phone.

With the Crazy Eyes emails, the trading software, and now the videos, the team knew it was game over. Zink, who had a reputation for being an aggressive prosecutor, marveled at his predecessor's foresight and guts in charging Sarao when so much crucial evidence had emerged *after* the arrest. Before they parted ways, the conversation turned to their perennial favorite subject: who was going to play them in the movie. Le Riche bagged Colin Farrell, O'Neill had the studious demeanor of a young Guy

Pearce, while Wible, in absentia, was assigned John Goodman. Harris got the last laugh when she insisted she be portrayed by Steve Buscemi.

Walking into the Bond Building, a place he knew well from his previous life with the Justice Department, Burlingame must have been conscious that he and his client had little leverage. By now, the evidence against Sarao was so overwhelming it was hard to imagine the trader getting anything other than crushed at trial. The only chink in the DOJ's armor was how sympathetic Nav was as a defendant, particularly in comparison to some of his supposed victims at the HFT firms. Even some of the individuals who worked on the case were starting to feel deeply uncomfortable about the idea of sending Nav back to jail. Burlingame had spent years on the other side of the table and, sensing an opening, he asked Zink, an ambitious prosecutor on the DOJ management fast track, whether he really wanted to be remembered for taking down Rain Man. If the Fraud Section was willing to recommend a more lenient punishment when it came to sentencing, Burlingame said, Nav was prepared to plead guilty to some of the charges and help the authorities with their ongoing investigations. At this point, the government's grasp of electronic trading was still limited, and having an insider explain what he was doing and how the markets really worked could be invaluable. Nav had also collaborated with a bunch of different programmers and brokers over the years whom the authorities might want to target.

Zink and O'Neill went away and considered their options. Flexing their muscles in a high-profile trial was tempting, but it carried some risks. Accepting Burlingame's offer, on the other hand, would lock in a win and send a message to the markets while also demonstrating some sensitivity as to who they were dealing with. After talking it through internally, the prosecutors agreed to the deal on the condition that Nav confess to everything, show remorse, and prove he had something of value to impart.

For Nav, it was a remarkable outcome, a shot at redemption and clemency that seemed unthinkable a few weeks before. If he didn't deliver the goods, though, Zink warned, they would be going to trial.

NAV ARRIVED at Heathrow Airport uncharacteristically early on Monday, November 7, 2016, where he and Burlingame were met by two FBI agents. During the flight to Chicago, Nav grilled them on what it was like to work for the Bureau and whether they'd ever hunted a serial killer. It was the week of the presidential election, and, touching down in the United States, images of Donald Trump were ubiquitous. Nav was taken to the Metropolitan Correctional Center, a notorious high-rise lockup in downtown Chicago a block from the CME. Buffeted by noise and activity, he couldn't sleep. The next morning, he was escorted to the Dirksen Federal Building, a blacked-out thirty-story monolith nearby that houses both the federal courthouse and the U.S. Attorney's Office. Nav's plea hearing was scheduled for the following afternoon in a courtroom on the twenty-third floor. Before that, he had back-to-back meetings with the DOJ and the CFTC in an interview room on the fifth.

Nav's first debriefing was with Zink and O'Neill from the Fraud Section as well as the FBI agents. Burlingame was also in the room. The opening ten minutes in any such encounter are critical and, based on what they'd heard about Sarao's mental faculties, the government was unsure what to expect. They needn't have worried. Nav answered the crucial early questions about his conduct and why he was there articulately and without equivocation. Asked if he knew that what he was doing was illegal, he replied, "Yes." Asked if he placed orders that were intended to deceive others for money, he said he did. With the confessions in the can, the next several hours were spent talking through the indictment line by line. Nav filled in the gaps in the DOJ's knowledge and pointed out where they'd got it wrong with a veracity that made it seem like he had truth serum running through his veins. After the stress of the past few years, he said he was relieved it was finally over. They touched on Nav's brokers and programmers, his competitors, his thoughts on HFT, and what he did with all the money. Nav was adamant that manipulation and spoofing were endemic in the markets, and he said he knew how to identify them. The frank and lucid way he spoke left the DOJ in no doubt that he was someone they could work with. When it was over, they bought him some food: Nav was excited to try a real American burger.

Waiting patiently to strike his own separate settlement with Sarao was the CFTC's Le Riche. There's a danger for the civil authorities in any multiagency investigation that they get steamrolled by their criminal counterparts, and the CFTC had been somewhat blindsided to discover that the DOJ had provisionally agreed to a plea deal. Deprived of a trial, Le Riche and his colleagues—the ones who had kick-started the investigation—wanted to at least make sure they had a settlement of their own to announce when Sarao pleaded guilty. When Burlingame, Sarao, and Le Riche eventually sat down over coffee, the focus of the conversation was money, or more specifically, how much Nav would have to cough up. CFTC penalties are made up of disgorgement, which is a defendant's ill-gotten gains, and a civil monetary penalty, which can be up to three times that amount again. The DOJ had already agreed on a disgorgement figure of $12.87 million as part of the plea deal, so it was up to Le Riche to decide how much extra to levy. Burlingame said he wanted to make sure that when Nav was out of custody and no longer allowed to trade, he would have something to live on. Le Riche countered that Sarao shouldn't get to keep anything he'd made from cheating. In the end, they agreed on a CMP of two times the gains, bringing a total of $38.6 million. It was an eye-watering sum, but if IXE ever actually returned Nav's money, he would still be left with a few million in the bank.

By now, Nav had been awake for more than forty-eight hours, and as another sleepless night in jail loomed, Burlingame pressed the DOJ to show some compassion and let his client spend the night in a conference room while an FBI agent stood guard. The prosecutors and agents considered the request, but in the end they concluded that the security risk was too high and sent Nav back to the lockup.

The following day, November 9, 2016, the plea hearing began at 2 p.m. News of Donald Trump's election as president cast a surreal pall over proceedings. The gallery at the back of the vast, windowless courtroom was little more than half full: a handful of government attorneys, a smattering of tired-looking journalists engrossed by their phones, some futures industry hawkers. Jessica Harris, who had recently left the CFTC, made the trip from Washington. None of Nav's family or friends were there. Nav emerged from a door at the front in an orange jumpsuit and ankle chains and took his place on the stand. "Yes, your Honor . . . No, your Honor . . . Yes, your Honor," he mumbled, as the judge asked him about his mental state and whether he understood the ramifications of his decision to plea. He then pleaded guilty to two of the twenty-two counts he was originally charged with: one for wire fraud, which covered his conduct over the entire five-year period, and a second for a single instance of spoofing in March 2014. The commodity fraud and manipulation counts were dropped.

Sentencing in the United States is calculated using the Federal Sentencing Guidelines, a points system that involves allocating a defendant an offense, adding and subtracting levels according to the specifics of their crimes, and taking into account their criminal history. For Nav, this exercise resulted in a recommended jail term of between seventy-eight and ninety-seven months. Under the terms of the deal, however, Nav would be given an opportunity to "earn off" part of his custodial sentence—perhaps even all of it—by providing assistance to the government in any civil or criminal investigation they needed him on. Normally, a defendant would provide such cooperation while they were in prison, but the DOJ had agreed to allow Nav to return to the UK and help them from there. When the judge expressed some skepticism about this highly unusual arrangement, Burlingame stepped in: "Basically, he has some extraordinary abilities with respect to pattern recognition and certain sorts of mathematical abilities, but he has some fairly severe social limitations and other limitations, and his ability to fulfill the cooperation terms of the agreement I think would be non-existent if he were to be incarcerated."

The judge agreed, on the proviso that Nav give up his passport, desist from trading futures, avoid drinking too much, steer clear of any potential witnesses, and keep an 11 p.m. curfew. His sentencing would be postponed until the DOJ no longer had any use for him. The judge asked Nav to confirm he agreed to forfeit the $12.87 million, and Burlingame said he did, although so far Kobre & Kim had still only managed to retrieve $6.5 million—essentially what was seized from the R. J. O'Brien trading account. "Judge, if I might, we've been engaged in a process with the CFTC for the last sixteen months of attempting to collect the defendant's assets all of which have been stolen from . . . I mean, he invested in a Ponzi scheme," the lawyer explained. In lieu of the full amount, the judge agreed for Nav's parents and brother, Jasvinder, to place a lien on their homes to the value of $750,000. To confirm the arrangement, she placed a call to Hounslow that was played on the courtroom's speakers.

"Good evening. My name is Judge Kendall, and you are on the record and in open court. Can you please tell me who is on the phone?"

"My name is Nachhattar Sarao."

"And do you also have Daljit with you?"

"Yeah, she is here as well."

"Okay. All right. Mr. Sarao, I am here in my courtroom in Chicago where your son has just pled guilty to the charges against him, and I am considering releasing him with some significant conditions of release . . . He has as a proposal here that your home that you live in with your wife will be part of a bond package, meaning that if your son violates one of the conditions of bond that I put on him, you could lose your home. Do you understand that?"

"Yes. Yes, ma'am."

After walking Nav's parents through the terms of his release, the judge asked Nav's father if he had anything to add. "I just want to say most everything, he doesn't take any sort of intoxicant at all. He doesn't even drink tea or coffee," Nachhattar said, and his son shook his head with embarrassment. The judge had a similar conversation with Jasvinder, then brought the proceedings to a close. Nav's lawyers and the DOJ agreed to come back in a few months' time to provide an update on how the cooperation was going. For the time being, Nav was free to leave. Watching him shuffle out of the courtroom at a little after 3:30 p.m., the investigators, agents, and lawyers who had worked so hard for this moment were struck by a strange combination of deflation and relief. Someone asked if Nav knew how to get to the airport and what flight he needed to catch. Then they went for dinner and raised a toast to the notorious Flash Crash Trader.

■

CHAPTER 25

CATCH ME IF YOU CAN

After one of IXE's investors threatened to impale his head on a spike, Alejandro Garcia called a creditors' meeting at the Marriott Hotel in Zurich for November 21, 2016. It was a Monday, and that morning between fifteen and twenty participants and their advisers traveled from the UK and elsewhere to hear Garcia explain what he'd done with their money and why he'd stopped paying interest. If they weren't satisfied, they had agreed in advance, they would go to the authorities. The Marriott, which overlooks the Limmat River in Zurich's picturesque old town, is a popular venue for weddings, and the conference room was set up for a reception. Garcia and another IXE director sat at a long table at the front with two lawyers, including a large, glowering Swiss-German with a thunderous voice named Dr. Felix Fischer. Behind them, and dotted around the room, were security guards. The investors, who had to show ID before they were allowed in, occupied half a dozen or so round tables draped in white linen.

Garcia thanked everyone for making the trip and then launched into a PowerPoint presentation. He clicked quickly past a "Disclaimer" that stated IXE gave no "representation or warranty" into the "accuracy . . . completeness or fitness for any purpose" of what he was about to say. Landing on a slide with the heading "Current Situation," Garcia said that IXE had been hit by a global downturn in commodities that was "impossible to predict." That was why, in 2014, the company had diversified away from backing the "riskless" trades of others to making its own direct investments in the agricultural sector. This change in tack would have "preserved capital" and brought "stable returns," he said, if it hadn't been for "a legal issue, related to a major Investor Participant" that resulted in "the company and related companies" facing "a collateral reaction within banking and commercial relations." Sarao's legal problems, in other words, had thrown an international conglomerate with, according to its own literature, seventy-two thousand employees and $5 billion in annual revenues, into disarray.

By now, exasperated investors had started heckling: "Where's our money!" IXE was in the midst of a "cash liquidity constrain," Garcia went on. The company had assets all over the world, he said, including thirty million square meters of land in Bolivia worth as much as $192 million. It had also recently entered into a contract to supply quinoa to a "major agricultural Company in the Republic of China," which, combined with its assorted other agricultural interests, would culminate in "potential consolidated income of about $86m" a year. To help illustrate these prospects, he pulled up a slide containing a selection of photographs of verdant landscapes, and another with images of a tractor, a smiling Garcia in a field, and some packets of quinoa with labels in Mandarin. In terms of actual investments, the presentation indicated that IXE had transferred 65 million Swiss francs ($66 million) into four privately owned entities in Florida, Singapore, Switzerland, and Bolivia, none of which produced audited accounts. The takeaway, Garcia explained, was that there would be more than enough cash to repay the $75 million invested by those in the room and Sarao, as well as the $10.5 million in commissions owed to introducers like Adamson, Sawicki, MacKinnon, and Dupont. The only problem, he said, was that liquidating the assets would take months, maybe even years, so if investors wanted their money back, they would have to be patient. In the interests of transparency, he offered to take a delegation to South America to see how their funds were being used.

When Garcia finished talking, the room erupted. A lawyer representing one of the investors stood up and asked what evidence there was that the money was where Garcia said it was. Another individual asked why his funds had been moved from Arner Bank to these other entities when he'd signed a contract stating it would be used for "trades executed solely by way of non-speculative transactions with real end purchasers already in place." One member of the audience said that he'd never authorized for his money to be taken out of Morgan Stanley. As the questions rained down, Garcia stayed quiet, allowing Dr. Fischer to respond on his behalf. Meanwhile, his wife, Ekaterina, dressed in designer clothes, passed from table to table handing out vol-au-vents nobody wanted. Eventually, a frustrated creditor asked why they shouldn't simply walk out of the hotel and into the nearest police station. On this point, IXE's response was crystalline: if anyone took any legal action, the company would fold and they would never see their money again. Better, Garcia said earnestly, to trust him.

The investors discussed the matter among themselves for a while before reluctantly agreeing to give IXE more time. When all was said and done, what choice did they really have? Garcia thanked them for their patience and, flanked by bodyguards, made his way to a side entrance where a blacked-out Mercedes was waiting to whisk him away.

THEY CALLED it "Home Videos with Nav." In the first week of February 2017, Rob Zink and Mike O'Neill from the Fraud Section, two agents from the FBI, and Jeff Le Riche from the CFTC flew to London to spend a week squeezing as much information out of Sarao as they could. The setting was Kobre & Kim's offices in Tower 42, a six-hundred-foot skyscraper in the heart of the financial district—exactly the kind of place Nav had spent his career avoiding. After the tension and high drama of the plea hearing a few weeks earlier, the mood in the conference room was relaxed and convivial. Now that he was working for the government, Nav asked, would he be allowed to draw the Justice Department seal on his notebooks?

"Stop, go back a bit!" Nav cried out as a video of his trading was played on a large TV. Every once in a while, when they got to something that sparked his memory, he jumped up from his seat and his eyes lit up like an old sportsman reminiscing about his career highlights. "So, what are you looking for here, Nav?" one of the Americans asked, struggling to keep up with what was happening on the ladder. Bids and offers came and went, and prices hopped around so rapidly it was hard for mere mortals to keep up. "Come on, mate," replied Nav with a smile, and took them through it one more time.

Over several days, Sarao gave the U.S. government a crash course on scalping, the intricacies of market structure, and how to identify when somebody was spoofing. His knowledge base was narrow but incredibly deep, and he spoke with a jargon-free, unvarnished clarity that was easy to comprehend. The interviewers took notes and asked questions while he talked about strategies and the footprints market participants leave behind. When they were done with the videos, they asked Nav how much his brokers knew and what role they played in his exploits. They had "no clue," Nav replied. "They just wanted the money." When it came to software developers like Jitesh Thakkar, the answer was less clear-cut. If you make a bespoke weapon for somebody, how much responsibility do you have for how they go on to use it?

One day, toward the end of the week, the group went for lunch in one of the building's upscale restaurants. There were no burgers on the menu, so Nav ordered a steak, swearing he'd never heard of Béarnaise sauce. They chatted about London tourist spots, and the food they'd order if they were on death row. Nav made the table roar with laughter recounting how his mum would call upstairs, "Navinder, what are you doing?" as he pulled off another million-dollar trade. And, for those few minutes, it was easy to forget why they were there.

EPILOGUE

Nav returned to Chicago to be sentenced on January 28, 2020. More than three years had passed since he'd pleaded guilty to fraud and spoofing in the same courthouse the day after the presidential election. As part of the plea deal, he'd agreed to help the authorities build other cases, and he'd been working hard to earn their favor and minimize any jail time ever since.

The weeklong debriefing Nav gave members of the DOJ, the CFTC, and the FBI in London in 2017 transformed their understanding of spoofing and market microstructure. He was only the second individual to be criminally charged with spoofing, and the government was still relatively naïve about the dark arts of electronic markets. Nav's insights into identifying cheating in the order book were incorporated into the agencies' detection software, helping lead to the convictions of more than two dozen traders from banks, hedge funds, and even the HFT firms he so despised. Nav's "home videos" are still shown to investigators and prosecutors in training programs across the United States. The CME and other exchanges have reported a sharp decline in spoofing and other forms of manipulation (although skeptics suggest market participants have just got better at hiding it).

As useful as Nav's intelligence proved to be, defendants are supposed to provide information on *specific* crimes if they want to gain any real credit for cooperation. That opportunity arose in January 2018, when the DOJ arrested Jitesh Thakkar, the software developer whose firm, Edge Financial Technologies, had built the NAVTrader program. Despite having never met Sarao in person, Thakkar was charged with conspiring with the trader to spoof the market as well as two related counts of aiding and abetting, offenses that each carry ten-year maximum sentences. Thakkar wasn't a trader himself, and the case raised important questions about the extent to which developers can be held responsible for how clients use their software.

Nobody disputed that Sarao had utilized the NAVTrader program to make millions of dollars by misleading other market participants about supply and demand. The issue was whether Thakkar had any culpability, given that he was never present when Nav was trading and didn't receive a share of the proceeds (Edge was paid a flat fee of $24,000 for the project). At trial in April 2019, prosecutor Mike O'Neill argued that, while Sarao didn't explicitly talk about how he planned to use the system, his intentions were clear from the blueprints and would have been glaringly obvious to a seasoned professional like Thakkar. O'Neill took the jurors through emails between the pair, and highlighted a contract that seemed to spell out Sarao's desire to cancel some orders before they were hit. Thakkar was represented by Renato Mariotti, the theatrical local attorney who, as a government prosecutor in 2014, had secured the first-ever spoofing conviction, against ex–pit trader Michael Coscia. "Ladies and gentleman, can you imagine a world in which ordinary people were charged with a crime just for doing their jobs?" Mariotti asked the jurors, before going on to compare Thakkar to a phone retailer who sells a handset to a drug dealer, or a car salesman who inadvertently supplies a getaway car.

Much rested on Sarao's shoulders when he lolloped through the courtroom in a red sweater to take the stand as a witness for the prosecution. Over several hours, he answered questions about his trading activities and interactions with Edge calmly and without prevarication, his eyes rarely lifting to make eye contact or take in his surroundings. Yes, he was a convicted fraudster, he said; no, he didn't discuss spoofing with Thakkar; yes, he was there to try to reduce his sentence. On the critical question of his relationship with Thakkar, Sarao conceded: "At the time, I didn't consider that we were colluding to commit crimes."

A few days later, after Sarao had flown back to Hounslow, the judge took the unusual step of throwing out the conspiracy charge against Thakkar on the grounds there was no evidence that the trader and his developer had ever struck up a nefarious pact. It was an embarrassing blow for the government, and a few days after that the case collapsed when the jury failed to reach an agreement on the remaining counts. Ten of the twelve jurors reportedly favored an acquittal, and, seeing an uphill battle ahead, the DOJ dropped the charges rather than pursue a retrial. It wasn't the outcome they were looking for, but Sarao had done what was asked of him. (At the time of writing, Thakkar was still in settlement talks with the CFTC about the civil charges against him.)

The clampdown on spoofing that followed Sarao's arrest was largely good for the big HFT shops, but beyond that life had grown harder. Increased competition, low trading volumes, and rising data and technology costs had squeezed profits, while a prolonged volatility drought, brought on by the intervention of central banks in global markets, was undermining a strategy that relied on big market moves. HFT continued to be involved in two-thirds of all futures trades, but the industry life cycle had spun and firms were increasingly looking at other strategies to make money. Artificial intelligence and machine learning, whereby robots continuously modify their tactics with little human interaction, were supplanting earlier forms of HFT, which relied more heavily on engineers to write and rewrite the algorithms. The result was even faster markets: trade speeds were now measured in nanoseconds, one billionth of a second.

At the time of Nav's sentencing, the hunt for his missing fortune was still ongoing. Hamstrung by a lack of jurisdiction outside the United States, the government had retrieved just $8 million of the $38 million it was owed. Mr. X, who stood to receive between 10 percent and 30 percent of whatever was collected, waited patiently for his reward. The biggest recipient of Nav's money, Jesus Alejandro Garcia Alvarez, still hadn't returned any of it and was said to be pursuing new business opportunities in Zurich. Meanwhile, Lynn Adamson and Chris Sawicki, the couple who introduced Nav to IXE, put their company into liquidation in December 2017. Iconic Worldwide Gaming, Damien O'Brien's online gaming venture, also folded. (O'Brien is now involved in crypto currencies.)

Miles MacKinnon and John Dupont, Nav's closest advisers, struggled to rebuild their business after his arrest. They said in a statement: "From 2010 to the time Nav was arrested, we had a great working relationship with Nav. He was making substantial amounts of money trading and asked us to alert him to any potential opportunities that gave large returns with minimum risk, which usually meant speculative investments in early stage businesses. Nav knew and appreciated this. Our role was to act as an introducer and at no time have we ever had any management or control over his assets or where his funds were invested. MD Capital Partners suffered substantial losses in the aftermath of Nav's arrest." The pair asked that it be made clear that they had no involvement in Nav's trading activities and that they had always urged him to cooperate with the authorities.

In the days leading up to Sarao's sentencing, the Justice Department, the probation office, and Nav's lawyer, Roger Burlingame, each filed memos to the court on what they considered to be a fair punishment. Burlingame painted his client as a kind of idiot savant who was barely able to function in the world without his parents. In a sprawling forty-one-page report, he recounted stories of Sarao leaving the house in his pajamas and keeping spiders as pets, and he quoted family members, including Nav's brother, Jasvinder, who wrote: "We all start life as innocent and inquisitive beings. As time goes on, due to numerous factors, we lose this quality, but Nav hasn't." Simon Baron-Cohen, an autism expert, said Sarao's condition made it impossible for him to distinguish between what was and wasn't allowed in a nuanced way and warned that sending him back to jail would be highly damaging because he was so sensitive to light and noise.

In a remarkable development, the Justice Department agreed, asking the judge in its memo to show leniency and let Sarao go home—a huge departure from the sentencing guidelines, which suggested he serve a minimum of six and a half years. O'Neill and Rob Zink cited Sarao's "extraordinary cooperation," and wrote that he had "substantially assisted and informed the government's nationwide efforts to detect, investigate and prosecute these crimes." The prosecutors had gotten to know Sarao since his arrest and maintained there was nothing to be gained by putting him behind bars, a conclusion shared by the probation officer.

With all sides pushing for a release, it was now just down to the judge to acquiesce. Back in Chicago, O'Neill and Burlingame took turns laying out their reasoning at a bench at the front of the court, while Nav waited alongside them grasping a sheet of paper with both hands. When it was his turn to talk, he spoke quietly and slowly: "I spent 36 years trying to find happiness on a path built on a lie," he told the judge. "I made more money than I could have imagined. I did the things society says will give you happiness, and when they didn't I didn't know where to look." Sarao had been addicted to trading, he said, but during his time in prison he came to realize that trading wasn't bringing him "deeper meaning." After his release, his brother gave him a spiritual book that opened the door to a new way of living. "Money doesn't buy you happiness," Sarao said. "And I'm glad I know that now."

Summing up the case, Judge Kendall said that when she first heard the facts she assumed she was dealing with some kind of criminal mastermind. "Now, here I am looking at this report of someone with autism who lives with his parents in a bedroom that looks like it hasn't been changed since he was 13 years old." Sarao may have treated markets like a computer game, she said, but "that does not impact the seriousness of what happened" on the day of the Flash Crash. "Your actions contributed to abusing the integrity of the market, something that's essential to maintaining a healthy economy." Kendall was adamant that Sarao face some kind of punishment beyond the four months he'd already served, and, in recognition of his medical situation, ordered him to serve a year of incarceration at his parents' house. If Nav wanted to leave— for a funeral, say, or a religious service—he would need to seek permission from the court first.

It wasn't exactly what they were seeking, but both the DOJ and Nav's lawyer appreciated it was an incredible result under the circumstances. That night Sarao arrived back at Heathrow Airport and prepared to hole up in the same bedroom where he had committed his crimes. The Hound of Hounslow was grounded.

AUTHOR'S NOTE

This book started with a twist of fate. In April 2015, I was work-ing as a reporter at *Bloomberg* in London when Navinder Sarao was arrested. Calling around, I was amazed to find out that an old friend of mine had rented a desk at Futex at the same time as Nav. He told me some now-legendary anecdotes, and I started working up a profile. Everyone I interviewed remembered Nav vividly thanks to his out-landish abilities and his death-or-glory attitude. It was one of those rare finance stories that cross into the mainstream—the genius kid from the wrong side of the tracks who finds himself in the crosshairs of the U.S. government—and I watched with fascination as the Hound of Hounslow butted up against the UK and U.S. legal systems. Then his lawyer revealed in court that, despite making tens of millions of pounds, the master manipulator of the S&P 500 couldn't pay his fine because he *himself* had been the victim of a Ponzi scheme, and I knew someone had to write a book.

This is a work of nonfiction. All the characters and events I describe are real, and no details have been changed or exaggerated for effect. The narrative was built using both public and private docu-ments, which I detail extensively in the notes, as well as interviews with over 150 people from every facet of the story, many numerous times. Owing to the sensitivity of the subject matter, the majority of interviews were carried out anonymously. Where there is dialogue, it is based on the recollections of one or more people who participated in or witnessed the conversation and has been run by all participants for accuracy. Everyone who is referenced in the book was contacted and asked about the veracity of the material pertaining to them as part of the fact-checking process. Outside of my own reporting, I relied extensively on the work of academics, authors, lawyers, finance professionals, and fellow journalists, particularly in the sections on HFT and the Flash Crash. They are cited in the notes. Before I wrote a word I read Michael Lewis's *Flash Boys,* Scott Patterson's *Dark Pools* and *The Quants,* John Sussex's *Day One Trader,* and Edwin Lefevre's *Reminiscences of a Stock Operator,* which all proved invaluable.

When I embarked on this project at the start of 2018, Nav had already pleaded guilty to spoofing and wire fraud. As part of his plea deal he agreed to provide the U.S. government with ongoing assistance in building other cases, and his sentencing was delayed. By the time the book was completed twenty-four months later, Nav still hadn't been sentenced, meaning there was no possibility of interviewing him. I did, however, provide a detailed list of facts to Nav's camp, and I am grateful for the feedback they provided ahead of publication. The manuscript has been neither seen nor approved of by Nav. I look forward to the day he can tell his own story.

ACKNOWLEDGMENTS

First and foremost, I'd like to thank my wife, Suzi Vaughan, who walked every step of this journey with me and probably deserves a joint byline. Not only was she a constant source of strength and love but she was also the first person I turned to for advice on questions of reporting and writing, and I am eternally grateful for her grace, patience, and impeccable journalistic instincts.

I'd like to thank my editors, Yaniv Soha and Cara Reilly at Doubleday and Tom Killingbeck at William Collins, who elevated the manuscript in countless ways and made the entire process enjoyable and collaborative. Thanks to my agent, Richard Pike at Conville & Walsh, who immediately saw the project's potential and has been a fantastic advocate ever since; and to Luke Speed at Curtis Brown for working miracles on the film side. Thanks, too, to Katherine Bridle and Simon Gillis at See Saw Films and to Jonny Perera, who have been a pleasure to work with.

A huge thank-you to everyone who gave up their time for interviews and contributed to my reporting in other ways. In particular, I'd like to extend my gratitude to Tom Dante, Leif Cid, Mr. X, and Ingo Malcher for their considerable input; to Robert Friedman for his insight and encouragement; to Nathan Smith for his wise counsel; and to Haim Bodek, who was a fount of knowledge. A special mention to Kit Chellel, who told me what I needed to hear at exactly the right time.

I am indebted to Bloomberg News for giving me the freedom and support to pursue this project. At a time when the news business continues to struggle and the work of journalists is routinely undermined, it is a privilege to work for an organization where standards are unwavering, employees are valued, and ambitious and important stories of all stripes are pursued.

Special thanks to my parents and the rest of the Vaughan and Ring clans for their love and support. And a final word of appreciation for Ellis and John, who introduced me to the wonders of email. It really is a great resource.

NOTES

PROLOGUE

4   That afternoon, both the DOJ and the CFTC: "Futures Trader Charged with Illegally Manipulating Stock Market," Department of Justice, April 21, 2015, www.justice.gov.

4   "CFTC Charges U.K. Resident Navinder Singh Sarao and His Company Nav Sarao Futures Limited PLC with Price Manipulation and Spoofing," Commodity Futures Trading Commission, April 21, 2015, www.cftc.gov.

5   Why was there no suggestion of market manipulation: "Findings Regarding the Market Events of May 6, 2010," a joint CFTC and SEC report, September 30, 2010, www.cftc.gov.

5   only the second individual to be criminally charged: The first was a former pit trader from Brooklyn named Michael Coscia who was indicted on October 2, 2014, by the U.S. Attorney's Office for the Northern District of Illinois with commodities fraud and spoofing in seventeen different markets including gold, copper, and currency futures.

5   those entities Michael Lewis dubbed: Michael Lewis, *Flash Boys: A Wall Street Revolt* (New York: W. W. Norton & Company, 2014).

6   "How One Man Crashed the Stock Market": Michael Maiello, *Daily Beast*, April 22, 2015.

6   "I don't know about computers": Marcus Leroux and Harry Wilson, "British Trader Accused of Sparking Wall St 'Flash Crash' from West London Semi," *The Times* (London), April 22, 2015.

CHAPTER 1: WORK WELL UNDER PRESSURE

9   "Wanted. Trainee Futures Traders": Classified ad in the *Evening Standard* newspaper, early 2003.

10   "a very likeable young man": Louise Eccles, "Wolf of Wall Street? More Like Hound of Hounslow," *Daily Mail*, April 23, 2015.

10   "prankster" who "got away with things": Camilla Turner, James Titcomb, and Gordon Rayner, "Flash Crash Trader a 'Prankster Who Always Got Away with It,' Friends Say," *Daily Telegraph,* April 22, 2015.

11   burgeoning number of arcades: The terms "trading arcade" and "prop shop" are often used interchangeably but, strictly speaking, the business models are different. Traders in a pure prop firm trade for a firm-wide account and the profits are divvied up by management, whereas in an arcade they trade for their own account and hand over a percentage of their profits.

11   a small sum on each trade: The life cycle of a trade is actually two transactions—a trader buys some futures then sells the same number to close out their position or vice versa. Thus the term "round-trip."

11   *Wall Street*: Directed by Oliver Stone (Los Angeles: 20th Century Fox, 1987).

11   *Trading Places*: Directed by John Landis (Los Angeles: Paramount Pictures, 1983).

14   "rude manners": Wikipedia entry on "Royal Exchange, London."

14   "Day One Traders": Special thanks to John Sussex, whose firsthand account of his experiences in the Liffe pits, recounted in the excellent *Day One Trader: A Liffe Story* (New Jersey: John Wiley & Sons, 2009), proved invaluable.

15   known as "liquidity": Liquidity is defined by the website Investopdeia as "the degree to which an asset or security can be quickly bought or sold in the market at a price reflecting its intrinsic value." In markets, it refers to how easily an asset can be bought or sold at "stable, transparent prices." The market for a one-off painting, for example, is less liquid than that for medium-size family homes, which is less liquid than that for shares in Apple.

15   according to myth: John Sussex, *Day One Trader* (John Wiley & Sons, 2009).

16   even in 2018, women only comprised: Anna Irrera, "Wall Street Wants More Female Traders, but Old Perceptions Die Hard," Reuters, June 14, 2018.

16   In 1997, a statue was erected: The bronze sculpture, *The Liffe Trader,* was made by Stephen Melton to commemorate fifteen years of Liffe. Today it is displayed at the south ambulatory of Guildhall, Gresham Street, London.

17 Most historians of financial markets: Allan Grody and Hughes Levecq, "Past, Present and Future: The Evolution and Development of Electronic Financial Markets," NYU Stern School of Business, November 1993.

17 The postmortem revealed: Mark Carlson, "A Brief History of the 1987 Stock Market Crash with a Discussion of the Federal Reserve Response," Finance and Economics Discussion Series, Federal Reserve Board, Washington, DC, November 2006.

17 The industry's reputation: Eric Berg, "46 Commodities Traders Indicted After a 2-Year F.B.I. Investigation," *New York Times,* August 3, 1989.

17 Then, when volumes started sliding: Estelle Cantillon and Pai-Ling Yin, "How and When Do Markets Tip? Lessons from the Battle of the Bund," Working Paper Series No. 766, European Central Bank, June 2007.

18 Liffe's share of the all-important: Cantillon and Yin, "How and When Do Markets Tip?"

19 used to call him "The Chav": "Chav" is a British insult meaning someone of low social class.

19 classic texts: *Market Wizards* by Jack D. Schwager contains interviews with high-profile traders. It was first published by HarperCollins in 1989. *Reminiscences of a Stock Operator* (Wiley), first published in 1923, is a fictionalized account of the life of trading legend Jesse Livermore by Edwin Lefèvre. *Steidlmayer on Markets: Trading with Market Profile* examines the use of charts to recognize patterns and identify trading opportunities. It was written by traders J. Peter Steidlmayer and Steven B. Hawkins and first published in 2003.

CHAPTER 2: THE BOY PLUNGER

21 coined the term "flow": Mihaly Csikszentmihalyi, *Flow: The Psychology of Happiness: The Classic Work on How to Achieve Happiness* (New York: HarperCollins, 1990).

23 "You'd hear people say . . .": Wherever Nav is quoted speaking to a friend, here and throughout the text, his words are based on that friend's detailed recollections of the conversation. In some cases those recollections are backed up by contemporaneous notes.

23 More than $200 billion of e-minis: E-mini S&P 500 Daily Volume, https://cmegroup.com.

27 a feature available on the CME called an "iceberg": Iceberg orders are used by market participants to execute large orders with minimum impact on the market. A fund looking to buy $1 billion of e-minis at a price of 1,500, for example, may use the feature to disguise the size of their overall position by executing the purchases in $50,000 install-

ments as and when the e-minis become available so the market doesn't spike while they're carrying out the trade, causing them to pay more.

27   This perpetual gamesmanship: Scott Patterson, "CFTC Targets Rapid Trades," *Wall Street Journal,* March 15, 2012.

31   "There is nothing new in Wall Street": Edwin Lefèvre, *Reminiscences of a Stock Operator* (New Jersey: John Wiley & Sons, 1994).

31   shooting himself in the head: Diana B. Henriques, "A Speculator's Life Is Still Elusive," *New York Times,* September 9, 2001.

CHAPTER 3: THAT'S A FUGAZI

34   Published a book called: Ralph Nelson Elliot, *The Wave Principle,* first published in 1938.

CHAPTER 4: THE TRADE I

39   If it wasn't the Chinese: The "Plunge Protection Team" is a moniker given to the President's Working Group on Financial Markets, a group of the foremost U.S. regulators and government officials. The group was set up by Ronald Reagan after the 1987 Wall Street Crash to foster better communication between government agencies in times of market stress. It is the subject of frequent speculation that it intervenes in markets to serve U.S. government ends. The Bilderberg Group is a group of around 150 leading global politicians, financiers, and businessmen who meet up once a year to discuss world affairs. It is also a frequent subject of conspiracy theories.

42   texted his boss: James B. Stewart, "The Omen," *New Yorker,* October 13, 2008.

42   Unlike most of the firm's elite traders: Stewart, "The Omen."

42   he'd made a profit of around $2 billion: Here and throughout the text, non-U.S. currencies have been converted into dollars using contemporaneous exchange rates unless specified.

42   Between January 2 and January 18: From "Mission Green," Société Générale's internal report into the Kerviel affair, May 20, 2008, www .societegenerale.com.

43   the bank had lost €4.9 billion: SG internal report, May 20, 2008.

43   the biggest fine ever levied on an individual: Kerviel was released from jail in 2014 after serving just five months. Two years later, his €4.9 billion fine was cut by a French judge to €1 million.

CHAPTER 5: RISE OF THE ROBOTS

44   The term is somewhat vague and ill-defined: A. Kirilenko, A. Kyle, M. Samadi, and T. Tuzun, "The Flash Crash: The Impact of High Fre-

quency Trading on an Electronic Market," Working Paper, October 1, 2010.

45   The first HFT firms: Getco—the Global Electronic Trading Company—was founded in 1999 by ex–Chicago pit traders Stephen Schuler and Daniel Tierney. Jump Trading was founded the same year by Paul Gurinas and Bill DiSomma, who both also started in the Chicago pits.

45   In 2003, HFT firms: Precise figures on the preponderance of HFT are hard to come by pre-2012, when the CFTC started publishing data. The 2008 estimate here comes from a May 3, 2010, report by Aite Group titled "High Frequency Trading in the Futures Market." The 2012 figures come from a Reuters report dated August 23, 2013, titled "CFTC Finalizes Plan to Boost Oversight of Fast Traders: Official," which cites New York consultancy TABB Group estimates (although when I contacted TABB myself, they were unable to provide figures).

45   Jump, a firm of a few dozen employees: Saijel Kishan and Matthew Leising, "Don't Tell Anybody About This Story on HFT Power Jump Trading," *Bloomberg*, July 24, 2014.

45   The same year, Citadel: Jenny Strasburg, Scott Patterson, and Lavonne Kuykendall, "High-Frequency Gain: Citadel Unit's $1 Billion," *Wall Street Journal*, October 5, 2009.

46   the CME Group, which had only recently: The CME Group was formed in 2007 by the merger of Chicago's two main futures exchanges, the Chicago Mercantile Exchange and the Chicago Board of Trade. It has since added a number of other global exchanges to its portfolio. It consistently reports operating margins of around 60 percent, making it one of the most profitable members of the S&P 500. In 2010, it reported profits of $951 million on revenues of $3 billion.

46   William Shepard, another longtime: Kishan and Leising, "Don't Tell Anybody."

47   "Given that HFTs are very short-term intermediaries": "HFT and the Hidden Cost of Deep Liquidity," Pragma Trading, 2012, https://www.pragmatrading.com.

47   The small number of researchers: One example of such research is "High Frequency Trading—Measurement, Detection and Response," a research note by Credit Suisse analysts Jonathan Tse, Xiang Lin, and Drew Vincent, December 6, 2012.

47   "What happens if a major event causes turmoil": Joe Saluzzi, "HFT Roundtable," Themis Trading blog, June 17, 2009, https://blog.themistrading.com.

48   "never-ending socially-wasteful arms race for speed": Eric Budish, Peter Cramton, and John Shim, "The High-Frequency Trading Arms Race: Frequent Batch Auctions as a Market Design Response," *Quarterly Journal of Economics* 130 (November 2015).

49   HFT firms largely eradicated losses: Although that didn't necessarily mean they were profitable, since the cost of technology and data were high and rising.

49   They also helped create a situation: I was unable to source figures for cancelation rates in 2010, but by 2015, as many as 95 percent of orders on the CME were canceled before they were executed, according to University of Southern California professor Larry Harris's testimony during Nav's extradition hearing.

50   electronic trading pioneer Thomas Peterffy: In March 2019, Peterffy, the founder and CEO of Interactive Brokers, was ranked the sixty-third-richest American by *Forbes* magazine, which estimated his net worth at $17.1 billion. Timber Hill was sold to a rival in 2017.

50   "We feel like Robin Hood": Michael Stothard, "Norway's Day Traders Take on the Algos," *Financial Times*, May 16, 2012.

CHAPTER 6: END OF AN ERA

54   according to Nav's recollection: Paolo's recollection is slightly different. He says he did call Nav, but his concern was that Nav had left such a large position on overnight when he wasn't in a position to get out of it quickly. He wasn't worried there was no stop-loss in place.

55   where he shared the fairways: Lawrence Donegan, "Golf Goes for the High Rollers," *Guardian*, May 11, 2005.

55   "Legend has it that just outside London": *Trader Monthly* was shut down in 2009 and is no longer available online. This extract was taken from a Facebook page called "Great Traders" operated by a firm called Varchev Financial Services. It is also referenced on various trading forums.

CHAPTER 7: THE TRADE II

59   CFT was founded by a high-rolling day trader: Braveheart's real name is Andy Priston. The "premiere issue" of *Trader Monthly* was dated 2004.

CHAPTER 8: A BRIEF HISTORY OF SPOOFING

63   "'Tis a trade founded in fraud": Defoe's essay, "The Anatomy of Exchange Alley" (1719), is available on *The Literary Encyclopaedia*, www.litencyc.com.

64   Spoof was the name of a card game: Word History, Merriam-Webster, www.merriam-webster.com.

65   One of the earliest references to spoofing in relation to financial mar-

kets: Gretchen Morgenson, "Chasing Ghosts at Nasdaq," *New York Times,* December 12, 1999.

65   orders and front-running: Front-running is the prohibited practice of placing a trade based on nonpublic information regarding a pending transaction. A broker-dealer, for example, may place a trade for its own account before executing a large transaction on behalf of a customer that it knows is likely to move the market; or a local in the pit may get wind of an incoming order and position himself to benefit. Since the emergence of electronic trading and HFT, what does and doesn't constitute front-running has become less clear-cut.

66   a new function called: "Avoid Orders That Cross" is a legitimate function offered by TT that allows traders with positions on both sides of the market to avoid trading with themselves. It works by automatically canceling a trader's resting orders if the same entity tries to hit into them. For example, imagine that the current best offer for wheat futures is $100.00 a bushel and a firm has placed a resting order to sell ten lots for $100.25 in the ladder, where they sit behind another forty lots at that price. If that same entity suddenly decided it wanted to *buy* wheat and placed a hundred-lot order at $100.25, above the prevailing price, the program would simultaneously cancel its own ten sell orders and pick up the other forty lots.

66   Rotter's cover was blown on a forum in 2004: Imogen Rose-Smith, "Flipping Out," *Trader Monthly,* date unknown. A copy of the article is available at https://largecaplinks.files.wordpress.com/2015/04/paul-rotter-trader-monthly.pdf.

69   But in March 2009: Criminal complaint against Navinder Sarao, U.S. Department of Justice, April 21, 2015, www.justice.gov.

70   The brokers at GNI were officially supposed to: This requirement is contained in "Rule 166.3—Supervision" of the Commodity Exchange Act.

CHAPTER 9: BUILDING THE MACHINE

71   On Friday June 12, 2009, Nav emailed his broker: Correspondence contained in the appendix to the CFTC's Motion for a Statutory Restraining Order, filed in the Northern District of Illinois, April 17, 2015.

74   thereby limiting any potential damage: In fact, to avoid suspicion, Nav wanted the program to allow one-lot orders to trade into his resting orders; any more than *that* and his spoofs would be modified and sent to the back of the line.

CHAPTER 10: THE CRASH

76   The previous day, over a few hours: *USA v. Navinder Singh Sarao,* DOJ Criminal Complaint, April 21, 2015, www.justice.gov.

77   seven times what his hero, Lionel Messi: According to CNN, Messi was earning around $45 million a year in 2010, including endorsements and sponsorship deals. That amounts to about $125,000 a day. "Messi tops Beckham in football rich list," CNN.com, March 24, 2010.

77   "This order is not in the book": DOJ complaint, April 21, 2015, www .justice.gov.

77   Unemployment was up by 50 percent: "UK Unemployment Increases to 2.51 Million," BBC, May 12, 2010.

78   Nav bided his time until 3:20 p.m.: DOJ complaint, April 21, 2015, www.justice.gov.

80   That barrage sat in an order book that was already severely imbalanced: "Preliminary Findings Regarding the Market Events of May 6, 2010," CFTC and SEC, May 18, 2010, www.sec.gov.

81   Terrified market participants: "Findings Regarding," CFTC and SEC, September 30, 2010, https://www.cftc.gov.

81   The S&P 500 jumped from a low of 1,056: "Preliminary Findings," CFTC and SEC, May 18, 2010, www.sec.gov.

81   Proctor & Gamble, Hewlett-Packard, General Electric, and 3M: "Preliminary Findings," CFTC and SEC, May 18, 2010, www.sec.gov.

82   "kiss my ass": DOJ complaint, April 21, 2015, www.justice.gov.

CHAPTER 11: THE AFTERMATH

86   Since 2005 and the introduction of a set of rules: The Regulation National Market System, or "Reg NMS," rules were introduced by the SEC to try to foster competition in U.S. stock markets and ensure investors received the best possible price for their orders. One consequence was a significant rise in the number of exchanges and alternative trading venues and, in response to *that,* an explosion in the number of HFT firms seeking to capitalize on the opportunities thrown up by the fragmented new market structure.

87   "High-Speed Trading Glitch Costs Investors Billions": Nelson D. Schwartz and Louise Story, *New York Times,* May 6, 2010.

87   "A temporary $1 trillion drop in market value": Mark R. Warner, senator from Virginia, "Investigating the Wall Street Freefall," May 7, 2010, https://warner.senate.gov.

87   It was an illustrious group: The committee's members were Brooksley Born, ex-CFTC chair; Jack Brennan, ex-CEO of investment company the Vanguard Group; NYU Stern professor Robert Engle; Richard Ketchum, former director of market regulation at the SEC; Cornell

professor Maureen O'Hara; ex–Federal Reserve board member Susan Phillips; ex–SEC chair David Ruder; and Joseph Stiglitz from Columbia Business School. At fifty-five, Brennan was the youngest.

88   One article in the *Wall Street Journal:* Scott Patterson and Tom Lauricella, "Did a Big Bet Help Trigger 'Black Swan' Stock Swoon?," *Wall Street Journal,* May 10, 2010.

88   Another, on CNBC's website, cited chatter: "Stock Selloff May Have Been Triggered by a Trader Error," CNBC.com with Reuters, May 6, 2010.

88   Mike McCarthy, an unemployed father: Lauren LaCapra, "How P&G Plunge Derailed One Investor," *The Street,* May 17, 2010.

88   a small hedge fund called NorCap: "Dallas Hedge Fund Suing over 'Flash Crash' Losses," *Dallas Morning News,* December 22, 2010.

89   "We'd watched the S&P completely fall apart": "Reliving the 2010 Flash Crash with a Veteran Floor Trader," *Stocktwits,* May 8, 2015, available on www.medium.com.

90   discovered that one entity: The CFTC never actually named Waddell & Reed, referring to it only as a "mutual fund complex." Its identity was first revealed in the May 14, 2010, Reuters article "Exclusive: Waddell Is Mystery Trader in Market Plunge," by Herbert Lash and Jonathan Spicer.

90   Waddell & Reed's flagship investment vehicle was: E. S. Browning and Jenny Strasburg, "The Mutual Fund in the 'Flash Crash," *Wall Street Journal,* October 6, 2010.

90   Normally, the firm's head trader: Jenny Strasburg and Jeanette Neumann, "As Markets Sank, Waddell Traders Were at an Event," *Wall Street Journal,* October 7, 2010.

91   However, Waddell & Reed had failed to incorporate: "Findings Regarding," CFTC and SEC, September 30, 2010, https://www.cftc.gov.

91   Under normal conditions: According to the CFTC/SEC joint report, the firm had recently carried out a number of similar orders, including one of about the same size that took five hours to complete (although on that occasion, the algo was programmed to factor in price and time as well as volume).

91   markets were severely out of whack: At 1:30 p.m., the Chicago Board of Options had stopped routing orders to a NYSE platform after identifying price anomalies. In the e-mini, resting bids far outweighed offers and the chasm was growing. All day, sellers had been willing to "cross the spread," a warning sign for market makers to get out of the water.

91   The CFTC would later conclude: "Findings Regarding," CFTC and SEC, September 30, 2010, https://www.cftc.gov.

92   "auto pilot(ing) into a ravine": Tom Lauricella, "Debate on 'Crash' and Its Causes," *Wall Street Journal,* October 5, 2010.

92   On May 6, the researchers found: A. Kirilenko, A. Kyle, M. Samadi, and T. Tuzun, "The Flash Crash: The Impact of High Frequency Trading on an Electronic Market," Working Paper, October 1, 2010.

93   "During the Flash Crash, the trading behavior": These quotes are taken from an updated version of the Kirilenko, Kyle, Samadi, and Tuzun paper published on January 12, 2011.

93   when the e-mini collapsed, it triggered stock traders: "Findings Regarding," CFTC and SEC, September 30, 2010, https://www.cftc .gov.

93   exchange-traded funds: An exchange-traded fund, or ETF, is a publicly listed basket of securities that tracks an underlying index.

93   In a few minutes: "Preliminary Findings," CFTC and SEC, May 18, 2010, www.sec.gov.

94   "no evidence to suggest": Carey Gillam, "Waddell & Reed Says Not Cause of May 6 Flash Crash," Reuters, May 17, 2010.

94   "Who puts in a $4.1bn order without a limit price?": Courtney Comstock, "Read the Email an HFT Chairman Is Forwarding Around About Firm That Caused Flash Crash," *Business Insider*, October 4, 2010.

CHAPTER 12: MILKING MARKETS

96   Nav signed up for a plan: The dividend scheme was later closed down by HMRC, which wrote to Nav demanding repayment of unpaid taxes.

99   the company was shut down and two thousand customers: Charles Walmsley, "HMRC Secures Victory in £200m in Double Taxation Loophole Scam Trial," *Citywire*, October 6, 2015.

99   "expected return over 5 years is 300%": From an advertisement placed on the website of OTS Solicitors, https://www.otssolicitors.co.uk.

102 he'd reportedly brought the inhabitants of Ayrshire to tears: According to an anti–wind farm campaigner quoted in the *Ayrshire Post* on November 16, 2013, Davie had, during one consultation meeting, "belittled those with genuine concerns, laughed at some of the points raised, was extremely rude to others and reduced some local residents to tears."

CHAPTER 13: THE DUST SETTLES

104 CBS's *60 Minutes* aired a segment: Steve Kroft, "How High Speed Traders Are Changing Wall Street," *CBS 60 Minutes*, October 7, 2010.

104 stocks like Cisco Systems and the Washington Post Company: The Washington Post Company changed its name to the Graham Holdings Company in 2013 after it was acquired by Jeff Bezos.

104 "Stock Market Flash Crash: Causes and Solutions": A video of the hearing is available on https://c-span.org.

105 To remedy the issue: As of November 2019, the Consolidated Audit Trail was still not completed.

105 The SEC's budget in 2010: It's worth noting that the agencies usually bring in considerably more money for the government in the form of fines than they ever spend.

105 HFT giant Citadel's founder Ken Griffin: "Hedge Funds Make Hay," *New York Times,* April 3, 2010. Citing a survey by *AR: Absolute Return + Alpha* magazine.

107 senators asked the owner of an HFT firm named Manoj Narang what risks: At the time Narang was CEO and founder of Tradeworx Inc. Today he owns and runs a trading firm called MANA Partners LLC.

107 creaming more than $10 billion: There are no precise figures on HFT profits. TABB Group estimates HFT firms made $7.2 billion trading U.S. equities alone in 2009, so $10 billion across all asset classes is a conservative estimate.

107 The CFTC launched a public consultation: In February 2012, the CFTC announced the creation of a new subcommittee of its long-standing Technology Advisory Committee to focus on HFT. In September of the following year it published a "Concept Release" on how it viewed and planned to regulate automated markets, and requested comment from market participants and the wider public.

107 The SEC undertook its own review: The SEC had actually already begun an overarching review of the equity market structure in January 2010, before the Flash Crash.

108 funneled donations to their political allies: "Emanuel's Rare Political Reach Fuels Fundraising Machine," *Chicago Tribune,* February 2, 2015.

108 Within the CFTC itself: Bart Chilton, a much-loved figure in futures markets, passed away in 2019.

109 Their influential 2012 book: Sal Arnuk and Joseph Saluzzi, *Broken Markets: How High Frequency Trading and Predatory Practices on Wall Street Are Destroying Investor Confidence and Your Portfolio* (New Jersey: FT Press, 2012).

109 A mysterious commentator writing: R. T. Leuchtkafer's comments, from April 16, 2010, are published on the SEC's website, www.sec .gov.

109 noticed that some exchanges were intermittently being bombarded: "Analysis of the 'Flash Crash' . . . Part 4, Quote Stuffing," June 18, 2010, www.nanex.net.

110 Intriguingly, one occurred as the e-mini collapsed: "Nanex Flash Crash Summary Report," September 27, 2010, www.nanex.net.

110 In July 2010, Hunsader was invited to Washington: Herbert Lash,

"'Flash Crash' Report Ignores Research: Nanex," Reuters, October 4, 2010.

110 "Why would SEC regulators deny": "Quote Stuffing Bombshell," December 14, 2012, www.nanex.net.

110 no multimarket "Splash Crash": The term "splash crash" was coined by John Bates, a senior director at Progress Software and an adviser to the CFTC, to describe a situation whereby a Flash Crash–type event spills over into markets and asset classes around the world with potentially catastrophic effects.

111 The CME and other exchanges: The CME increased the penalties it levied on firms that breached its fill-ratio thresholds from $1,000 to $2,000 within a thirty-day period (after two warnings).

112 In the fall of 2012: Adam Clark-Joseph, "Exploratory Trading," Harvard University, January 13, 2013 (a version of this paper circulated in late 2012).

112 And in November: Matthew Baron, Jonathan Brogaard, and Andrei Kirilenko, "The Trading Profits of High Frequency Traders," University of Chicago Booth School of Business, November 2012 (first published October 2011), www.chicagobooth.edu.

112 On December 3, 2012: Nathaniel Popper and Christopher Leonard, "High-Speed Traders Profit at Expense of Ordinary Investors, a Study Says," *New York Times,* December 3, 2012.

112 The *Wall Street Journal* published its own account: Scott Patterson, "High Frequency Trading Arms Race Has Plenty of Drawbacks," *Wall Street Journal,* December 3, 2012.

112 Amid pressure from the HFT lobby: "Review of the Commodity Futures Trading Commission's Response to Allegations Pertaining to the Office of the Chief Economist," prepared by the Office of the Inspector General of the CFTC, February 21, 2014.

113 An inquiry into the CFTC's handling: "Review of the CFTC's Response," Inspector General, February 21, 2014.

CHAPTER 14: THOUGHT CRIME

114 King Jack Sturges: Jerry Markham's sweeping history of skullduggery in the futures markets, "Manipulation of Commodity Futures Prices: The Unprosecutable Crime" (*Yale Journal on Regulation,* 1991), as well as interviews I conducted with him, were invaluable for this chapter.

114 In the late nineteenth century, it was gold: Jerry Markham, "Manipulation of Commodity Futures Prices: The Unprosecutable Crime," *Yale Journal on Regulation* 8, no. 2 (1991).

114 when three brothers from Texas monopolized: Nelson, William, and Lamar Hunt successfully cornered the silver market in 1979, pushing

prices from $6 per troy ounce to $50. After the authorities intervened, however, the price collapsed and the brothers lost over a billion dollars.

115   one manipulation case at trial: 2008's *DiPlacido v. CFTC*—and even then, the case was decided by a so-called administrative law judge rather than at a full trial in federal court.

115   After one particularly high-profile failure: Letter to CFTC Chairman Timothy Massad dated October 8, 2014, by Senators Dianne Feinstein, Maria Cantwell, and Carl Levin after energy trader Brian Hunter was fined just $750,000 by the agency compared to the $30 million originally sought by the Federal Energy Regulatory Commission for alleged manipulation.

116   When Gensler was appointed: Gensler had held a number of senior positions at Goldman Sachs, as well as in the Clinton administration, and Democratic senators including Levin and Cantwell worried he would be too soft on Wall Street in the aftermath of the financial crisis.

116   These included what's colloquially known: "Banging the Close" is the practice of trading in such a way as to try to move the market during key moments. For example, imagine a bank has built a large oil derivatives position by buying up contracts whose value is determined by the oil price at 4 p.m. on the last Friday of the month. That bank may be inclined to trade as aggressively as it can in the buildup to and during the 4 p.m. window in an effort to move the so-called "cash" market and maximize the profits on its derivatives trade.

116   with little fanfare an amendment was inserted: A legislative history of Dodd-Frank is available on the Law Librarians' Society of Washington, DC's website at www.llsdc.org.

116   The existing manipulation statutes in the Commodity Exchange Act were also tweaked: Daniel Waldman, "Has the Law of Manipulation Lost Its Moorings," April 7, 2017, www.arnoldporter.com.

116   practices like placing stop-losses: A stop-loss is an order that a trader places *hoping* that it will never actually be hit. A trader who believes the e-mini will rise, for example, might place a stop-loss order to sell at 50 points below the current price to minimize his potential losses if he's wrong. At the time he placed the trade, he *intended* to cancel it. One concern was that the use of stop-losses would inadvertently be caught by the broad language of the new rules.

117   "make the market more liquid and more efficient": Adam Nunes was speaking at the CFTC's roundtable on Disruptive Trading Practices on December 2, 2010. A transcript is available on the CFTC's website, www.cftc.gov.

117   "This is not a moral issue": Ronald H. Filler and Jerry Markham, amicus brief to the U.S. Supreme Court on *Michael Coscia v. United States,* March 8, 2018.

118   three years later, the CFTC issued a document: Interpretive Guidance

and Policy Statement on Disruptive Practices, CFTC, May 20, 2013, www.cftc.gov.

118 spoofing was like pornography: John Lothian, publisher of the John Lothian Newsletter, made the analogy during the CFTC's December 2, 2010, roundtable on Disruptive Trading Practices.

119 several HFT employees and firms have been sanctioned: Traders from leading HFT firms Jump Trading and Tower Research have been charged with spoofing, for example.

119 firms such as Citadel and HTG Capital Partners: Citadel and HTG both testified against Igor Oystacher, who was charged by the CFTC on October 19, 2015, with spoofing in multiple markets.

CHAPTER 15: PIMP MY ALGO

121 "It was as if a manager of the New York Yankees": Peter Lattman and Nelson D. Schwartz, "In Corzine Comeback, Big Risks and Steep Fall," *New York Times,* November 1, 2011.

121 Convinced the authorities would never let that happen: Bryan Burrough and Bethany McLean, "John Corzine's Riskiest Business," *Vanity Fair,* January 10, 2012.

121 former high school quarterback: Burrough and McLean, "John Corzine's Riskiest Business."

121 In October 2011: Paul Peterson, Department of Agricultural and Consumer Economics, University of Illinois, "Behind the Collapse of MF Global," August 2, 2013, www.farmdocdaily.illinois.edu.

121 In the frenzied final hours: The CFTC alleged in its June 27, 2013, complaint that MF Global's assistant treasurer, Edith O'Brien, "directed, approved, and/or caused numerous illegal transfers." On January 5, 2017, she agreed to pay $500,000 to settle the matter. Corzine, who was accused of either not acting in "good faith" or "knowingly" inducing the violations, was fined $5 million.

123 *Secrets of the Millionaire Mind:* T. Harv Eker, *Secrets of the Millionaire Mind* (New York: HarperCollins, 2005).

123 *The Secret*: Rhonda Byrne, *The Secret* (New York: Simon & Schuster, 2006).

124 "I received your message regarding TT": These messages are included in the appendix to the CFTC's Motion for a Statutory Restraining Order, April 17, 2015.

124 Nav sent Thakkar an email: Nav sent an identical message to two other software providers. At least one of them expressed an interest in working on the project, but Nav opted to work with Edge.

126 Nav wanted Edge to make him a program: Sarao talked through a video of himself trading when he was giving testimony during the trial

of Jitesh Thakkar in Chicago in March 2019. Sarao agreed to testify against the software developer as part of a plea deal with the U.S. government. The description of his strategy contained in this section is largely based on that testimony.

127 Thakkar took Nav's plans and instructed his developers: DOJ Criminal Complaint against Jitesh Thakkar, January 19, 2018, www.justice .gov.

127 "this is sort of below cost for us": CFTC complaint against Jitesh Thakkar and Edge Financial Technologies, January 28, 2018, www .cftc.gov.

127 a modest sum: Thakkar would later tell investigators that the reason he charged so little was because he had no idea how big or profitable of a trader Nav was. Sarao was stingy from the outset, and it's considered almost gauche among developers to ask your client about their trading size. The government would argue at trial that the entrepreneur knew how desirable the machine would be to other traders, which is why he structured the deal so that Edge retained "all rights to modify, use or sell any code, or derivative work."

127 He didn't feel comfortable having such a controversial system named after himself: The "MASTERCHIEF" email was entered into evidence during the Thakkar trial. Sarao was asked why he made the request on the stand.

128 The subcommittee Thakkar was a part of: Testimony of CFTC economist Richard Haynes during the Thakkar trial.

128 One day a few months later: Evidence presented at Thakkar trial, April 3, 2019.

CHAPTER 16: JESUS ENTERS

129 an Aztec word apparently meaning: Helmuth Fuchs, "Interviews: Alejandro Garcia, CEO IXE (English)," www.moneycab.com, September 18, 2013.

130 a supplier in China would accept: This activity is commonly known as "trade finance."

130 IXE was already making big profits: Details on the opportunity were laid out in a document titled "Frequently Asked Questions" distributed to potential investors and introducers in late 2012. Further details were contained in a three-page brochure dated August 2012.

130 "We are offering alternative investment vehicles": The same pitch was laid out in a Q&A with Garcia on IXE's website, www.ixe-group .com.

131 Asked about IXE's pedigree: "Frequently Asked Questions," IXE, 2012.

131   IXE also claimed to be regulated: The reality was more nuanced. Under Swiss law, financial intermediaries are given the choice of either registering with FINMA or becoming a member of one of a handful of authorized "self-regulatory organizations." After agreeing to pay an annual fee of $2,400 and attend some compliance classes, IXE opted for the latter.

131   MacKinnon and Dupont weren't legally licensed: Introducers are not authorized to provide financial advice in the UK. FCA rules state it must be clear that the investor "is not seeking or has not sought advice (from an introducer) on the merits of his entering into the transaction."

132   The investigator had found a 2010 legal complaint: *Bank of Mongolia v. M&P Global Financial Services Europe, AG, GT International Holdings Inc., Burton Greenberg et al.*, Second Amended Complaint, U.S. District Court for the Southern District of Florida, March 31, 2010.

132   who would later serve an eight-year stretch: "Florida Man Sentenced to Eight Years in Prison For Investment Fraud Conspiracy," U.S. Attorney's Office, Northern District of New York, February 19, 2016, www.justice.gov.

132   he signed off on the transfer of $17 million: Appendix to the CFTC's Motion for a Statutory Restraining Order, Northern District of Illinois, April 17, 2015.

133   they were now receiving a residual $500,000 a year: Between them, Nav's introducers actually received around $750,000 a year, but Paul James, the accountant, also took a slice.

133   Shortly after Nav made his first deposit: "EU Imposes New Sanctions on Iran," BBC, October 15, 2012.

134   Garcia was invited to join the board of the Swiss arm: Listing for Robert F. Kennedy Foundation, www.business-monitor.ch.

134   "Switzerland's most important farmer has an urban workplace": Markus Stadeli, "Mexikanische Grossgrund-besitzer ziehen in die Schweiz," *Neue Zurcher Zeitung*, November 3, 2013. This translation from the original German-language article was carried out by IXE and published on IXE's website.

135   Garcia was invited onto Al Jazeera, CNBC, and Bloomberg: The interviews were available on the "Publications" page of IXE's website, www.ixe-group.com.

135   one publication estimated Garcia's worth at 250 million Swiss francs: Stefan Luscher, "Familie Garcia Alvarez: Superkorn fur Bolivien," *Bilanz*, April 1, 2014.

135   "Our fathers' businesses and deals were based on a handshake": Fuchs, "Interviews," www.moneycab.com, September 18, 2013.

CHAPTER 17: MR. X

138 He'd read about how nine stock traders: "Finra Sanctions Trillium Brokerage Services, LLC, Director of Trading, Chief Compliance Officer, and Nine Traders $2.26 Million for Illicit Equities Trading Strategy," September 13, 2010, www.finra.org.

139 A preliminary version of the report states: "Preliminary Findings," CFTC and SEC, May 18, 2010, www.sec.gov.

139 whose $2 billion of profits in 2011: The CME's net income was $1.8 billion in 2011. The CFTC's annual budget was around $200 million.

139 As Mr. X considered his next move: Scott Patterson and Jenny Strasburg, "For Superfast Stock Traders, a Way to Jump Ahead in Line," *Wall Street Journal*, September 19, 2012.

140 full negative alpha: Alpha is trader-speak for a strategy's ability to beat the market, or its "edge."

140 Bodek started using Hide Not Slide orders and his profits improved: Patterson and Strasburg, "For Superfast Stock Traders."

141 Bodek, who eschewed his right to anonymity, now stood to receive: Bodek's complaint resulted in the SEC levying a $14 million fine against the BATS exchange in January 2015, of which he received 25 percent. Today, he works with prospective whistle-blowers looking to bring claims under the Dodd-Frank Whistleblower Program via his company Decimus Capital Markets, LLC.

CHAPTER 18: NAVSAR

149 In the twelve days the CFTC ended up selecting: Report by CFTC expert witness Terrence Hendershott of the Hass School of Business at the University of California, Berkeley. Contained in the appendix to the CFTC's Motion for a Statutory Restraining Order, April 17, 2015.

149 On the day of the crash, the algo accounted: DOJ Sarao complaint, April 21, 2015, www.justice.gov.

CHAPTER 19: CORNBREAD AND THE CME

152 "Lol, guarantee if I switch on my computer": DOJ indictment, September 2, 2015, www.justice.gov.

155 The first iteration: *William C. Braman, Mark Mendelson et al. v. The CME Group, Inc. and the Board of Trade of the City of Chicago*, U.S. District Court of the Northern District of Illinois, Eastern Division, April 11, 2014.

155 "The suit is devoid of any facts supporting the allegations": CME Group statement, April 13, 2014, www.cmegroup.com.

155 The previous month: Michael Lewis, *Flash Boys: A Wall Street Revolt* (New York: W. W. Norton & Company, 2014).

155 "The U.S. stock market was now a class system": Michael Lewis, "The Wolf Hunters of Wall Street (an adaptation from *Flash Boys*)," *New York Times Magazine*, March 31, 2014.

156 insider trading 2.0: Eric Schneiderman, "Cracking Down on Insider Trading 2.0," *Albany Business Review*, October 11, 2013.

156 Joseph Stiglitz, the Nobel prize–winning economist: Joseph E. Stiglitz, "Tapping the Brakes: Are Less Active Markets Safer and Better for the Economy?," presented at the Federal Reserve Bank of America, April 15, 2014.

156 Charlie Munger, Warren Buffett's right-hand man: Alex Crippen, "Buffett, Gates and Munger Criticize High-Frequency Trading," cnbc .com, May 5, 2014.

157 in May the CME filed a motion: *CME Group Motion to Dismiss, Braman et al. v. The CME Group*, May 31, 2014.

157 The bedrock of the amended complaint: Scott Patterson, Jenny Strasburg, and Liam Pleven, "High-Speed Traders Exploit Loophole," *Wall Street Journal*, May 1, 2013.

158 just one losing day out of 1,238: Virtu Financial Inc. IPO prospectus, filed with the SEC on March 26, 2014, www.sec.gov.

158 CME Group promised to try to minimize: Jenny Strasburg and Scott Patterson, "Exchange Vows to Trim Data Loophole," *Wall Street Journal*, May 1, 2013.

158 Citing confidential witnesses: *Braman et al. v. The CME Group*, Second Amended Class Action Complaint, July 22, 2014.

158 The CME maintained that the deals were essential: Matthew Leising, "Perks Live Forever at CME Amid Review of Trade Incentives," *Bloomberg*, June 14, 2014. The article reported that perks for some early firms were ten times greater than for new entrants in Eurodollar futures, one of the CME's highest volume contracts.

158 by 2013 it had become widespread enough: Ann Saphir, "US Regulators Examining 'Wash Trades,' CFTC's Chilton Says," Reuters, March 18, 2013.

159 an estimated ninety-five out of every one hundred: This estimate was provided by Larry Harris, University of Southern California professor and former chief economist at the SEC, during Sarao's February 2016 extradition hearing. The CME declined to provide figures.

159 "Over the past decade": *Braman v. CME Group*, Amended Complaint, July 22, 2014.

160 and on May 29, in lieu of an interview: This email is included in the appendix to the CFTC's Motion for a Statutory Restraining Order, April 17, 2015.

162   hard to square with the reality: CFTC Sarao complaint, April 21, 2015, www.cftc.gov.

162   Nav couldn't resist crowing: Although, as ever, Sarao didn't actually know who he was trading against.

CHAPTER 20: MINDGAMES

164   To help cut through the noise: Jeff Le Riche also engaged a firm called Analysis Group to expedite the gathering and processing of data—something that, until then, had been largely handled by Harris alone.

164   The professor examined Sarao's use of the algo: Hendershott's report, Appendix to the CFTC's Motion for a Statutory Restraining Order, April 17, 2015.

164   "the layering algorithm . . .": Emphasis added.

166   an agent in Chicago: The FBI's point man on the Sarao case was special agent Greg LaBerta.

167   Martin Davie, the irascible Scotsman running things: Davie resigned from the other company, Willowind, in March 2014.

169   "Financial markets are on the news": Pitching document titled "Iconic Bet: The Next Generation of Online Gaming," October 12, 2014.

169   He had also attracted some big names: The company's chairman was Sir David Michels, who was previously CEO of the Hilton Group as well as chairman of Ladbrokes. High Court judge Sir Robin Jacob was also on the board.

172   At the time, the enforcement division was working on a fairly typical case: "CFTC Charges Florida Residents Anthony J. Klatch II and Lindsey Heim, along with Their Company Assurance Capital Management, LLC, with Fraud and Misappropriation," January 27, 2017, www.cftc.gov.

173   Inside, they presented a judge: *USA v. Navinder Singh Sarao*, Criminal Complaint, filed under seal on February 11, 2015, www.justice.gov.

173   Ever since Jesus Alejandro Garcia Alvarez appeared: Ingo Malcher, "Bezahlt wurde noch nicht," *Brand Eins*, October 2016.

173   four hundred bank branches: "Bankenplatz Zurich," *Zahlen und Fakten*, Ausgabe 2017/2018. According to the report, there are 536 branches in the canton of Zurich, of which the majority are based in the city itself.

174   Arner had been struck low: Guy Dinmore, "State TV Discloses Berlusconi Bank Deposits," *Financial Times*, November 16, 2009. The article cites claims about Arner's ties to Berlusconi first made in the Italian documentary show *Report*.

174   Garcia purchased a 9.8 percent stake: "IXE Group acquires BANCA ARNER," December 16, 2014, www.legal-monitor.com.

174 He also found a new chairman: "Michael Baer Nuovo Presidente Di Banca Arner SA," January 7, 2015, formerly available on Arner Bank's website, www.arnerbank.ch. (In April 2019, Arner merged with Geneva Swiss Bank to form a new entity, ONE Swiss Bank.)

174 Rather than everyone having their own individual accounts: The information in this section is taken from internal IXE documents and interviews with multiple direct witnesses. IXE Group and Alejandro Garcia declined to comment.

174 would receive even more interest: Where previously IXE paid investors interest on a percentage of their total deposit—usually 85 or 90 percent—it was now offering to pay them on the full amount.

CHAPTER 21: WHERE'S THE MONEY, NAV?

180 "Nav was always going to be the kind of person": "Flash Crash Trader 'Potentially Legendary': Rossi," *Bloomberg,* April 24, 2015.

181 Wandsworth houses roughly 1,700 inmates: Wandsworth Prison information, www.justice.gov.uk.

182 Nav's funds were subject to strict lock-up clauses: Nav had also signed up to a multiyear currency swap that guaranteed his interest payments would be exchanged from dollars to pounds at an agreed exchange rate each quarter.

183 One of his favorites was *The Celestine Prophecy*: James Redfield, *The Celestine Prophecy* (New York: Hachette Book Group, first self-published in 1993).

183 The judge was unmoved: *Sarao v. United States of America,* England and Wales High Court, May 20, 2015.

184 A 2015 study by the University of Cambridge: "Study of Half a Million People Reveals Sex and Job Predict How Many Autistic Traits You Have," November 3, 2015, www.cam.ac.uk.

184 The CFTC agreed: *CFTC v. Nav Sarao Futures Plc and Navinder Singh Sarao,* Consent Order of the Preliminary Injunction and Other Ancillary Relief in Resolution of Plaintiff's Motion for Statutory Restraining Order, Preliminary Injunction and Other Equitable Relief, June 29, 2015.

184 a sixty-second action-movie-style advertisement: "Iconic Faceoff—Commercial with Conor McGregor 60 sec," YouTube, July 10, 2015.

185 A month after the bout: Iconic Worldwide Gaming Limited was placed into administration on January 15, 2016.

CHAPTER 22: #FREENAV

186 "The simple idea that a chap in West London": Paul Murphy, "Saving Trader Sarao," *Financial Times,* April 22, 2015.

186 the *New York Times* published an op-ed: Rajiv Sethi, "The Trader as Scapegoat," *New York Times,* April 28, 2015.

187 In *Bloomberg,* Michael Lewis questioned: Michael Lewis, "Crash Boys: How Did a Kid from Hounslow Grow Up to Cause a Crash?" *Bloomberg,* April 24, 2015.

187 particularly since the "disruptive trading" provision: The relevant amendments to the Commodity Exchange Act became effective on July 16, 2011.

187 The DOJ's indictment stated: *USA v. Navinder Singh Sarao,* DOJ Indictment, September 2, 2015.

187 However, all those layers of nuance were lost: "Futures Trader Charged with Illegally Manipulating Stock Market, Contributing to the May 2010 Market 'Flash Crash,'" Justice Department press release, April 21, 2015.

188 Speaking to the *Wall Street Journal:* Bradley Hope and Andrew Ackerman, "'Flash Crash Investigators Likely Missed Clues," *Wall Street Journal,* April 26, 2015.

188 the trader's program was switched off: Tim Cave, Juliet Samuel, and Aruna Viswanatha, "U.K. 'Flash Crash' Trader Navinder Sarao Fighting Extradition to U.S. Granted Bail," *Wall Street Journal,* April 22, 2015.

188 We "should have seen this": Hope and Ackerman, "'Flash Crash' Investigators."

189 "Yes, Sarao's conduct was dodgy": Craig Pirrong, "A Matter of Magnitudes: Making Matterhorn Out of a Molehill," *Streetwise Professor,* April 24, 2015, www.streetwiseprofessor.com.

189 After analyzing e-mini and SPY trading data: Eric Aldrich, Joseph Grundfest, and Gregory Laughlin, "The Flash Crash: A New Deconstruction," January 25, 2016. Aldrich is at the Department of Economics, University of California, Santa Cruz; Grundfest is at the School of Law, Stanford University; Laughlin is in the Department of Astronomy and Astrophysics at the University of California, Santa Cruz.

189 "A front-runner profits by gleaning the intentions": John Arnold, "Spoofers Keep Markets Honest," *Bloomberg,* January 23, 2015.

190 "gross misuse of the term": "Spoofing Corrupts Markets: A Reply to John Arnold," *Mechanical Markets,* April 12, 2015.

CHAPTER 23: ALL IS LOST

193 That faith was tested on September 2: *USA v. Sarao* indictment, September 2, 2015, www.justice.gov.

194 "If I am short I want to spoof it down": *USA v. Sarao* indictment, September 2, 2015, www.justice.gov.

195 was charged by the CFTC with spoofing: "CFTC Charges Chicago

Trader Igor B. Oystacher and His Proprietary Trading Company, 3 Red Trading LLC, with Spoofing and Employment of a Manipulative and Deceptive Device," October 19, 2015, www.cftc.gov.

195 in the case of Oystacher: Although, unlike Sarao, Oystacher was never criminally charged. The DOJ looked into the case but ultimately decided not to bring charges, to the chagrin of some CFTC enforcement staff.

195 Oystacher's MO: *U.S. CFTC v. Igor B. Oystacher and 3Red Trading LLC*, complaint, October 19, 2015, www.cftc.gov.

195 An affidavit written by the CFTC: Despite the crossover, CFTC management decided to keep the investigations into Sarao and Oystacher largely separate to minimize the risk of tipping off one of the defendants.

196 The defendant, who was also charged with commodities fraud: "High-Frequency Trader Indicted for Manipulating Commodities Futures Markets in First Federal Prosecution for 'Spoofing,'" October 2, 2014, www.justice.gov.

196 was a barrel-chested, fifty-three-year-old former pit trader: Brian Lois, Annie Massa, and Janan Hanna, "From Pits to Algos, an Old-School Trader Makes Leap to Spoofing," *Bloomberg,* November 12, 2015.

196 "pump the market": This email was presented as evidence during the trial. The coder, Jeremiah Park, was cross-examined about it on day three, according to court transcripts.

196 Coscia hired a Murderers' Row: The team from Sullivan & Cromwell included Steven Peikin, the current cohead of enforcement at the SEC, Kenneth Raisler, the CFTC's former general counsel, and Karen P. Seymour, who prosecuted Martha Stewart while at the Southern District of New York. She is now Goldman Sachs's general counsel.

196 agreed to pay fines of more than $3 million: On July 22, 2013, Coscia was simultaneously fined $1.4 million by the CFTC, $800,000 by the CME, and $900,000 by the UK's Financial Conduct Authority.

197 "I'm not dealing hot dogs, I'm dealing futures!": Kim Janssen, "Spoofing Trial Gets Testy as Defendant Faces Questioning," *Chicago Tribune,* November 1, 2015.

197 "You know, it reminds me of something": Coscia trial transcripts, day 7.

197 He was later sentenced: "High-Frequency Trader Sentenced to Three Years in Prison for Disrupting Futures Market in First Federal Prosecution of 'Spoofing,'" July 12, 2016, www.justice.gov.

197 "This Court's task is not to adjudicate": *Braman v. CME Group Inc.,* Memorandum Opinion and Order, United States District Judge John Robert Blakey, December 3, 2015.

198 is governed by a treaty: The UK-US extradition treaty of 2003.

198 There is a list of possible objections: They are laid out in the Extradition Act of 2003.

198 Lord Baker, who led the review, concluded it was: "A Review of the United Kingdom's Extradition Arrangements," the Right Honorable Sir Scott Baker, September 30, 2011.

198 David Gilmour, Chrissie Hynde, and Bob Geldof: The song, released in 2009, was a rerecording of Graham Nash's "Chicago."

198 The case might have provided a useful precedent: Theresa May statement on Gary MacKinnon extradition, October 16, 2012, www .gov.uk.

199 Arguing on Nav's behalf was Lewis: In 2007, for example, Lewis convinced the High Court to block the extradition of hotel magnate and alleged fraudster Stanley Tollman to the United States so he could care for his sick wife.

199 "The key question for this court is whether": Suzi Ring, "Spoofing Isn't a U.K. Crime, Attorney Says in Sarao Case," *Bloomberg,* February 5, 2016.

199 economist who wrote a book called: Larry Harris, *Trading and Exchanges: Market Microstructure for Practitioners* (Oxford: Oxford University Press, 2002).

200 "characterizes these orders as being bogus": Submission by Sarao's lawyers, *Government of the United States of America v. Navinder Singh Sarao,* February 2016.

200 Britain's financial regulator had fined a Swiss hedge fund: "FCA Secures High Court Judgment Awarding Injunction and over £7 Million in Penalties Against Five Defendants for Market Abuse," August 12, 2015, www.fca.org.uk.

201 treated for post-traumatic stress disorder: David Hellier, "'Flash Crash' Hearing Told Spoofing Does Not Justify Trader's Extradition to US," *Guardian,* February 5, 2016.

201 "It was American individuals": Suzi Ring, "Flash Crash Trader Headed to U.S. After Losing Final Appeal," *Bloomberg,* October 14, 2016.

201 Seven weeks after the hearing: Ruling of District Judge Purdy, *USA v. Navinder Singh Sarao,* March 23, 2016, www.judiciary.uk.

CHAPTER 24: COME TO JESUS

203 In August 2016, the German business magazine: Ingo Malcher, "Bezahlt wurde noch nicht," *Brand Eins,* October 2016.

203 flicking through the Swiss newspaper: Markus Stadeli, "Mexikanische Grossgrund-besitzer ziehen in die Schweiz," *Neue Zürcher Zeitung,* November 3, 2013.

204 Greenberg, who was seventy-five, had been imprisoned: "Florida Man Sentenced to Eight Years in Prison for Investment Fraud Conspiracy," February 19, 2016, www.justice.gov.

204 according to a complaint filed in Florida: *Bank of Mongolia v. M&P*

Global Financial Services Europe et al, Second Amended Complaint, March 31, 2010.

204 the complaint alleged that Garcia: IXE and Garcia declined to comment on a detailed list of facts sent to them in advance of publication of *Flash Crash,* including on the allegations made by the Mongolian Central Bank. Martha Forcucci, a spokesperson for the company, described the facts as "tendentious."

204 Greenberg and the rest of the defendants: *Bank of Mongolia v. M&P Global Financial Services et al.,* Final Judgment, September 23, 2010.

205 Malcher also spoke to Edgar Soliz: Ingo Malcher, "Bezahlt wurde noch nicht," *Brand Eins,* October 2016.

205 the head of the National Board of Salt Rocks: Ingo Malcher, "Bezahlt wurde noch nicht."

206 the *Wall Street Journal* ran a piece: John Letzing, "Failure of Swiss Bank Deal Leads to Finger-Pointing and Confusion," *Wall Street Journal,* July 19, 2016.

206 "Businesses that need money often don't look hard enough": Ingo Malcher, "Bezahlt wurde noch nicht."

206 persuaded the U.S. government to insert an amendment: "Order Granting Joint Motion for Entry of an Addendum to the Consent Order of Preliminary Injunction," *CFTC v. Navinder Singh Sarao,* December 12, 2015.

207 But it was a desperate plea: *Navinder Sarao v. USA,* Approved Judgment, November 3, 2016.

209 whether he really wanted to be remembered: The 1988 film *Rain Man* stars Dustin Hoffman as an autistic savant with a photographic memory who is put to work by his brother, played by Tom Cruise, counting cards in a casino.

211 they agreed on a CMP of two times his gains: "Federal Court in Chicago Orders U.K. Resident Navinder Sarao to Pay More than $38 million in Monetary Sanctions for Prince Manipulation and Spoofing," November 17, 2016 www.cftc.gov.

212 He then pleaded guilty to two of the twenty-two counts: "Futures Trader Pleads Guilty to Illegally Manipulating the Futures Market in Connection with 2010 'Flash Crash,'" November 9, 2016, www.justice .gov.

212 For Nav, this exercise resulted in: Court transcripts of Sarao plea hearing, U.S. District Court for the Northern District of Illinois Eastern Division, November 9, 2016.

212 "Basically, he has some extraordinary abilities": Sarao plea hearing transcripts, November 9, 2016.

CHAPTER 25: CATCH ME IF YOU CAN

215 He clicked quickly past a "Disclaimer": IXE Trading PowerPoint presentation, given by Alejandro Garcia on November 21, 2016, and emailed to nonattendees the following day.

216 according to its own literature: These figures are included in a document titled "IXE Group Due Diligence Presentation" from around 2013. It states, "IXE STAR employs over 72,000 people" and has "turnover in excess of USD 5 billion per year."

216 "potential consolidated income of about $86m": IXE presentation, November 21, 2016.

216 In terms of actual investments: The four entities listed are IXE I&T, TBZ Farms, Innomarket Pte., and Grupo Agricola IXEQUIN.

216 The takeaway, Garcia explained: According to the presentation, Sarao was owed a total of £39.5 million, the other investors £17.2 million, and the introducers £8.1 million, for a total of around £65 million, or a little over $80 million.

217 "trades executed solely by way of non-speculative transactions": This language was included in the contracts issued by IXE to investors when they transferred their funds from Morgan Stanley to Arner Bank in 2014.